Who Stole Our Game?

The Fall and Fall of Irish Soccer

Who Stole Our Game?

The Fall and Fall of Irish Soccer

Daire Whelan

Gill & Macmillan

Gill & Macmillan Ltd
Hume Avenue, Park West, Dublin 12
with associated companies throughout the world
www.gillmacmillan.ie
© Daire Whelan 2006
ISBN-13: 978 07171 4004 6
ISBN-10: 0 7171 4004 0
Index compiled by Cover To Cover
Typography design by Make Communication
Print origination by TypeIT, Dublin
Printed by ColourBooks Ltd, Dublin

This book is typeset in 11 on 13.5pt Minion.

The paper used in this book comes from the wood pulp of managed
forests. For every tree felled, at least one tree is planted, thereby
renewing natural resources.

A CIP catalogue record for this book is available from the British Library.

5 4 3 2 1

The quotation (on page 13) from 'The Sheltered Edge' by John
Montague is taken from *Poisoned Lands and Other Poems* (London:
MacGibbon and Kee, 1961).

'Doesn't it disturb you when the natural order
of things
Shakes like something that is unstable?'
asked Casca the night Caesar's senators conspired
to have him murdered.

JULIUS CAESAR, WILLIAM SHAKESPEARE

Contents

Foreword

Munster rugby. Leinster rugby. The GAA. Croke Park. The Irish soccer team. Roy Keane. Aidan O'Brien. Kieran Fallon. Padraig Harrington. Paul McGinley.

There's no doubt about it: Irish sport is sexy and full of winners, glamour and entertainment. The Celtic Tiger has taught us we want to be winners and achievers. Money and winning defines our psyche nowadays; it's a well-matched pairing.

What place is there, then, for a League of Ireland that is derided and scorned; which attracts less and less people to its fixtures; where those in charge are openly ridiculed; and where those playing are seen as second-rate. What place, then, for the League of Ireland amongst the Munster rugbys, the GAAs, the Padraig Harringtons and the Kieran Fallons of Irish sport? That is the most vexing question facing the League of Ireland in the twenty-first century.

For fifty years or more soccer and the League of Ireland had an undisputed place in Irish hearts. The local heroes packed out the local grounds, the crowds turned out in force, the bets flowed in, the shouts rang out or fell silent, depending on the kick of a ball: it was a reliable, heart-warming symmetry of people and sport. But then, as society changed, so too did our sporting tastes. Discernment and comfort, glitz and glamour, these were the temptations we saw on display abroad, and we wanted them for ourselves. The Celtic Tiger announced itself with a roar, and the country was caught up in a gold-rush frenzy that consumed the population.

In the twenty-first century the money and ambition are still there, but now we are witnessing a return to the local and a celebration of community and parish. This swing back to our roots has been helped in no small part by the success of the GAA Club Championship, but is also a reaction to the global homogenisation affecting our society. As a result, playing your part, mattering in your small pond and belonging to the local community have once again become desirable characteristics.

The League of Ireland was built on local strengths, but it has lost its link to the local communities. Is it too late to turn back the tide and recover some of what has been lost? After forty years of mismanagement and small-mindedness, many observers would say it *is* too late. Irish people have changed their outlook and now embrace the GAA for what it says about the unique Irish identity in a chaotic world; similarly, they embrace rugby, golf, horse racing and international soccer because they copperfasten our new ability to succeed beyond the shores of this island. The GAA and the international sports reflect back to us a pleasing picture of ourselves—and we've become hooked on looking.

So what can the League of Ireland do to catch up and cash in? Ongoing improvements to the sporting infrastructure might just help the League's cause. The sale of Dalymount to facilitate a new, purpose-built, 10,000-seat stadium on the edge of the M50, plus a €25 million cash bonus, have been hailed as a fresh start for Bohemians. The mooted sale of Tolka Park could do likewise for Shelbourne FC, while the development of the stadium in Tallaght for Shamrock Rovers means they too, finally, have a place they can be proud to call home. But will bedding down on the edge of the city and trying to incorporate themselves as part of the commuter belt actually work? Bohemians may be able to fit 10,000 people in a new stadium, but if they couldn't fill it before, how will they do it in three years' time—and on the edge of the M50? It's going to be a long slog: identity and attachment have to be recreated all over again.

The sorry truth may well be that the only legacy of League of Ireland clubs will be the goldmines their patched-up grounds are sitting on. Bohemians had been playing at Dalymount Park for 105 years, but barely an eyebrow was raised at the plan to sell the ground to developers. Think back, for a moment, to the fierce resistance when Shamrock Rovers sold Milltown in 1987, and then fast forward nearly twenty years: when the home of Irish soccer was sold, the ground that was home to the Irish soccer team and that had seen the debuts of Carey, Giles and Brady, all people talked about was the money. The €50 million. The groaning coffers. The lucre. The Rovers story and its legendary opposition blazed for over a year in 1987; the sale of Dalymount was gone from the sports pages by the second day.

In 2006, do we care about the League of Ireland anymore? We want winners and we want them to make us feel good about ourselves. What chance of that, sitting in a jaded old ground with 1,000 other foolhardy souls?

The fall of the League of Ireland from its heyday in the 1950s has been a long and tortuous descent. To find out the why and how of it, one has to look at the country as a whole and see how poverty, emigration, economic policies and other sports and lifestyle choices all impacted on the League. Before sport took over the headlines, and our lives, it used to exist in the background. As a post-colonial nation, we inherited the traditional British snobbery to sport: it was something the working-classes did while the intelligentsia got on with the important matters of politics, society and culture. As a result, sport was seen as peripheral, not part of the make-up of society and national identity.

What we now see in the modern world is that sport is an important element in a society, and has much to contribute. It deserves its place in the front-row of our national and international performance. This book is therefore as much about charting the politics and culture of the time as it is about half-time scores and high hopes. Nor is it meant to be an extensive factual record. The aim was not to set out in detail the achievements of teams and players, but to talk to former players, administrators, fans and commentators, to find out their perceptions and opinions. At base, it is about giving Irish soccer a voice and a platform from which to speak. Once the League of Ireland was important, but over the course of fifty years it lost its heart and its energy, and it lost its fans. *Who Stole Our Game?* looks for some answers. It's the least football fans deserve.

Acknowledgments

Where to begin? One of the first things you realise when writing a book (and working in journalism as well) is how much goodwill we writers rely upon. We ask people who are just trying to go about their daily lives to stop for a few hours and tell us their stories. Not all are willing or comfortable with that, and to those who did so, despite their initial reservations, my utmost thanks.

I wish also to thank my editor, Fergal Tobin—a man who was willing to meet for coffee on the back of some vague ideas. From our first meeting in 2004 to the time I completed my first book, none of it would have happened without his help, guidance and, most of all, his patience. My deepest gratitude.

Thanks also to Rachel Pierce for her sterling work on the text.

Thanks to the guys at Ceart for the transcriptions and other business services.

Finally, to my family. To Mum, Dad and Aoife for being there every step of the way and encouraging my writing when I was younger.

And, of course, to my dearest Trina. You make me believe in me and what I can be. With all my heart, thank you. This book is just part of our journey and our dream.

Introduction: Soccer and Society

'Those were the days. The floodlights all lit up to be seen for miles around, beckoning people to come for another night of excitement and thrills. And the crowds. What crowds they were! Streams upon streams all converging to meet in the great bay of the ground. Fathers, sons, granddads, uncles—nare a woman in sight. All giddy with the nervousness of what the next two hours could bring. People walking, people cycling, some even driving. And as the crowds filed by our house, I knew it was time to head on up myself. One quick glance out the bedroom window to check. Yes, the lights were standing tall and all lit up—the team's own way of letting me know that they were waiting for me. A quick shout to the Ma that I was going. And then I was gone. Filing in with the steady flow, catching pieces of conversation, "Can we do it tonight without Byrne?" "Hope Murphy doesn't miss the sitter like last week." "Imagine it, a win tonight and we're top of the table!" And so it went, all the five minutes of walk from my house to the ground. To our Mecca. My field of dreams.'

It's hard to believe it now, but many of us were brought up on tales like these of the glory days of the League of Ireland. Those days when soccer had a unique hold on the city. Crowds upon crowds of people jostling to get into Tolka, Dalyer, Milltown, bursting the old stands at their seams and creaking them to their very foundations. Some days the crowds would spill onto the pitches, such was the demand for space. Imagine! People thirsting for, craving for and aching for League of Ireland matches. Their weekly football fix didn't come from across the water and involve exotically named players they would never meet in real life. No, the legends of the game were the Ambroses, the Tuohys and the Coads who came from down the road and would cycle by your house during the week. They were our very own, but so very special as well. Gods in our lifetime. Gods from the East Wall!

Now it's all different: 2,000 spectators per match on average and very little enthusiasm, very little pride—certainly not enough to test the structures of the old stadia. The current state of play makes it almost impossible to picture the crowds of 20,000-plus that turned up weekly at League games in the 1950s. How can youngsters today appreciate just how much the Drums–Rovers rivalry meant to the fans and to the city—Northside v Southside, bus specials leaving from O'Connell Street, kids and grown men cycling the length of the city to be there two hours before kick-off just to be sure of getting in?

Fast forward to the 2000s: fifty years and an unfathomable distance. It's a chilly November evening. Not rainy though. Not bitter. Just chilly. Not enough to keep you by the fire or in the pub. A brisk night is what it's called, isn't it? Nonetheless, here in Tolka Park there are barely 1,500 souls: big bald patches of red and blue seating yawn behind the goals; the old stand across the way is scattered with a mixture of away support and some curious neutrals; while around me is the 'hard core', the 100 or so who are here every week—even if it is more than just chilly or brisk. Just 1,500 people—not even enough to drown out the sounds of the city on a Friday night: ambulance sirens, police cars and the shouted ramblings of a passing drunk all intrude on our attempt to recreate some sort of magic.

We watch as Shelbourne become the League Champions. Again. Shelbourne are the strong and emerging face of Irish soccer, even harbouring hopes of some success in Europe. As the captain lifts the trophy of champions and the team celebrates in exuberance, I clap warmly but half-heartedly; happy for the team to have worked so hard and done so well, but embarrassed, saddened to be one of just 1,500 football fans who cares enough to witness it. Where are all the others?

My mind wanders back to the stories I heard from my Dad: '...*Those were the days. The floodlights all lit up to be seen for miles around, beckoning people to come for another night of excitement and thrills. And the crowds. What crowds they were! Streams upon streams all converging to meet in the great bay of the ground. Fathers, sons, granddads, uncles ...*'

I found myself there in the stands of Tolka, clapping for the new League of Ireland champions, but looking wistfully at the spectators scattered about the ground: how many stories do these diehard fans have to tell about the game? How far have they come? And do they remember way back when this stadium was creaking to the rafters? Do they gaze down in the corner and see Paddy Ambrose scoring that famous forty-yard winner? Or the goal-mouth that saw so many heroics, and which do they recall? Or the dugouts filled with the legendary players from every part of Dublin?

The few kids around me had jumped onto the pitch and were running to the players to get their autographs, or just to have a run around; I was getting ready to leave. Another season over, but tonight something clicked: I needed to find out how and why the League of Ireland had gone from 20,000-plus crowds to this, tonight. Why thousands upon thousands had forgotten about soccer in the city. How many never even knew that the Drums–Rovers rivalry was once like a Manchester, Milan or London derby?

It had been fifty years since the 'golden age' of League of Ireland soccer—fifty years of forgetting. All epochs must wane, of course; Rome wasn't built in a day, but it didn't last forever either. The problem was, this was different. Irish soccer was in freefall, not waning but plummeting. That November night it really struck home just how truly the game was dying on its feet. The League itself may not have declined—full-time professionalism was seeing to better footballing standards—but the crowds had the enthusiasm and the love, and without those, there was nothing.

Down below, the last of the players were leaving the Tolka pitch. Three and four nights of training a week plus a match. Countless hours of sacrifice and slog and all for the love of the game. It wasn't much different from players of the 1950s, but in the interim Irish society had moved on. The culture and the people had changed irrevocably.

That night I decided to find out just who, or what, was responsible for what had happened in the last half a century. And why it had happened. After all, the GAA and rugby are thriving and soccer internationals are sell-out events, so why have soccer fans turned their backs so resolutely on the home game? There was, it seemed, a story to be told and it was the story of the fall and fall of Irish soccer. While the economy had risen, dipped, fallen further and then miraculously soared higher than ever before, the League of Ireland's curve was easier to track: down, down some more and then past rock bottom. All the while the GAA is moving further and further away, taking with it the badge of identity and Irishness. And all the while football in Europe is becoming a world away— not only from our lives and realities but from the League of Ireland's own little sphere. The chances of Ireland ever again hosting Real Madrid or Manchester United are now so slim as to be non-existent: you're better off saving the fare to go see them in Old Trafford or the Bernabeau yourself.

Someone once said that the League is Old Ireland caught up in New Ireland—and being strangled by it, it would seem. Just take Shamrock Rovers, for example, as apt a symbol as any for the League: once great, Rovers has since had an examiner appointed to it and was saved only by its diehard support, but also suffered the ignominy of relegation for the first time in its history. People inevitably talk about 'good times' in the past tense. In the present, there's a shrug of the shoulders, a sigh that signifies resignation to the fact that it's just the way things are now. New Ireland tolerates the League of Ireland like a piece of old, cumbersome furniture: it's not used anymore, but it can't be thrown away because, well, it's always been there, and what else would cover that stain on the carpet?

So, what can the past fifty years teach us? Even more to the point, how can we explain football and its hold over us in just six chapters? We will have to start with the first glimpses of decline in the 1960s to the difficulties stemming from the arrival of television, to the bad old days in the 1970s when the terraces were emptying and there was little appetite for the game. Then on to the 1980s when people were 'queuing for a living', as Paddy O'Gorman had it, and Irish soccer reached its nadir with the sale of Milltown, the spiritual home of soccer. There is no more resonant symbol of the decline of the game than Glenmalure Park: next time you drive by the concrete jungle it is now, try to imagine 30,000 people crammed into a fine football ground with a carpet for a pitch, where dreams were made and hearts broken during ninety minutes and over the course of decades. And what, too, of Dalymount? History and heritage comes at a price these days: €50 million.

The question we inevitably come to is: did no one notice? Did no one try to stop the rot? And that, of course, just as inevitably brings us to the sport's governing body: the Football Association of Ireland (FAI). Through it all, and in spite of themselves, the FAI and the clubs are still in existence. Merrion Square still stands, despite all the back-stabbing, petty rivalries, feuding, shafting and 'nights-of-long-knives'. Soccer in Ireland was once described as 'a professional game run by amateurs' and while no one can dispute the hours and effort officials and volunteers put into their clubs, it is fair to say that there has been no vision, no long-term planning. As Dublin and Ireland were changing in the 1960s and 1970s, as people moved out of their communities to newly built and ever-expanding suburbs, there was no attempt to ride with these developments and encourage in the young families starting new lives a sense of the pride and history of League of Ireland clubs. The new communities in places like Tallaght and Lucan were left unsown, fertile grounds that they were, with huge populations ready to be distracted and entertained.

Compare and contrast this with the philosophy and approach of the GAA and its awareness and acknowledgment of the urbanisation of Dublin and of towns across the country. Into these suburbs the schools and churches came first, followed quickly by the GAA clubs, their community halls becoming focal points for the areas and establishing a bond and an identity between people and team—from under-10 to senior level.

As the GAA thrived, things got worse for the League of Ireland: it was slowly being engulfed by the backbiting and the continuous, exhausting firefighting. The perennial struggle of making ends meet, paying wages and raising money became ever more difficult as recession hit hard in the 1980s. It was obvious that an overhaul was needed, but the League's response was to give four points, three points, two points for wins. No attempt was made to smarten up the grounds, improve the experience for spectators. The football fans were no longer willing to put up with being treated shoddily when there were plenty of other options available, and so they drifted away.

It's not like the opportunities weren't there: John Giles' return in 1977, post-Italia 1990, Celtic Tiger monied days … Irish football hit euphoric levels with Italia '90 and USA '94, but despite the new-found wealth and sense of optimism in the country, it never translated itself into the League of Ireland. People still preferred their Riverdance to their Richmond Park. New Ireland found itself in new money, but people would venture more to Old Trafford or Anfield than travel across their dirty old town. They were all opportunities for things to be put right, but the domestic game hit the post, scuffed its shot or just plain missed the open goal.

So who is right and who is wrong? While it wouldn't be fair to lay all the blame at the FAI's door—so much time has been spent putting out fires from week to week there was no time for long-term planning—nonetheless a culture has been allowed to breed whereby getting through committees and getting the votes to climb high enough on the blazers' ladder has become the mark of true progress. Instead of being measured on foresight and ability to administer, it seems the real kudos lies in which rung you are standing on. As a result of this inward-looking approach the FAI is like the corner shop that is taken unawares by the arrival of the supermarket down the road: it was genuinely blind-sided by the fall-off in popularity of the game in the 1960s. But it was plain to see that Irish society was changing, with people's habits, tastes and lifestyles being altered continually, it's just that no one in charge of the League of Ireland clubs thought to wonder if it was going to affect them too. The prevaricating and the fulminating meant that by the 1970s they were too far behind to be able to do anything worthwhile to catch up. There was tinkering and plastering over, but those attempts only showed up the game's administrators for what they were: men without vision or imagination. They had old scores to settle and were focused on that, so the intra-club rivalry became paramount, even as the terraces emptied. In the end, the fans became superfluous to the imagined or otherwise power struggles between the clubs and their officials.

That is the crux of the matter: me and you. The fans. We are the glue that holds this game together. We are part of the problem— falling attendances—and we are also the solution. John Byrne, a fanatical Shamrock Rovers fan, explains it well:

'I am not a League of Ireland fan, I am a football supporter. People tend to categorise us as being different, as if it is a different sort of sport or something. It is just football. I just love football. Let me try and explain . . . Rovers have played Charlton Athletic a few times and in actual fact there was a few Charlton lads on holidays and they came to the match and all that. They came for a few pints with us afterwards and we did the whole "Charlton, Charlton give us a song". And they sang some old bollocks and bored us all to tears and we had to give a standing ovation at the end of it. But at the end of it all, they want to know what is going on with our club and we want to know what is going on with their club. They want to go to the bar with us and have a chat because you have something in common. You are just football fans. Then you get the Irish people who come along to support the English clubs, they are looking down their noses at us. But in England or anywhere else we get mutual respect—if I am in Manchester they know you are from Dublin and you support Shamrock Rovers—it makes sense. It makes total sense to other supporters, but here at home we are mad people. When you go to Europe with Rovers you can see the respect that is there. They respect you are representing Ireland, you are representing Poland, or Sweden or whatever the hell. And, okay, they are better than us ninety-nine times out 100, but following your local club is what is normal in other countries, but here it is not. People grow up supporting United or Liverpool and well, let's face it—it is a lot easier. What do you have to do? You have to go down to the pub and have to drink beer. That is hard work, that.'

What we're asking is: is the League of Ireland dying, and therefore capable of being revived? Or is it dead, flatline, no hope? Probably not. Football has a strange way of letting our hearts rule our heads, and people will always be willing to stump up money to keep their club going. But somewhere along the line, time will be called on what it stands for and where it stands in our recent past. The further we travel from the golden days and the more we know only of empty grounds, internal rows and poor facilities, the more our disdain will grow. When the memories get tarnished and lost, then the League will die.

Note: I have used the generic term League of Ireland throughout the book rather than use a lot of different terms. Football and soccer are used interchangeably throughout, but the term 'soccer' is more generally used when also discussing Gaelic football so as to avoid any confusion.

Part One

The 1950s: A golden era in a grey landscape

THE PLAYER

'... A shilling in or whatever it was, I remember coming to Tolka in 1957. I think Shels were playing Shamrock Rovers in a replay of the Cup, and there were 22,000 people in Tolka Park on a Wednesday afternoon at a quarter-past two. The bicycles were out ten deep along the railings of the park . . . They were up on the roof of the terrace. I couldn't take a corner-kick because the people were all around. They were all spilling over the wall and they were around the inside of the pitch and you had to move them back to take your corner-kick. You couldn't move to the touchline, you would be tripping over feet.'

I. The defences are not strong enough to resist a soccer invasion

The Football League of the Irish Free State was born on 1 June 1921 in Molesworth Hall, Dublin, and, ominously, it was born out of a split with the Irish Football Association (IFA). According to Peter Byrne in his book, *The FAI, 75 Years*, the Irish Football Association, based in Belfast, was perceived by many as a puppet of the FA authorities in London. With the nationalist fervour that swept the country after 1916, relations between the IFA and the football bodies in the South were deteriorating. When the 1921 Cup final between Glentoran and Shelbourne in Belfast ended in a draw, convention meant that the replay was to be held in Dublin, but with the South in the midst of a Civil War, the IFA ordered the replay to be held in Belfast. Shelbourne refused. Within a year, clubs in the South had decided to form their own football association, and its officials became the new power-brokers of Irish football in the Republic. The hierarchical structure of the game meant that club officials got to run the international side of things as well and this was, of course, where the real power and influence lay. Trips abroad, wining and dining with international counterparts, meeting and greeting titular heads, hob-nobbing with Presidents, Lord Mayors, Government Ministers and Taoisigh all became part of the role of making it to the top in Irish football circles. The increasing popularity of the game and the increased internationalisation of it through the inauguration of the World

Cup tournament in 1930 also meant an increase in standing for FAI officials. Little wonder, then, that the parish-pump politics of priest and publican quickly came to include club official as well.

By the 1940s and 1950s the League of Ireland was playing to packed houses each week at League grounds, as well as a moderately successful international side. The FAI never had it so good. Thirty years on, their decision of 1 June 1921 looked like a stroke of genius.

Eamon Dunphy was just like the thousands of other kids around the country who slept, ate and dreamt football. He was luckier than most, however, because he grew up in the 1950s, opposite Tolka Park, and spent his days bunking in to see the mighty Drums, kicking a ball around after school in the shadow of the Tolka stands.

'There were three places I went to: Croke Park, Tolka Park and the Library. In my case we were living so adjacent to Tolka you couldn't ignore it and we would go there all the time and the place was packed. And when the floodlights came we had midweek matches as well because it was the only place in Dublin with floodlights. So Tolka Park . . . that was ideal place to be.

All the guys that played in those times they were local heroes, they were huge men and they were wonderful footballers. I used to go in and watch them training at night and with a couple of other buddies we used to just watch them train. The idea of ever getting onto a pitch and playing, that is what nurtured it in me. The notion of playing football, the idea that you would actually ever get onto a pitch with a real ball and a set of jerseys and nets—nets were the big thing because we all played with coats. So it was wonderful and it did nurture the passion in me.

And of course we had to bunk in—there was never any tickets — I would get a lift over the stile, "give us a lift over the stile, mister" we'd ask and there would be guys going up who would be arseholes, but you would always get a lift over the stile from someone. You could be standing there for half an hour asking and eventually, it was just like your heart was pumping, saying, "please God, someone lift us over" and someone would come up and they would lift you over the stile and away you would go and the guys on the stile wouldn't bother you.

But you were lucky if you got in at all. Once, I remember ripping me hand trying to get into Dalymount to see a Cup Final between Drums and Evergreen. I cut me hand on the barbed wire and ran all the way home in the pouring rain because I couldn't get in. I was crying to me Ma so I could hear it on the radio. You had your good days and your bad days I suppose.'

When the League of Ireland is spoken of with fond nostalgia, this is the period referred to. Post-war and into the 1950s was the golden age for the League. The famous 'Coad's Colts' emerged as one of the greatest teams ever and a thrilling inter-city rivalry sprang up between the southside Shamrock Rovers and northside Drumcondra. Their respective grounds of Glenmalure Park and Tolka Park would heave when derby day came around. It was a time when Irish soccer, Irish players and Irish teams had the nation transfixed.

Interestingly, this 'golden age' stemmed from a 'dark age' for Irish society. While the rest of Europe enjoyed a post-war boom, the Irish government's misguided policy of self-sufficiency left Ireland with a stagnant economy and increasing emigration. Ireland of the 1950s was a drab place, as poet John Montague so eloquently described it in 'The Sheltered Edge':

'Standing at the window, I watch the wild green leaves
Lurch back against the wall, all the branches of the appletree
Stretch tight before the wind, the rain lash
The evening long against the stubborn buildings
Raised by man, the blackened rubbish dumps,
The half-built flats, the oozing grey cement
Of hasty walls, the white-faced children
Deprived of sun, scurrying with sharp laughter
From point to point of shelter,
And arched over all, the indifferent deadening rain.'

Perhaps it is hard for many people now to appreciate what Ireland was like then. Reading contemporary descriptions and reports, it truly sounds like another country, a different place— somewhere you wouldn't be keen to visit. In the final issue of the influential *The Bell* magazine, in July 1954, Anthony Cronin described the greying pallor of an ailing people:

> 'One looks out of the window at the wet Sunday morning, ineffable grey above melancholy deep green and dull red bricks; at the girls hurrying to mass in their glowing mackintoshes, at the man with the six soaked Sunday newspapers under his arm and a face as grey and expressionless as the sky. Here, if ever was, is a climate for the death wish.'

The *Belfast Telegraph* levelled a stinging criticism when it wrote that 'the government of Eire is more kind to the rich and more harsh to the poor'. From beyond the border the view was clear, and they saw a country where between 1949 and 1956 real national income rose by only 8% while the European average was 40%; where between 1951 and 1961 412,000 people emigrated; where between 1951 and 1959 employment in industry fell by 38,000, or 14%; where between 1941 and 1961 the agricultural workforce fell by 200,000. There was an inexorable slide downwards, and it was pulling the people down with it.

Was it any wonder, then, that with jobs so scarce and living so tough, sport boomed and became the panacea to take away the misery once a week? Attendances at soccer, GAA, athletics and even speedway events reached record figures as people sought refuge from the drabness and toughness of life through their local sporting heroes. Soccer and GAA, in particular, were the opiates of the working-man's pain, the one escape—for a few hours at least—from the fear of losing one's job, the fear of not being able to provide for a family and the fear of not being able to pay the bills.

> 'The fundamental options and the cheaper options were to get a bit of happiness and a bit of diversion,' says Dunphy, recollecting what it was like for his family. 'That was what people did, they went to the matches, they had a few drinks afterwards, the pubs were packed and they rowed and talked about the matches. In the Dublin that I was in and I observed, I would see that these were the happiest days of people's weeks and lives and their love and passion for football and for the local game was extraordinary.'

Soccer was very much based around local communities and local heroes; when going to the game meant more than being able to watch it from afar; when an aura surrounded the clubs and players and when the limits of one's horizons might stretch as far as across the other side of the city.

The war years from 1939 to 1945 were also a help as it meant that, with the lack of competition in England, League of Ireland clubs were able to capitalise by bringing across English star players. It all helped to swell the crowds and provoke greater interest, and with the ending of the war in 1945, the post-war boom for soccer in England was to provide a further fillup to Irish clubs through the increased transfers of Irish players to England. Upon such fees were club's futures and survivals guaranteed, for example, in 1947 Dundalk were able to wipe out debts and end up £7 in the black thanks to the transfer of Peter Corr for £2,500.

There was no doubt that Shamrock Rovers were the League giants: 'Coad's Colts' were the Busby Babes of Ireland, capturing the imagination of football fans and creating a legend and a folklore that still exist to this day. Under the guidance of Paddy Coad, the 1950s were the boom time for Rovers, with three League titles and two FAI Cup wins. Paddy Coad, Paddy Ambrose, Liam Tuohy, Gerry Mackey, Noel Peyton—the names still run off the tongue for fans like a teamsheet from today and people still talk about 'Coad's Colts' with admiration and satisfaction.

'A passionate Shels supporter,' Dunphy continued, 'would hate Shamrock Rovers. A passionate Drums supporter would also hate Shamrock Rovers. Everybody hated Shamrock Rovers. And of course Shamrock Rovers was actually where the vision and the dreams were and that was certainly to some extent down to Paddy Coad who was the player-coach there and he was a wonderful player. He created the great Rovers side that would go back to Paddy Moore and the '20s. Rovers always had great sides. Rovers was the place. They were the Man Utd there was no question about that.'

Of course, a golden age needs more than one team—it requires a competitive edge. The Dublin clubs regained the upper hand in the League after Cork's dominance during and after the war; St

Patrick's Athletic, Shelbourne, Shamrock Rovers and Drumcondra were all to win League titles in the 1950s. The defining rivalry, however, was that of Rovers and Drums. It captured the imagination of the entire city and propelled the League into the heart of people's affections. It was a Northside–Southside rivalry with the River Liffey as its dividing line. (Although Shelbourne people, like their Chief Executive Ollie Byrne, will hotly dispute this, arguing that Shels–Rovers is the real derby: 'factually and historically and whatever else terminology you want to use,' Byrne says, 'because both clubs were from Ringsend, Shelbourne would have been more Pearse Street, the upper end of Ringsend, Bath Avenue and Sandymount and Rovers, I suppose, was in the heart of Irishtown rather than Ringsend. Rovers was basically formed out of pettiness and a little bit of envy of Shelbourne because it came some years later, but the rivalry between the two clubs was horrendous.')

Shamrock Rovers carried the legend and the aura—in much the same way as Manchester Utd do in England—but it was Drumcondra on the northside who were leaving their imprint on the football honours list in the 1950s, and giving northsiders something to crow about to their southside neighbours. Three League titles, five runner-up spots and three Cup victories post-war had brought the glory years to Drumcondra FC. Around such rivalries are successes built, and the derby matches would capture the imagination of the city in the days before and after the game and often neither Tolka Park or Milltown could accommodate the numbers trying to get in.

If one game was to epitomise the era at its peak, a height it would never again scale, it was the first ever all-ticket League clash between Drumcondra and Shamrock Rovers, which took place in January 1958. As well as having a heated fan rivalry, Drums and Rovers were becoming fierce rivals on the pitch and since the 1946 Cup Final (which Drums won, 2-1), the rivalry had increased and every single League, Cup and shield game was of huge significance. While it would be too much to claim that the two teams were carving up the game's honours between themselves, they were undeniably the most dominant, the best supported and the most bitter of rivals. By the late 1950s the demand to see key Drums–Rovers games was far exceeding their ground's capacities, but it didn't stop the clubs from squeezing them in—and onto—the pitch, if necessary.

The days leading up to that Sunday afternoon League clash in January 1958 saw huge demand for tickets at Tolka Park, as had been expected, with Drums owner, Sam Prole, reporting that '20,000 have been sold already'. This did not deter the many thousands who were determined to see the game, come what may.

Rovers had pipped Drums to the League title the previous year, but this time Drums were leading the way at the top of the League and Rovers were a further five points behind them, in fifth place. The scene was set for a pulsating afternoon's entertainment in Dublin.

The official turnstile returns reported that 19,053 fans passed through into the ground that January day, but by kick-off it was obvious that many more thousands had squeezed into the ground, ticket or not. There was ominous swaying in the stands as they creaked beyond capacity, then the spectators solved the problem themselves by scaling the surrounding wall and hopping down onto the pitch, finding places inside the wall and all along the touchlines. This sort of overcrowding wasn't unusual, so there weren't too many causes for concern. It was just another hugely important fixture that was having trouble accommodating all those who wanted to see the game.

When the game got underway, Rovers took the lead in the thirty-fifth minute when Ronnie Nolan hit a left-foot shot into the top of the net from outside the box. Then, right on the stroke of half-time, Rovers went 2-0 up when Paddy Coad was put through into the box and beat Alan Kelly with a shot into the bottom corner. Drums came back out fighting and ten minutes into the second half Willie Coleman was brought down in the box and Stan Pownall converted the penalty. It was 2-1: game on!

For the next eight minutes Drums and Rovers drove at each other at a high pace, looking for the all-important next goal. It seemed as if Rovers would gain a decisive third when Tommy Hamilton was put through by Noel Peyton. He tried rounding

Alan Kelly, but then appeared to be tripped before hurtling into the crowd, which was just inches from the play. Hamilton had difficulty extricating himself from the crowd, and soon trouble was threatening to flare up.

'The police force present, utterly inadequate for the occasion, failed to shift the crowd and Drumcondra chairman, Mr Royden Prole, pushed out and heaved a couple of youngsters to the touchline,' wrote WP Murphy in the *Irish Independent* the next day. 'Then he was attacked by another youngster and when a Garda came to his assistance the crowd gathered, and Mr Prole, with fists flying around him, raced frantically for the pavilion, jumped over a would-be trip, and reached safety. The referee, availing of this diversion, took his chance to escape.'

Referee Sgt Tommy Cannon quickly realised that it was pointless trying to force the crowds back behind the touchlines and, sensing trouble in the air, called a halt. Dublin's first ever all-ticket League game ended in recriminations and accusations. As a result, it was the aftermath and the post-mortem discussions in the media and amongst the fans that would generate most column inches:

'What a pity it was that such a grand game should have had such an unfortunate finish,' continued Murphy in his report, 'however, the ingredients of trouble were there from the start. Indeed, a more experienced referee might have refused to start the game until the crowd was behind the surrounding walls.'

Adding to the surrealism of the day, as fans made their disgruntled ways home after the debacle, the city was being enveloped by one of the worst fogs experienced for many years: so bad, in fact, that traffic was halted by 7.00pm; visibility was reduced to just three yards; drivers abandoned their cars; and buses were led through the streets by their conductors on foot in front of them, which practice in turn had to be stopped as the drivers were unable to see their conductors leading the way from just a few feet away. Dublin that night was like a scene from

Sherlock Holmes' London. Like the fog, word of the match spread quickly. In the pubs and houses on the north and southside of the city, lights were lit and people pulled closer to the fire, shutting out the darkening world outside and leaning into the intense discussions about 'the match'.

Were Rovers still the better team, or would Drums be able to overcome their bitter rivals in the Leinster Senior Cup? It became the only talking-point across the city for days afterwards. Would the result stand? was what fans were eager to know and, more importantly, what could be done to address the all-too-common crowd incursions onto the pitches? How much longer could clubs and spectators afford to ignore their own safety before addressing this issue?

'Now you lot of hypocrites, what can you say about Windsor Park, it's a pity the Continental Press didn't see Tolka Park yesterday,' was how WP Murphy followed up the incidents of Sunday's match, quoting a gentleman friend from Belfast. 'Then I met a man who had paid the increased price of 5/- for a stand seat and felt that he had not got good value despite a great first half, and then a follower who paid a ticket tout 3/- for 1/6 entrance ticket—his view was that he had been robbed. Then I met a Shelbourne follower who asked me a straight question and really put the League of Ireland officials on the spot, "Why was our (Shelbourne) League game with Waterford in 1956 taken to Dalymount Park by the League? Then we were tenants at Tolka Park and we decided to make our match with Waterford all-ticket. We printed 15,000 tickets which we thought was enough, but the League swept down and changed the game to Dalymount in the interests of the game and public safety. If an all-ticket game in 1956 with a 15,000 ceiling was out in 1956, why do nothing in 1958 when the Drumcondra club announced that they are taking in an extra 6,000 customers?"'

The problem facing the League was, ironically, how to keep the spectators out rather than how to get them in. The fencing at the Drumcondra end had been left in ruins thanks to the hundreds of ticketless fans who raced down the Tolka Bank and took the fences apart in order to gain entry to the ground. The demand to see

Drums–Rovers clash again was such that their next game against each other, in the Leinster Senior Cup Final replay, was called into question. 'It is obvious,' wrote WP Murphy, 'that Tolka Park will not hold the spectators who want to see these two sides and what was a near riot in daylight could be a disaster at night . . . the Drumcondra defences are not strong enough to resist a soccer invasion.'

It was obvious that something needed to be done. There was much criticism of the League and its officials because they had not learnt from previous incidents over the years. For example, in the 1940s, Billy Mulville of Drums broke his leg after colliding with spectators. The officials has failed to take the issue of overcrowding and crowd incursion seriously, leading the famous English international Raich Carter to express his horror at the lack of stewarding in place on the afternoon of the Drums–Rovers match. There were only six gardaí present that day, compared to an equivalent ground in England where 100 police, Carter said, would be stationed. In the interests of public safety, it was time for the Gardaí to get more actively involved in crowd control, said the soccer writers and supporters; the official word from both Drums and Rovers in the aftermath was, predictably enough, 'no comment'.

The next potential flashpoint came just a week later when both sides met in the replayed final of the Leinster Senior Cup, but this time officials were taking no chances. 'Drumcondra are taking every possible precaution to avoid a repetition of the scenes which caused an abandonment of their League encounter,' wrote Murphy. 'Tonight a strict check will be kept on the turnstiles so that when the required number have passed through, the stiles will be closed . . . and on the advice of Gardaí there will be no schoolboys gate.' This, it seemed, worked and 'Tolka Park was a happily congested area, and with an adequate number of Gardaí on duty and sufficient stewards to give them authority.' The attendance this time was a strictly adhered to 16,500 and the turnstiles were again clicking merrily. And for the record, Rovers retained the trophy for the third successive year.

So, things were looking up for soccer and for sport in general, because people needed something to captivate them and games were an accessible, affordable option. Sport was thriving across the country: GAA matches were hitting record highs, as were athletics meets; 25,000 turned up to the opening of a new athletics stadium out in Santry, North Dublin (Morton Stadium); and the League of Ireland reported a profit of over £1,200 for the 1952–53 season. However, lack of forward-planning or fiscal stability meant that success was growing on shallow ground. The inter-League game against the English League was the main profit-earner, and the precariousness of the situation was noted by the League itself, which recorded that it depended on St Patrick's Day falling on a Tuesday or Wednesday for the teams to be able to travel to play each other.

Just before the start of the 1953–54 season, it was announced that ticket prices were to be raised by six pence. Given that it was a feat in itself for the average working man to save the ticket price, everyone wondered what effect it would have on the support. 'This should be an interesting weekend for it will be the first under the 1s 6d regime,' wrote Frank Johnstone of *The Irish Times*, 'the League of Ireland having decided during the close season to raise the admission prices by six pence. Public reaction is being awaited eagerly—and not without a little trepidation I imagine by the clubs.'

The clubs had little to fear. Even though the six-pence raise was an increased hardship for the fans, it was a burden they were willing to bear to see their heroes in action. With precious few other distractions available to them, football fans kept coming back to the League of Ireland grounds for the next season, and in increased numbers for the rest of the decade.

Perusing the newspaper clippings of the time shows just how good the clubs had it at this stage, with regular comments of 'record gates', 'record attendances' and 'clicking turnstiles' popping up in any number of match reports from across the country. The League was cresting a wave of faithful support: Cork Athletic recorded a League attendance of 11,356 at the Mardyke for the visit of Shelbourne in 1953, grossing a gate of £670; Evergreen Utd's biggest gate of the season was against St Patrick's Athletic; in 1958

Cork Hibs attracted its biggest crowd of the season, with gates of over £500; while Shelbourne sent their directors home happy after beating Evergreen Utd 2-0 and pocketing the biggest gate of the season in the process, with over 10,000 attending.

Although criticism was, and has, been levelled at the League of Ireland for lack of vision at this time, on the ground many club managers were working hard on the League's behalf. The two most successful clubs—Rovers and Drums—were headed by the Cunninghams and Proles, respectively.

Sam Prole was one of the most respected men in Irish soccer. In 1953 he brought Drums from the Hunter family and moved from Dundalk to Dublin's northside. He had been with Dundalk for more than thirty years and his move to Dublin was met with sadness and regret from the Co. Louth team, who said he had been central to stabilising the club's finances; by 1953 a dozen players had been transferred, banking over £23,000 for the club.

'To state just how much the club owes Bob [Sam] Prole would be difficult,' wrote those in the club that he was leaving behind, 'but it might not be too much to say but that for him, the club would not now be in existence. In the difficult years that have passed, when mounting costs made the running of a professional team yearly more difficult, he showed extraordinary talent in the transfer of players whose fees provided the lifeblood of the club; in fact his talent went back earlier than the transfer dates, for in many cases the players had been discovered by him. In many respects, soccer football owes him a debt which cannot easily be discharged.'

Rovers were seen as the more glamorous and successful side, but when Sam Prole arrived at Drums in 1953 the club became the most innovative and progressive club in the League. They were, for example, the first to have floodlights, which were introduced for a friendly against St Mirren in 1953.

'Drumcondra's first floodlit match, played at Tolka Park last night, provided spectators with grand entertainment,' wrote Frank Johnstone in *The Irish Times*. 'The crowd was disappointing, a cold evening probably keeping many at home, but I am sure that the undoubted success of this game will ensure a much bigger attendance for Drumcondra's next floodlit attraction against Glenavon . . . The novelty of the event possibly tends to make one exaggerate somewhat on the potentialities of soccer by floodlight, but it was certainly good football to watch.'

At Drumcondra, the Proles created a football club that northside Dubs associated with and that was at long last able to rival Shamrock Rovers. The Proles were looking to take the club forward, both on and off the pitch. Robert Prole, Sam's son, notes that Drums were Bovril's biggest customer in Ireland after they introduced the drink as a half-time refreshment for fans. Even such things as pitchside advertising were new foreign concepts until Sam Prole introduced them at Tolka.

In spite of all this effort, including record gate receipts, clubs still found themselves just managing to scrape by. Even though players' wages were paltry—on average £3 a week—professional soccer management was considered to be fraught with risk. Bohemians, Dublin's amateur club, held tenaciously to their cherished status: 'no player who shares the slightest professional intentions will be allowed become a Bohemians player' the club maintained and the directors were determined to stop the club being used as a 'stepping stone to the professional ranks, the amateurs will screen all applications for playing membership'. For investors, the cash flow was all one way, even when they devoted their energies to redirecting it.

The support was there, the games were there and the money was there to copperfasten the League's success. But that is not what happened. Looking at the graph of the League's performance in the following years, the logical question to pose is: where was the money invested? It doesn't appear that it was used to solidify the success and build on it for the future. So what happened?

This became a recurring question from fans and officials alike and as the League faced into darker times in the years to come, it was to be a question raised even louder. Not a penny, it seemed, was being put away for a rainy day, a decision the clubs would, in time, rue dearly. When it came to the financial affairs of the clubs, nobody really knew what happened to the money they appeared to be making. The payment of players' wages and the upkeep of grounds would have been the biggest liabilities, but no matter how much the gate receipts, it seemed it was never enough. Most likely, no tribunal of inquiry could ever find a paper trail to answer the questions people still have to this day.

Robert Prole, whose father, Sam, bought the club from the Hunters in 1953, is adamant that no money was made from the club and that all profits were put back into the club's coffers. For Ollie Byrne—Shelbourne's Chief Executive and a man who knows only too well the trials and tribulations of keeping a club afloat having seen it first-hand through his father's involvement with Shelbourne when Chairman from the 1940s to the mid-1950s—the reason for the League's and the clubs' failures in the long-term was the fact that they were led by working-class men who simply didn't have the necessary knowledge or experience to make a business profitable.

> 'The majority of soccer is working class. They had a love for the game and either for one reason or another became attached either through their sons or their family to particular clubs or they just took a shine to it and worked up into the hierarchy of the club. But the clubs weren't backed with any business acumen or whatever. It would be fair to say that the first one of those clubs that had the business acumen, and they had it from the early part of their history, would have been Rovers because the Cunningham family, Eoin, Joe and Mary Jane, who were arch rivals of my father in a football sense but in a personal sense were reasonably good friends … had a business acumen about them and that is why they were in a position to run Rovers very successfully whereas most of the clubs were working-class people and worked on a committee basis.'

Can the answer really be that simple: because of circumstance and education, the working-class person who was attracted to the game just did not have the awareness or *nous* to run a club properly? For many it is an overly simplistic argument and doesn't hold up when compared to the GAA and the poor, rural backgrounds of many of those involved in its success. However, Brian Kerr, Ireland's former International manager and a man who

was involved in the League of Ireland for many years, would agree
with this theory.

> 'Soccer in this country was a working-class game. It was not for the
> middle-class, Fianna Fáil types. How many soccer pitches did you
> ever see in the schools? Sport was controlled by the religious and
> powerful, whereas those running football had little business
> acumen—they'd be second-hand car salesmen or electrical
> engineers—that class of people. Although now things have
> changed. But these were the kinds of people who didn't have
> knowledge and foresight to look ahead. I remember being told once
> that the problem with the FAI was that there was too many bicycles
> chained to their gates. That sums it up really.'

Whether the League officials were doing a good job or not, there
was little soccer to be had elsewhere, so fans were dependent on
their League of Ireland fix and flocked to the grounds. But if clubs
were struggling financially while the grounds were packed, what if
something happened to take the fans elsewhere? Long-term
planning was not part of the soccer agenda, and it was in this
regard that the GAA was able to gain an important advantage over
its soccer rivals. In response to this criticism, League of Ireland
people point to the fact that while they were trying to make ends
meet to pay players' wages, the amateur ethos of the GAA meant it
had the luxury of being able to concentrate on the development of
Gaelic games throughout the country and how best to respond to
changes in Irish society and culture. They may have a point, and
perhaps they shouldn't be criticised for failing to foresee the major
changes that took hold in society, but nonetheless the fact remains
that there was little appetite for forward-planning in soccer circles
at the time.

II. The GAA threat

So what exactly was the GAA doing in the 1950s that the League of
Ireland failed to do? A comparative study of the two organisations
is very revealing.

The GAA is an amateur organisation, but it had vision. It saw
itself as an integral part of Irish society, with a duty to work with

and among the people, and to give them pride in their national sport. Their HQ, Croke Park, was the jewel in their crown, and they understood from the outset its symbolic importance. As a result, they were always looking to improve and modernise it. In their Jubilee Year, 1934, for example, plans for a new double-deck stand (the Cusack Stand) as well as terracing on the Hill for 16,000 spectators were unveiled, 'as much for the public image of the Association as … for the morale of the rank-and-file members' wrote Marcus de Burca in his *History of the GAA*. 'The Cusack became, on its completion, at once a symbol of the new prosperity and permanence of the Association and solid proof of the leading position in Irish sport attained by the GAA.'

Part of the GAA's vision always included moving the stadium onto the next grand level. In 1948 there were plans for the venue's capacity to be increased to 100,000 people, but the dilemma was whether to accommodate the maximum number of spectators, or the maximum amount of seating. A record number attended the All Ireland football final that year between Cavan and Mayo, and it was noted by some that restricting the capacity of Croke Park to a 'mere' 100,000 would be a big disappointment to GAA fans: such confidence, such ambition! Contrast this with the 'vision' of the FAI in 1956 with regard to developing its centrepiece and international HQ: Dalymount Park. It was hoped to increase the ground by 1,000, with an extra room added beneath the stand for 'social purposes', and all to be ready for the much-anticipated clash with England in May of the following year. The plan was ruled out as no funds existed to meet the £30,000 project fee. At that same FAI Council meeting, Bohemians pointed out that since 1932 their club had spent £24,000 on Dalymount, yet had only received £10,000 in fees from the FAI. Shelbourne's John Traynor proposed that the Ireland–England game be moved to Lansdowne Road where, with a 52,000 capacity, they would net £7,000 more in gate income. Traynor fell ill during the meeting, however, and had to leave the room, whereupon the proposal to keep the game at the more restricted venue of Dalymount was voted on and passed.

While both soccer and GAA were thriving throughout the 1950s, there were already hints that the GAA would win the battle for people's hearts—and money. Long regarded as a 'country' sport, GAA now got a foothold in the urban stronghold of Dublin, and it wasn't about to cede the ground gained to the League of Ireland.

Kevin Heffernan, a man who played in and captained the Dublin teams of the 1950s and 1960s, winning an All-Ireland in 1963, and then managed the great side of the 1970s and created the legendary 'Heffo's Army', describes how the seeds were sown in the city:

> 'The fifties was a good period for Gaelic for Dublin, they had a team that somehow caught the imagination of the city—just as the teams of the seventies did—with the type of football that they played and the fact that they were nearly all St Vincent's and all that was new. That gave a major leg-up to Gaelic Football in the 1950s.'

In 1953 Dublin won the League title for the first time with fourteen St Vincent's players, and captured the Leinster title two years later to eventually set up their meeting with Kerry in a final that was attended by 87,000 people. Predating the Heffo's Army phenomenon by twenty years, the resurgent Dubs were generating increased success while also tapping into the market of country people who now lived in the capital.

Legendary RTÉ commentator Micheál O'Hehir wrote about that 1955 final in his autobiography:

> 'No final in modern times had such a build-up of excitement—and, indeed, tension. It was the ultimate 'country versus city' clash: Kerry, the traditionally strong football super-power . . . Dublin, the recently crowned National League winners . . . Dublin missed a lot of chances early on and by half time Kerry were two points ahead before a record crowd of 87,102 and they went four up soon after the resumption. There was only one goal in it—ironically scored by Dublin when Ollie Freaney's 14-yard free was booted straight through the packed goalmouth into the net—but it was too late to save the Dubs.'

Three years later though, the Dubs did manage to capture the All-Ireland by beating Derry in the final and they were finally able to lay the ghosts of 1942 to rest.

The Diamond Jubilee Year for the Association was in 1959, and despite packed crowds for its games and increased club numbers, the GAA was under no illusion about its success: it realised its current dominance of Irish sport could be reversed in a moment—indeed, the 1952 Annual report noted how emigration had killed off an entire parish team in one fell swoop. Forward motion and forward-thinking were pegged as the main priorities, thanks to the vision of General Secretary Paddy O'Keeffe, a man who had the remarkable distinction of being Secretary from 1929 until his death in 1964. 'The architect of the modern GAA', as he became known, was central in ensuring that the Association moved with the times, an action that left an important legacy: it ensured that Gaelic games remained at the heart of suburbanisation in the late 1960s and 1970s.

> 'Questions of championship and finance are important,' wrote O'Keeffe in his 1958 Annual Report. 'In numbers and club strength the Association continues to flourish despite the effects of emigration . . . and it is precisely because of its strength and prestige that we must be on our guard against the danger that always beset such organisations.'

As O'Keeffe was worrying about the future, the GAA was hitting peaks not previously seen: the 1955 All-Ireland between Dublin and Kerry drew a record crowd of 87,000, only bettered in 1960 by the largest-ever attendance of 90,000 for the match between Down and Kerry (and that figure was probably swelled by the fact that it was the first appearance of an Ulster county in the final and thus had a curiosity factor). Hurling and football reached peaks of attendances in the 1950s while the numbers of GAA clubs rose by 30%, from 2,226 in 1950 to 2,850 in 1960. In the Diamond Jubilee Year 2,833 clubs existed compared to 1,908 in their Golden Jubilee Year in 1934—an increase of 49%.

O'Keeffe's 'paranoia' and worrying was often derided by the GAA's detractors, but it would prove to be the quality that gave strength and endurance to the Association, especially in seeing it through difficult times in the 1960s. The GAA was not an organisation that was sitting on its hands, smiling smugly to itself at the full grounds. Instead it constantly wondered about what might lie around the corner; the FAI and League of Ireland were more concerned about next week's gate and paying wages. Is it any wonder, then, with the massive social changes about to occur in the 1960s, that it was the GAA that was best prepared and able to adapt?

III. European standards

The other obstacle that would soon trip up the League of Ireland was the matter of players' ability on the pitch. While domestic club rivalry and domestic domination was one thing, proving one's worth on a bigger stage was quite another. At this time, with the beginning of the European club competitions and a general raising of the bar all round, the standard of play in the League teams was brought into sharp focus.

Tommy Roe, Drums' striker at the time, summed up the differences:

'We played against Atlético Madrid once in the European Cup. Over in Atlético's ground. But they were laughing at our boots. And they were laughing at our stockings and our jerseys because we had woollen stockings that would see us through the whole season. We had the big studs that you would nail into the sole of your shoe. You know they thought that was hilarious, but there you are.'

International football was always there, on the periphery, but it would become increasingly important during the 1960s (in spite of attempts to clamp down on it), heralding one of the many changes that would challenge the League and threaten its existence. Ireland's track record internationally wasn't terribly inspiring. After a particularly galling defeat to Switzerland in 1948, 'Soccero', writing in *The Irish Press*, called on more League of Ireland players to be included in the International team so as to halt the side's decline:

'The time has arrived for our Association to look to League of Ireland clubs for players for their international matches . . . The

entire structure of our football should be examined . . . League of
Ireland clubs must not be nurseries for cross channel clubs . . . The
Association and clubs exist on public support. That will not be
forthcoming unless attractive fare is provided.'

The League's participation was increased, and by 1956 achieved
its greatest heights when seven League players started against the
reigning World Champions, West Germany. The winners of the
World Cup two years previously, the West German team had
arrived in Dublin just days before the November game and
without their most experienced player, inside-left Fritz Walter,
who was not in the squad due to a family illness. While this gave
some hope to the Irish squad, the game would in fact be a
watershed for Irish soccer. Before a capacity crowd of 45,000, the
Irish team and its seven League of Ireland players conjured up a
magical 3-0 victory. The victory cannot be underestimated: this
was a win over the World Champions, in Dalymount, by a team
made up of mostly local players, all of whom were known to their
supporters, or who worked down the road from them. Irish
football was on top of the world—but come Monday morning,
Gerry Mackey was back in the petrol company office, clerk Jimmy
McCann was in the stockbroker's office, Ronnie Nolan was in the
glass bottle factory, while plasterer Alan Kelly was working on a
school building scheme. And all less than forty-eight hours after
humbling the reigning World Champions.

The sense of Ireland having arrived on the international sports
stage was cemented when just a few weeks later Ronnie Delaney
captured gold at the Melbourne Olympics, becoming the first
Irishman to win gold since Bob Tisdall in 1932. Surely now,
anything was possible for Irish sport? Couldn't soccer take the
great leap into the big time?

Prior to this, inter-League matches were the best gauge of how
good Irish players really were, and although they were beaten by
their English counterparts more often than not, the occasional win
did occur and victories over the Welsh, Scottish and Northern Irish
were not so infrequent. Now, it was how clubs fared in Europe that
was the real eye-opener. As Brian Kerr says, our ways, which were

close to those of the British teams, were not going to be effective against European teams. Indeed, for the first few years English clubs abstained from the competitions, believing they had nothing to prove on the Continent. The League of Ireland was also slowly realising its folly, and its close connection to English soccer was about to show up its failings as well.

In 1957 Shamrock Rovers were set to be the League of Ireland's first ever representatives in European club competition, and coincidentally were drawn against Manchester Utd. Predictably enough, Rovers were outclassed 6-0 in the first leg, but did make a better showing of themselves in the second by managing to score two goals against Man Utd's three. It would be another six years, however, before a League of Ireland side would win over two legs in European competition—when Drumcondra achieved two notable feats in the Fairs Cup. They won 4-1 at home, beating an Odense Select xi, and then held on to record a 4-2 victory away to become the first Irish side to win a European leg. Their victory at home was also the first time an Irish side had won a game in Europe.

The Irish crowds had always been enthralled by their club's League campaigns, but now defeat to European teams planted a seed of doubt. Fans and players suddenly realised that Irish clubs were not as good as they had thought, or hoped, and when the likes of Nice or Zurich were in town to play, they were treated to a sample of the higher level of football that was being played elsewhere. This led fans to look on their own domestic League with fresh eyes, and to question its value and standing. Questioning led to doubt and doubt to skepticism, with the inevitable consequence that fans began to turn away from their own League and clubs.

Football, in fact, mirrored much of Irish society in its dependence on England. De Valera's isolationist policy of the 1950s kept Ireland away from European influences and its post-war social, political and economic developments, as a result of which Irish society—and Irish soccer—fell even deeper into the embrace of its English neighbours. Cut off and on the periphery of Europe, Ireland had only one country to look to, and it wasn't the most forward-thinking country in Europe—not by a long shot. Even in football terms, English soccer was light years behind what Europe was able to do and how it was thinking about the game. England and Ireland languished in Europe's wake, although, unlike England, Ireland was unable to catch up with European football thinking until the 1990s, when Irish under-age teams came to dominate the world and European stages under the guidance of Brian Kerr.

Back in the 1950s, when the possibility of learning from its European counterparts was most open and the game was at its zenith, the Irish League's closeness to the English culture and game would be paid for dearly. Given the popularity of League football domestically and the fact that keeping fans *away* from the games was a concern, the League of Ireland's entry into Europe should have marked a watershed, a point when the domestic game was vastly improved. At that stage, proper training and coaching methods could have been imported from across Europe, as happened in similar-sized countries on the Continent. Unfortunately for Irish football, by allowing itself to be dominated by the English game and allowing a stultifying culture to pervade its management structures, no ground was gained at this critical juncture.

IV. Archbishop McQuaid and the visit of Yugoslavia
Before Irish football could freely engage on an international level, there were some obstacles to be overcome first: in 1955, one of those obstacles was the Church. The Church–State relationship in Ireland at this time has been well-documented, and it is no secret that the Catholic clergy had a stranglehold on most institutions. The GAA was an obvious bedfellow and as such was subject to various dicta, whereby 'Faith of our Fathers' had to be sung before major games, captains kissed the Bishop's ring before an All-Ireland and the throw-in was performed by religious dignitaries. (These practices weren't scrapped until 1979.) Sport was a direct link with the people, and the Church wanted to ensure it remained in the loop.

The Church wasn't so interested in soccer, but that was about to change. In 1955, Church and soccer clashed in a head-to-head. This was to be one of the few occasions when the two mixed, but was one in which fans came to express their true faith: to Irish soccer. The lightning rod in this case was an international match between Ireland and Yugoslavia, scheduled for 19 October 1955, in Dublin. The enigmatic and controversial conservative Archbishop of Dublin, John Charles McQuaid, endeavoured to prevent the match from going ahead on the basis that Catholics were being persecuted under the Yugoslav regime of Tito.

One week before the match, on the Wednesday, there was no sign of any problems: the papers were reporting that 'tickets were selling well' and that the President would be in attendance. By Monday 17 October, all hell had broken loose and the controversy over the game even featured on the front page of *The Irish Times*, which reported: 'FAI refuse to cancel game.'

'In spite of the request and the representations made by the Department of Justice, the Football Association of Ireland has decided that the match will be played on Wednesday at Dalymount Park, Dublin. Transport FC, however, has withdrawn its support and has announced that its members will not attend a dinner to which the Yugo-Slavs had been invited on Wednesday evening. The President, Mr O'Kelly, will not attend the game. The No. 1 Army band, which had been engaged to play, has been withdrawn.'

It emerged that opposition had arisen just seven days before the game:

'Difficulties about the Yugoslav team arose when an official of the Department of Justice telephoned the association and asked if it was aware that permission was necessary to bring the team to Ireland. Mr [Joe] Wickham [FAI Secretary] said he told the official that his association had never had to ask for such permission before and pointed out that during the past 20 years, visiting teams had always made their own arrangements.'

McQuaid's influence was obvious. On the Friday his Chancellor, Fr O'Regan, rang Joe Wickham to tell him that the Archbishop 'had heard with regret that the match had been arranged . . . that the association had not had the courtesy to obtain the views of the Archbishop on the proposed game as it had done when the Yugoslavs had wanted a game in Dublin in 1952.' To which Wickham replied 'that no discourtesy had been intended' and added that 'in 1952 the Archbishop, when approached, had said that he was not interested but suggested that if the association could get out of it discreetly, the match should be called off.'

Suddenly a storm of controversy engulfed the game. It was one of the few occasions when a football story made it from the sports pages onto the front pages of the Irish newspapers. And the opposition to the game was, it seemed, gathering pace. The Guild of Regnum Christi and the Knights of Columbanus both voiced protests, the Catholic Association for International Relations wrote of its unhappiness at the Yugoslavs' visit, stating: 'We are unhappy about it because we fear that you may think from the reception you receive as footballers that this Christian country condones the unjust treatment of Cardinal Stepinac, the Rt. Rev Mgr Cule, Bishop of Mostar and so many others of which the present Government of your country has been guilty.'

Most notable, however, was the personal decision of radio commentator Philip Greene not to take part in the game if Radio Éireann decided to broadcast it. However, Fred Cogley, former head of sport in RTÉ, says it wasn't a political decision by Greene:

'Phil wasn't a political person at all and it would have been done out of conviction. At the time that is what he felt and it was his personal belief and it wasn't one that was greeted with a great amount of joy from the broadcasters or the supporting people. But that was Phil, he wouldn't have thought, "Well, if I do this will I get into trouble with whoever". He did it just because he felt it was the right thing to do.'

The following day Radio Éireann announced it would not be broadcasting the match. The story continued on the front pages of the papers for the second day running, leading with RTÉ's decision, while the Yugoslav team arrived into Dublin, unaware of the brewing storm. The Irish greeting party and the security arrangements were somewhat comical though: it seemed as if the

State was waiting for Communist torturers to step off the planes with the heads of Yugoslav Catholics in their hands. 'Uniformed civic guards and plain-clothes detectives were on duty at the airport when the party arrived, but no members of the general public were present.' It seemed the gardaí who took up vantage points on the airport balcony and along the tarmac wouldn't have to hold bloodthirsty Irish Catholics at bay after all.

The response from the Yugoslav ambassador in London was predictably strident and hit the nail on the head in targeting McQuaid:

> 'It is regrettable that the Archbishop of the Catholic Church in Dublin has used the friendly meeting between the football representations of Yugoslavia and the Republic of Ireland as an occasion for a campaign of intolerance . . . The campaign of intolerance is particularly regrettable as it comes at a time when the overcoming of racial, ideological and religious prejudices in international relations gives rise to the entire world to the spirit of optimism and hope for a long period of peace.'

'Letters to the Editor' from the general public voicing opposition to the game were filling up the pages of the newspapers, and one could easily have thought that Dublin was a city stringently opposed to the Yugoslavs' presence. As match day approached, there was a lot of tension and expectation in the air as people wondered if the footballing public would indeed heed McQuaid's calls to stay away from the match. Dublin Bus denied reports that it was cancelling its bus specials from O'Connell Street, while Joe Wickham reported that tickets were selling briskly. Meanwhile, the Yugoslav team was being accompanied by detectives to and from their base at the Gresham Hotel to training at Dalymount Park, while gardaí were also posted on duty both inside and outside the ground.

Wednesday 19 October 1955 dawned and the whole country knew that Ireland were playing Yugoslavia in an international soccer friendly in Dublin that evening. Except Radio Éireann that is, which acted as if no event were happening at Dalymount Park; only its preferred broadcasts of 'Wild Week' and 'It's our country' were on offer for the discerning wireless listener. People knew of the Church's opposition to the game and that a request had been made to the public to stay away. As kick-off approached the question on everyone's lips was: would the Irish soccer public obey their religious leaders? And would there be trouble with protesters outside the ground?

Despite the week-long hype, there was just one Legion of Mary protester reported to be on duty outside the ground, holding a solitary vigil. More notably, 21,399 fans filed past his lonely picket, defying Archbishop McQuaid's express wishes. While not a full house by any stretch of the imagination, the 22,000 or so who did turn up represented a healthy attendance figure for an international friendly-double, a figure that could normally be expected for the visit of England; an average attendance would probably be about 32,000. The only hiccup on the day occurred when the playing of the National Anthems had to be delayed when it was noticed that the Yugoslav flag had been raised upside-down. The situation was remedied by a Yugoslav official.

For the 22,000 spectators, they watched an Irish side outclassed and beaten 4-1, but the atmosphere suggested this was more than just a soccer match and that their presence said more about their attitude to the Church and sport than anything ever had before then. Walking out onto the pitch to meet the teams—a duty normally out carried by President O'Kelly—Oscar Traynor, TD and FAI President, received an especially wry cheer from the crowd. Soccer people just weren't used to Church interference—that was what the GAA was there for—and the week of controversy and hype surrounding the game was a novel distraction from the real matter at hand: improving the lot of the Irish soccer team.

The whole fiasco said more about Archbishop McQuaid's inflated sense of power and influence: he believed himself capable of cancelling an Irish soccer international because he had not been consulted. For the last time that week, the match made the front pages and all that could be headlined was: 'Crowd of 21,400 sees Yugoslavia beat Irish team'. The tone of the crowd was noted though and with typical dry Dublin wit it was recorded that there were 'prolonged cheers for the blue-clad Yugoslav eleven as they followed the Irish team on to the field.' But the biggest cheer of the night came at the final whistle: despite the comprehensive defeat they had just dished out, the Yugoslavs got a standing ovation from the crowd. As the teams had cleared the pitch and the fans were starting to make their own way home, the FAI officials were spotted still struggling to take down the Yugoslav flag, which had wrapped itself tightly around the flagpost. It seemed the controversy—and the Yugoslavs— just didn't want to go away.

The build-up to the Ireland–Yugoslavia game was unlike anything witnessed before in soccer circles, with what must have seemed an unwarranted and unwelcome intrusion by the Church and State into their affairs. Curiously, just nine days before the Yugoslav game, Pope Pius XII gave an important speech on sport and its role in society to 100,000 Italians in Rome. He warned of the 'over cultivation of technique' which destroyed Christian spirit and called for a return to the purity of sport, which had nothing to do with commercialism and the exaggerated cult of stardom. The care of the body, he told his flock, was not an end in itself but a means of protecting the soul, 'limits should be set on the right to use one's body' he warned, advising against the use of 'strong stimulants'. Whether it was the Pope's comments that thrust the sporting sphere into the foreground for McQuaid we may never know, but it was clear from the Pope's comments that the Church was becoming increasingly aware of the role sport was playing in people's lives—and how better to influence the masses than through their opiate of choice?

The match has long since entered Dublin folklore, seen as the night the Dublin working-class gave a two-fingered salute to Archbishop McQuaid, but the reality is probably a little different. Far from being political activists striking a blow, those 22,000 people were football fans first and foremost: they were just going to a game. Soccer may have made it to the front page, but for the fans it was on the sports pages where they preferred to have it and by the weekend there were league games to be fought and the normal visits to Milltown and Tolka to be made. Nonetheless, it did signal an era of change, which lay just around the corner.

V. The threat of television

Television. Who could have foreseen or imagined the effect this little set-top box would have upon our lives, our society, our habits and, most damagingly, on our live sports viewing. It was the vanguard of the modern world, laying waste to received wisdom and tradition and ushering in a brave new world.

In terms of media, radio was first to affect sport and its coverage. While radio had nothing like the impact TV would have, how sports organisations dealt with it and how Radio Éireann viewed sport in its early days is instructive and revealing for our look at the 1960s, when things really started to change. Despite being the first station in Europe to broadcast a field game when it covered the All-Ireland hurling semi-final between Galway and Kilkenny in 1926, Radio Éireann's attitude to sport in Ireland was at best snobbish, at worst downright hostile. 'The toy department' is how Fred Cogley, Head of Sport with RTÉ from the 1970s to the 1990s, said they were often described by others in the station, and yet while sneered at from within their own ranks, it was the sports programmes—particularly 'Soccer Survey'—that would gain the most interest and, some would say, provide the best service for the community.

> 'Certainly in broadcasting it was way down the priority list,' says Cogley. 'Drama and documentaries and all of that, they all ranked up there. And I would attend these idiotic production meetings with all the heads of the departments and it was totally . . . it was like slogging bricks about . . . are we going to get the big match on Sunday? Stuff like that. The toy department comments drove Micheál O'Hehir mad and even though Milltown or Tolka were jammed with people, that wouldn't have made any impression on our superiors.'

But the effect of radio was bigger than people thought. Radio Éireann's budget had quadrupled in the 1940s and active attempts were being made to create new sports, children's and music programmes. 'Radio in some ways became more interactive and controversial in the 1950s and did contribute to a liberalisation of public discourse,' argues historian Diarmaid Ferriter, whose

Transformation of Modern Ireland is a seminal account of Ireland in the twentieth century. Noel O'Reilly, former Assistant Manager on the International team and a man who grew up loving the League of Ireland recalls the effect of radio:

'I remember as a young lad supporting Rovers. I used to tune into 'Soccer Survey' with Tony Sheehan every Sunday evening after the half-six news and then Philip Greene would come on and he would always say, "Well my game today was at . . ." And at the end of it they gave the results—but they gave the reserve results as well, you see, but I didn't know what the word reserve meant. I knew Shamrock Rovers and Drums and Bohs had the amateurs but they all had reserves as well, you see—except I didn't know the word and the way they used to be called out, to me it was as though they were saying, "Shamrock Rovers deserves 2. Shelbourne deserves 1". This was me, just a kid growing up in Dublin, thinking the reserves was deserves! Years and years later I remember meeting Tony Sheehan and telling him that story and he nearly broke his heart laughing. Then I got to know Philip Greene and they were all heroes of mine from the wireless. They were on the wireless—they weren't on the radio, they were on the wireless. You had to tune them in and they took batteries and they were electrical. When the first of those other things came like transistors, people started walking around listening to matches. You would be at a match and that became a great thing of the day that if you went to Milltown, people would be listening to other matches.'

Aside from 'Soccer Survey', sports fans also had the opportunity to hear GAA matches, athletics, rugby or motor racing on Saturday and Sunday afternoons, while 'GAA Sports Results' with Seán Óg Ó Ceallacháin found its place on a Sunday night and, more than fifty years later, is still going strong. But sport on the radio wasn't just confined to Friday nights. 'Sports Stadium', presented by Eamonn Andrews, began in 1950 and covered weekend events. Following on from all the sporting action over the weekend came a Monday morning, American-style magazine sports programme, presented by Micheál O'Hehir and imaginatively titled 'The Vaseline Hair Tonic Programme'; and they say advertisers and sponsors intrude too much on today's media.

For Fred Cogley, it was an exciting time to be involved:

'There wasn't much of anything in fairness up to that. The budget that Radio Éireann used to have in totality was a pittance. They didn't broadcast in the morning, sometimes they only came on at one o'clock in the afternoon for about two or three hours and then they would close down and come on again at about five o'clock and go on until about half eleven. It was a part-time service and it only began to expand really in those days, about 1953/4, when Philip Greene was appointed as the first sports officer. Not sports editor mind you, but sports officer, and he had a budget of fourpence ha'penny. That was a tiny budget and he tried to expand the commentary service.

There were very few live reports at that time. Then 'Junior Sports Magazine' came on the air. This was developed by Harry Collier, scripted by Fred Cogley and presented by Liam O'Neill as a magazine for young sports people and it covered soccer as well. It was originally on a Thursday at half-past five. It was then moved to Saturday and it became a mini sports report. An imitation. And for the first time we were taking in reports from the venues and sometimes we recorded them on the rooftops on Henry Street, pretending we were in Cork and so on to give it a bit of atmosphere. Although anyone perceptive who had a good radio would have heard in the background of our so-called reports from Limerick chants of the traders coming up from Moore Street!

Even though 'Soccer Survey' and our soccer coverage were very popular and even though Phil [Greene] was a soccer commentator and his background would have been soccer there was always an antipathy towards them and the GAA would get preference. In the very early days, in the late 1930s, the GAA even insisted on having an input into who would actually do their commentaries on matches. And the broadcasting officers were kind of aware that they didn't want to upset the GAA. Although the soccer people wanted the same sort of attention . . . they never got the same sort of sympathetic hearing that the GAA got. I suppose because, largely, Radio Éireann in those days was peopled more by civil servants who were assigned to keep that going and behave themselves and they would have been largely rural people who had an interest in GAA and wouldn't have been that interested in soccer.

Mick O'Hehir, a GAA commentator, was appointed as sports

officer and he was perceived by the soccer authorities as having a leaning towards the GAA. I think that was more in the perception than in reality because essentially he was a journalist, first and foremost, and he knew the values of things and he would have been conscious not to go out of his way to stand on soccer's toes. Nonetheless, he was seen to be of the GAA and it came into focus in those early days, especially when the final of the National League between someone like Kerry and Donegal was listed and scheduled to take place on the same day as the FAI Cup Final. And that was a problem straight away.

On this occasion it was decided by the broadcaster, as had been the case previously, that the match between Shamrock Rovers and Cork would be broadcast on the Dublin/Cork wavelengths and the Kerry/Donegal match would be broadcast on the Athlone wavelengths. That way they would hit their respective audiences. But the Athlone wavelength was perceived as being the national one and the FAI said "we want to be broadcast on the national air as ours is the FAI Cup Final and this is the equivalent to the All-Ireland". So there was this clash and there were meetings going backwards and forwards. Eamonn Andrews was Chairman of the Authority at the time and Eamonn and Micheál O'Hehir had a meeting and said maybe we can resolve this. Micheál said maybe because I am being seen as having an axe to grind maybe you will go and meet the FAI. So Mick went to the GAA and said would you switch your time for your National League final until two o'clock and we will get the soccer people to switch their time to four o'clock so we can have both matches on the national wavelength. The GAA said sure, Eamonn Andrews went to the soccer people and they said "we begin our match at 3.00pm because that is the way it has always been" and so there was a stalemate.'

Far from helping their own causes, the FAI and the GAA were fearful that any coverage of their games would result in a drop-off in attendances, but, if anything, interest in the games grew, with people crowding around the wireless set to hear Tony Sheehan give out the scores from the rest of the Sunday afternoon League of Ireland fixtures. Did Rovers manage to beat Cork today? Would Drums come out on top after their visit to Sligo? Only 'Soccer Survey' could let the fans know that evening. While just back from seeing their own game live, they would know shortly afterwards where it would place their team with the rest of the results.

In Dublin City Centre, at O'Connell Bridge, at 7.00pm *The Independent* would post up in its window the results from all the games, and there would be a throng of up to 1,000 people waiting to read them.

'Traditionally the Sunday evening entertainment in Dublin was that everybody went to the cinema,' remembers Peter Byrne, former *Irish Times* soccer writer. 'Everybody, especially young people and courting couples, went to the cinema. There was no such thing as going to the pub and you had to book your seat by Thursday or Friday, you couldn't just go up and pay—you booked your seat. You could have what was called a regular permanency, say the same seats in the Royal or the Metro or the Capitol and you had the same seats but you had to book those by Thursday at the latest. There was also a tribe of black-market tickets as the touts would be going up and down flogging tickets at quarter to eight on Sunday. Money was very scarce at that stage but this all fitted into why people's values were so simple. And into all of this fitted football. It was a huge thing and you would have this huge throng of people standing outside what is now O'Connell Bridge House looking in the window, giving people the first inkling people had of who had won the matches down the country. So that was then a subject of conversation, you met people going to the pictures and they would say, "did you hear Bohs won in Cork today?"'

The radio had played a central role in Irish family and social life, but now it was challenged by an altogether more seductive medium. 'TV. The entertainment you can pluck out of the air!' trilled *The Irish Times'* headline in 1955, going on to marvel at this new contraption that was now available (expensive though it was):

'Seeing is believing. Under the compelling influence of that ancient truth the world is progressively turning its back on sound radio, joyfully to embrace the new and more convincing wonders of television. Soon, scarcely half a century since it came to revolutionise the life of man, wireless broadcasting, as we know it, will become obsolete. What of Ireland in this vital departure from the settled ways of communication and entertainment? What shape of things to come does the gleaming TV crystal hold for this country?'

By the late 1950s, 40% of the population in the Irish Republic could receive British TV broadcasts. 'There were warnings about the potential for decadence and moral corruption in television content, though politicians became more concerned with the idea that they could be called to account by truculent interviewers,' says historian Diarmaid Ferriter.

The shape of things to come, as *The Irish Times* had asked, was clear: 4,000 TV sets had already been sold in the Republic of Ireland, and 190 were going out of shops every week, with sets ranging from 60–70 guineas and the aerial an extra £20. While still out of most workers' reach, TV was going to become cheaper over the years and the influence and intrusion of cross-channel television was the talk of the country.

'What of those fireside evenings?' *The Irish Times* asked, rather quaintly. While de Valera's attempts at spinning a thatched cottage, self-contained, pure isle image of Ireland were failing, there were still some, it appears, who saw TV's arrival as a further step down the road of ruination of Dev's dream. Despite their fears, others claimed that TV was in fact bringing families closer together:

'Seldom now does father swallow down his tea,' wrote *The Irish Times*, 'and set off for the local or for a rendezvous with his pals at the club. Instead he remains at home and to a large extent the old form of family life has returned, bringing back the atmosphere of the days when many nights were spent at home.'

Here, in 1955, was the clearest sign yet of what lay ahead for the League of Ireland. In black-and-white print, commentators were writing how TV was making people—especially men—stay at home. While many were espousing the benefits to be had from this ('there is now no need to endure the ordeal of pushing and shoving in the arena'), in reality, club owners and sports officials could only but be scared for a future society based on the family all sitting around the TV: 'All that is needed is to bag the best easy chair in the room and the contest can be followed much more closely than would be possible from most parts of the modern stadium.'

Ask a random selection of people why they think the League of Ireland crowds declined and most, if not all, will point to the arrival of TV as the bell tolling doom. 'No one wanted to come anymore when they could watch football on the TV', 'It was 'Match of the Day' that done it', 'You could go to the pub and watch it in comfort' are all common accusations. Much like as was happening in America and Britain, in the 1950s people were predicting that Irish families would be sitting in front of the telly with their dinners on their laps. But still, crucially, the League of Ireland did not respond. Mesmerised by the clicks from the turnstiles, it turned a blind eye to the obvious: in future, the League would have to work to earn its fans' support.

Hindsight is a wonderful thing, of course. Back then, in the late 1950s, looking forward to a new decade, none of those who ran or attended games could have imagined that the League would begin to die away very soon after. They simply wouldn't have believed it. They thought the bubble could never burst. They were wrong. They might argue ignorance or innocence, but there were signs that things were not right, such as the clubs' inattention to the fans, the fact that spectators' comfort and safety were not of paramount concern and the arrival of European and English teams on the scene. De Valera's Ireland was a sealed box, but the modern world was encroaching on all sides, and although many failed to see it, Irish people would very soon be seduced by what the wider world had to offer. The greatest irony, of course, was that it was the League's immense popularity that marked the beginning of the souring of things for Irish soccer, but its board, basking in the warmth of success, was too cosy to notice. Before they realised it, 'next Sunday's game' soon became the 1960s, and what has been termed the 'Best of Decades' would turn out to be the beginning of the end for the League of Ireland. The heyday was going. League of Ireland clubs and officials were about to have a rude awakening.

Part Two

The 1960s: A changing Ireland and the beginning
of the end

'I would love if somebody said to me, "What would you like to do? Would you like to win the Nobel Prize for Literature or score three goals against Shamrock Rovers?" I would go for the hat-trick against Rovers any day of the week.'

I. 'They never saw the day'

'I must admit that sometimes when I think of television and radio and their immense power, I feel somewhat afraid. Like atomic energy, it can be used for incalculable good but it can also do irreparable harm. Never before was there in the hands of men an instrument so powerful to influence the thoughts and actions of the multitude . . . it can build up the character of the whole people inducing sturdiness and vigour and confidence. On the other hand it can lead through demoralisation to decadence and disillusion. Sometimes one hears that one must give the people what they want. And the competition is unfortunately in the wrong direction so standards become lower and lower.'

These were the words of Éamon de Valera, President of Ireland, upon the opening of Telefís Éireann on New Year's Eve, 31 December 1961. Snow was falling and piling up in drifts around the transmitter station on bleak Kippure Mountain in Co. Wicklow, while families gathered around their TV sets to hear the President's portentous words. In time his words would prove to bear much truth. But then, on New Year's Eve 1961, there was only excitement in the air as Ireland entered a new era.

As much as anything, TV would draw a dividing line between the new, younger generation of Irish people and the old, conservative order; a barrier of understanding was about to separate the new from the old. In this march ever onwards, TV was the medium to communicate a growing liberalism. While the 1960s in Ireland weren't as glamorous as in London or New York, Ireland too was affected by the new ideas, the new feeling of confidence and looking outward. More and more people were standing up and asking, 'Why?' Those in power wondered, 'Why should we?'

The de Valera age was coming to an end, too. Taoiseach Seán Lemass had taken the reigns. Although he was less conservative in some ways, Eamonn Andrews, then Chairman of the RTÉ Authority, found he had a double-edged approach to television: while he seemed to believe it should 'be an arm of government', he could just as soon distance himself and accuse programme-makers of being responsible for the breakdown of moral fibre.

'We were at once the destroyers of the national heritage, the national music, literature, sport, culture, the enemy of the Churches, the breaker of families, the weakeners of morals, the money-grabbers, who buy Mickey Mouse instead of Finn McCool, and Rambo—had he then existed—instead of Cú Chulainn,' Andrews once wrote.

The focus of much of this ire was 'The Late, Late Show', especially after the infamous 'Bishop and the Nightie' affair in February 1966, when a woman was asked if she could remember what colour nightdress she had worn on her wedding night, to which she replied that she 'didn't wear any nightie at all'. All of a sudden the authorities were up in arms, with Bishop Thomas Ryan of Clonfert in apoplexy and the Loughrea Town Commissioners, the Mayo County Board of the GAA and the Meath Committee of Vocational Education all denouncing the 'Late Late' as 'a dirty programme that should be abolished altogether'.

If that wasn't bad enough, the following month the programme provoked another furore when Brian Trevaskis, a student at Trinity College, called Bishop Michael Browne of Galway 'a moron' because of the money being spent on extravagances, like the new cathedral in Galway, while unmarried mothers were being shunned and treated as outcasts in society. Trevaskis was hauled back the following week to apologise, but compounded the insult by enquiring 'whether the bishop of Galway knows the meaning of the word *moron*? I doubt very much whether he knows the meaning of the word *Christianity*.'

The response was predictable enough: 'If the programme is to be allowed to develop along the lines on which it is moving in recent times, it would be better if it were taken off the air,' thundered Joe Brennan, Minister for Posts and Telegraphs. Eamonn Andrews defended the programme's freedom of expression and the programme survived, but Andrews quit as Chairman of the RTÉ Authority little over a fortnight later. He explained his resignation in a letter to Lemass:

> 'I am afraid the Authority as now constituted is too susceptible to outside pressures. I have tried to compromise to the point beyond which honesty will not permit me to go.'

Television—and the 'Late, Late' in particular—would radically challenge and change traditional perceptions of authority. The Irish nation had long been in thrall to the Catholic orders, who governed schools, churches, hospitals and communities with a rod of iron. Now, however, the emphasis was slowly shifting. Instead of dealing in orders and obedience, public figures were finding that they needed to convince, persuade, prove, argue—and they had to be entertaining and charismatic as they did so.

> 'I actually remember the first thing I ever saw on television was Cassius Clay when he had beaten Sonny Liston, and turning on the television and there was this huge black man shouting, "I am going to be the king of the world. I am the greatest!" And I was like, f**k, you know, this is what television is like and it was *Wow!* this is unbelievable.'

This was writer Fintan O'Toole's first memories of the box as a child.

> 'And you see, what was on Irish television was 'Champion, the Wonder Horse', 'Lassie', 'Matt Dillon'—it was entirely American—

plus a couple of news programmes and 'The Late, Late Show' and a few sort of add-ons, but you suddenly had direct access to American popular culture. In a way that, certainly as a child, then became your culture. It was much more powerful than Bible stories and traditional music and the Clancy Brothers and all that, you know. And the way it operated seemed at first kind of fairly safe, but gradually as it got going it began to change the nature of public authority. Previously, people who were in charge were way up there and they were entitled to enormous respect because of who they were, particularly the Church, because that was the big power. I remember John Charles McQuaid, who was the Archbishop of Dublin, coming to our parish to conduct a funeral mass for the parish priest. The sense of authority he held meant his visit was much more like the king or the queen arriving. Within a couple of years, however, bishops were going on 'The Late, Late Show' and you had to sing a song and you had to entertain people and you had to sort of earn your respect by being likeable in some way. They sent out Bishop [Eamonn] Casey for example and he was great and people loved him and it worked out fantastically well, but over time of course what that does is it shifts the nature of authority so now you have to be charismatic, you have to be kind of, tell a joke and sing the 'Rose of Tralee' and enter into that sort of world, which they never had to do before.'

This was an era when there was a shift from the grander, mass participation, communal event to the smaller, more private one that television could so intimately provide. It was a time when, for example, there was a distinct shift away from the dance halls to the lounge bar:

'People were going to grotty, dirty, filthy ballrooms around the country with no amenities at all and, by and large, listening to fairly indifferent musicians banging out their few chords.

The ballroom people were so short-sighted that they didn't realise they would have to improve their surroundings . . . people got a bit more sophisticated and time caught up with the ballroom owners.'

Thus did Gay Byrne describe the cultural shift away from the dance halls, but he could just as easily have been writing the epitaph of League of Ireland football. In exactly the same way, football fans were deciding against the grotty terraces and choosing instead to enjoy their football in the comfort of their own homes, with only the TV to shout at.

The League of Ireland may have been slow to comprehend the extent of the problem, but it was no longer just pitted against the GAA in the fight for players and spectators, now it had to face the Goliath of televised sports events, especially English soccer. The BBC began its first broadcast of 'Match of the Day' in 1964, while ITV kicked off its Sunday afternoon live match coverage in 1968, and it is safe to say that no two programmes (prior to the arrival of Sky Sports) have had such a detrimental effect on Irish sport. Before this, English footballing stars, such as Stanley Matthews and Wilf Mannion, were names spoken in reverential tones. *Imagine* was the watch word: imagine seeing them play. Imagine! Although the FA Cup final was broadcast live every year by the BBC and many stars came over for special, one-off appearances in the League of Ireland, the chance to see these footballing heroes play in the English Division One was something beyond fans' wildest dreams. Instead, they had to content themselves with accessible heroes: the Paddy Coads, the Liam Tuohys and the Bunny Fullams. From 1964, all that would change as the centre of attention shifted from down the road to across the water, via the BBC and ITV.

The bottomline was that English football was just so damn seductive. This was the decade of cool, and that notion now embraced football, too. George Best, Bobby Charlton and Denis Law at Manchester Utd, under Matt Busby, brought 'cool' to the game. Football was suddenly sexy, and everyone wanted a piece of this dashing squad. Ireland had always had a strong connection to Old Trafford, dating back to Jackie Carey and Liam Whelan, and this new, brash United team, which was picking up FA Cups and League Championships, was revered. These outstanding players not only dominated the English stage but also the European one, and they were capturing not only the fans' imagination but also a wider popularity. George Best was being proclaimed as 'the fifth Beatle' and his scintillating skill and absolute dominance of the game was to impact on Irish soccer fans in more ways than one. In the 1960s, for the first time, Irish fans could see Manchester Utd's exploits on TV every week. Having been reared on a restricted diet of Drums–Rovers, fans could now only marvel at what they had been missing all this time, for here was one of the greatest teams and the greatest players of all time coming into Irish homes on a weekly basis, with skills unsurpassed and unmatched.

By 1966 the majority of Irish homes had TV sets (in fact, a 1967 survey showed that 80% of urban households owned TV sets, but in parts of rural Ireland this figure was as a low as 25%; by 1978, 83% homes had sets—a figure that rose to 92% in Dublin). Alongside the English League, now, for the first time, the 1966 World Cup was being held in England. The world of Brazil, Pelé and Rivelino was revealed in gleaming technicolor. In this glorious period, which bred some of the best players ever to play football, the fever pitch that was building in Britain found its way into Irish homes. It was ironic: on the one hand, the country was celebrating the fiftieth anniversary of the Easter Rising with full military pageantry, on the other hand, we were cheering on the English soccer heroes of Bobby Charlton, Bobby Moore and Geoff Hurst. It was a breathtaking time, and Irish fans were entranced.

So what of League of Ireland fixtures and players: what hope did they have in the face of such brilliance? A coincidence of factors in the 1960s teamed up against the League of Ireland, and they were factors no one could easily have fought: the emergence of George Best, one of the greatest footballers of all time; the flamboyant, entertaining and successful Celtic and Man Utd teams who not only conquered Scotland and England respectively but also conquered Europe for the first time; and England's hosting and winning of the World Cup in 1966.

While we may choose to sweep the actual event of the 1966 World Cup under the carpet—preferring to pretend that England never actually won the Jules Rimet trophy—culturally, it was an event that would help to shape Ireland's fascination with football in England and thus contribute to the decline of the League of Ireland. It cemented the place of soccer in kids' imaginations, but it wasn't the soccer of local heroes. When the boys kicking a ball around the streets dreamed of being footballers, it was the teams of England, Brazil and Italy they were picturing—not Dalyer, not Tolka, not Ireland at all, in fact. Although, taken altogether, it wasn't a death knell for soccer in Ireland. While it did draw fans away and highlight the gaps in the home game, it also fostered a desire to play football, and that meant an influx into clubs and onto pitches. As Con Houlihan described it:

'The World Cup Final tournament of 1966 was, of course, the great watershed; it can be seen now as a fieldmark in the cultural history of this island. Even if the Pope of Rome himself had come over to preach about the evils of soccer, he would have been as helpless as Alan Dukes holding out that famous fork. Clubs sprang up like daisies in a moist May—and seemingly the country is none the worse for the revolution.'

Fintan O'Toole, author and *Irish Times* columnist, remembers it as an influential moment in his childhood:

'I remember deciding to support the Soviet Union in it because the Christian Brothers had told us that if they lost, they were going to be tortured and sent to the saltmines—there was all this big propaganda stuff. So I thought, "these poor guys" you know and I remember being devastated when the Soviet Union were knocked out. It was only a game, but these guys are going to be killed, I thought!'

The Soviet players may not have been killed, but the Christian Brothers' exaggeration did sum up one unchanging attitude: an abhorrence, among GAA fanatics, of anything other than Gaelic games. But for the kids growing up watching colour TV and seeing English soccer and World Cups, this was a world fast moving beyond the narrow confines of the Christian Brothers' teaching. It was, in a sense, to determine a kind of Irishness that wasn't willing to be a slave to Irish 'gaeldom', an Irishness that was looking beyond this shore. In his book *The Politburo has decided that you are unwell*, writer John Waters remembers it like this:

'Like boys all around who played in car parks and imagined themselves not at Milltown but at Wembley, we played at Hackers Lane and imagined ourselves in Rio or Mexico City . . . The life of Hackers Lane coincided roughly with the interregnum between the World Cups of 1966 and 1970, and then it died away as we became more interested in other things.'

II. The GAA and long-term planning

The impact of television and 'cool English culture'—the Mersey Beat, The Beatles, The Stones—was particularly felt within GAA circles. As an organisation founded on the desire to maintain a distinct Irish culture, language and games, the arrival of rock 'n' roll, TV, American programmes and the affectations of an Irish middle and upper class set alarm bells ringing for the Gaelic Athletic Association. How could an amateur organisation withstand such change, and what could it do to convince its flock to remain faithful? Adapt, change, foresight: these were the new keywords and they proved just how in tune with society the GAA was. Paddy O'Keeffe, Secretary General until 1964, was central in recognising the need for change and adapting the GAA to survive and to emerge from the decline of the 1960s even stronger than before.

O'Keeffe urged the Association to be cognisant of people's changing habits in a changing society. The increased urbanisation and migration of people from land to town was having a big effect on country clubs, and O'Keeffe was acutely conscious that it was vital not to lose these new urbanites. The sense of the club as the focus of the community was being preached far and wide, with the support of the Catholic Church. These two organisations—the GAA and the Church—were most aware of the need to tap into the emerging communities and to ensure their religious and sporting influences were of a Catholic and GAA kind. Massive suburbanisation wouldn't occur until the late 1970s, but even by the 1960s the GAA had recognised the pattern of change and was looking to cut itself from the same cloth. To this end, it established the Commission on the GAA and by 1964 had drawn up a twenty-year hurling development plan, which aimed to have hurling in every parish by the time of the organisation's centenary celebrations in 1984.

Nonetheless, just like soccer and athletics, in the 1960s the GAA suffered its worst decline in match attendance—the blame for which was laid squarely at the door of RTÉ, despite the fact that its coverage was limited to All-Ireland finals, football semi-finals and St Patrick's Day games. The hurling final drew a crowd of 65,000 only one more time—and that wasn't until the 1970s; the football finals dropped to a level of 71,000 and below from 1965; the football semi-finals showed a drop of 46% in attendances between 1958 and 1970; and even provincially the papers were reporting that county finals were seeing much smaller crowds—just 13,000 saw Cork's county hurling final, one of the smallest turnouts in years.

The firebrands of conservatism weren't going to give up without a fight, however. The Christian Brothers still ruled in the schools and made sure GAA was the number one sport. Remember that Liam Brady was expelled from his secondary school, St Aidan's in Dublin, for opting to captain the Ireland under-15 team against Wales in a schoolboy international soccer game instead of playing a Gaelic football match for his school. As the threats mounted, the resistance grew fiercer and more desperate. One memorable piece of invective came from 'An Fear Ciúin' in an article that appeared in the *Sunday Press* in 1965 after Ireland's play-off defeat to Spain. An Fear Ciúin wrote of his disgust at RTÉ for comparing such a game to the GAA: 'the apparatus and staff were exported to Paris where a foreign soccer game between a motley group of Irish and English-serving natives were opposing a Spanish collection'.

The defences couldn't hold out against modernity forever, however. The new generation of Irish people who knew about The Beatles instead of the Clancy Brothers, about TV instead of radio, were questioning the old ways more and more, and it was inevitable that the GAA's Rule 27 would eventually be brought down. The Rule forbid any GAA member from playing, attending, or promoting soccer, cricket, hockey, or rugby. Tomas MacAnna, former Artistic Director of the Abbey, remembered his days as a Dundalk fan and rule-breaker:

'I remember a whole class of us from the CBS facing instant expulsion for slipping away on an afternoon to see a Cup-tie replay

and it is something ruefully to recall that soccer and all its works
and pomps was strictly forbidden by the Brothers. Indeed, I was
refused the gold *fáinne* for this lamentable Sunday evening
obsession with the game.

I remember quite vividly the exhortations and threats hurled at
us in the classroom, indeed I was once slapped for attending a
soccer match, and there was a time when a certain cleric, staunch in
his allegiance to the GAA, could be seen Sunday after Sunday,
notebook in hand, standing by the turnstiles, diligently putting
down (more in anger than sorrow) the many names of the grinning
faithful.'

Once obeyed and enforced with rigour, Rule 27 now stood as an
outdated symbol of the old ways, an anachronism. TV meant the
errant GAA member could sit in the privacy of his own home,
without fear of reprisal, and watch soccer or rugby matches to his
heart's content.

By 1962 the GAA's Annual Congress had four motions before it
in relation to the ban on foreign games, but while change may have
been inevitable, they weren't quite willing to accept revolution at
this stage—all motions were rejected decisively. Tom Woulfe of
Dublin's Civil Service Club remained steadfast in his attempts to
get rid of the Rule. The Congress of 1965 came and went, again
without success in removing the Ban, but by 1968 Woulfe had built
up grassroot support across the country for his proposal, and the
Congress of that year saw the beginning of the end for the rule.
Motions to delete the rule failed, but a motion to set up a special
committee to report on it within three years was passed. Over the
next three years the Committee canvassed and gauged reaction
and feelings to the Ban, finally releasing a report in 1970
recommending no change be made. A Special Congress was called
for 1971, by which time thirty of the thirty-two county conventions
had voted on changing the Ban. Finally, the rule was abolished in
April 1971—nine years after the first Congress defeated the idea so
decisively.

It is interesting to note that it was the Dublin County Board that
led the call for outright deletion of the rule at each Congress in the
1960s. Their stance recognised the fact that it was in the capital that

the GAA was fighting hardest for playing members, as the country moved en masse from the land to the city. The Dublin board saw the potential danger for the Association: the people might move from Gaelic games to soccer, too.

III. No answers in sight

The GAA was fighting its corner, and League of Ireland had work to do too. The televised games, the skilled players being beamed into people's home, the sense that everything was happening somewhere else—all of these things affected the public's perception of and participation in League of Ireland matches. Did this swing away go unnoticed? Certainly, the soccer journalists were well aware of it and sounded warnings.

Con Martin was one of Ireland's leading international players, had a successful club career with Aston Villa and founded the *Con Martin Soccer Annual*, which had prescient articles asking how things could be remedied in the League of Ireland. Looking back on the 1962 season, those articles revealed just how much of a downward spiral Irish soccer was already caught in. *The People's* Frank Johnstone, in a piece headlined 'A Vicious Circle', posed the questions he claimed were on the lips of most people that year: 'How to answer our soccer ills?', 'What's to be done then to bring the crowds back? And they must be enticed back if senior football here is not to be slowly throttled to death.'

Eddie Boyle, Sports Editor of the *Sunday Review*, in a piece opposing a ten-club league, noted that the fans were declining steadily:

'Week in and week out the fans, steadily dwindling, are watching the same old teams, the same old faces, in action against one another. Sometimes the same clubs are competing against each other within a matter of days.'

The sad fact is, if you were to write about the current ills in the game, you would be writing the same things, asking the same questions and wondering the same things. And, of course, many of the answers given today would also be the same as those being suggested in 1962. Banning transfers to England was suggested as one possible solution, banning professionalism was another—and in light of the straitened financial circumstances, it probably would have made sense for many. At the time, however, Frank Johnstone believed 'we can try a 12 club League again; we can try a break in mid season; the players can help by showing more enthusiasm—so can the spectators . . . every little helps.' Eddie Boyle's argument was to scrap the ten-team league, which he called soccer suicide:

> 'Drumcondra v Dundalk. Three meetings within the space of 21 days! No wonder the fans prefer to stay at home . . . what they should have done, in my humble opinion, was to have increased the number of clubs; formed two leagues with say eight clubs in each and had promotion and relegation. I have been advocating this for the past five years and I am still convinced that it is the only solution to put life into our League of Ireland soccer . . . to save sport from coming to a premature death.'

The *Evening Herald*'s KJ Kenealy, writing on international club competitions, made a very astute point: 'While these games [European club ties] draw big crowds, they adversely affect gates in home competitions—that the public, having seen star-studded continental sides, are not prepared to pay to see the lower standard of play in local fixtures. There may be something in that and home gates certainly have fallen.'

Once again, skip forward forty years and the same holds true. Shelbourne's European adventure in 2004, which culminated in their tie against Deportivo la Coruña, with the first leg played in front of 25,000 spectators at Lansdowne Road. Just one week later barely 2,000 turned up to see their next League of Ireland match.

Kenealy went so far as to draw an analogy to what happened to speedway racing, which had gone through a boom period in the 1950s:

> 'When Speedway Racing was introduced to Shelbourne Park it fairly boomed. Crowds flocked every Sunday, as new star riders were introduced; but apart from the Irish Championship, there was

no real competition, and inevitably, the supply of new riders ran out. And having seen all the stars, spectators were not content with anything less. The sport is now a memory in Dublin.'

It's clear that fans, clubs and soccer journalists were extremely worried that the League of Ireland would go the same route. This means the board of management must have at least been aware of the concerns being expressed, so why wasn't anything being done about it?

Shelbourne Chief Executive Ollie Byrne's argument that soccer's predominant working-class background precluded it from having the type of people who could manage and run clubs and a League successfully has been rejected by many as a cop-out; GAA people point out that they weren't university graduates either. However, some of those who were very involved at the time continue to hold this view. Eamon Dunphy, now famed as a broadcaster and pundit, returned to Ireland in 1977 with John Giles to help establish a new set-up at Shamrock Rovers. He was, and has remained, dismissive of the League of Ireland and those who were and are in charge. In looking back at the game's administrators, Dunphy concludes that it does, in fact, come down to a class issue—and then some:

'It is a class thing. I mean the class of people who ran soccer then— and a lot of them are still hanging around—the class of person meant that it was not just a working-class thing, it was the worst of the working class. It was the most exploitative of the working class that had positions of influence through the junior leagues and the clubs and they had positions of influence in Merrion Square. So there has always been that sort of county councillor type—the slieveen—the "I don't give a damn about the sport or anything" type, that didn't have any governing ethos or vision the way the GAA guys do or even the rugby people.

The Gaelic Athletic Association, in contrast, if you go back to its founding ethos was a vision of a sense of Irishness or a culture, an Irish culture that would be distinct. They would link *céilís* and Irish music and Irish culture with the games so when people praise the GAA they often do it in a glib way, but actually where the GAA does deserve praise is the way it had a vision of Irishness. You wouldn't have to agree with the vision, but it was a vision. Soccer people

never had that. They couldn't have had a vision because they didn't
have that class of person around generally and that is to do with
education. It is not to do with class it is to do with education. The
working-class people with real vision, real ideas and real class were
actually playing the game, they weren't running the game, that is
the key distinction. They were fantastic men with a love of soccer
and there were lots of people like Liam Tuohy and all sorts of
people with great visions of what soccer could be and how it could
thrive, but they didn't run anything. They were just the employees.'

It was the club owners—who were also the FAI officials—who
counted and their attitudes to players was still steeped in boss-to-
worker contempt, just as it was in England. Jimmy Hill was leading
the charge to break the maximum wage in the game in England
and Ireland followed suit with its own professional footballers'
association, but it didn't really grow teeth until the 1990s. In the
meantime, players were treated poorly and, as Dunphy says, were
being exploited by their own. Worse still, by the very lowest of their
own: the exploitative working-class boss.

When it came down to it, League of Ireland players always fared
worst between themselves and those players based in England. Joe
Haverty explained in Sean Ryan's book, *The Boys in Green*, just
how drastically circumstances changed as one's career changed:

'When I was with Arsenal the FAI never questioned my expenses but
when I was with Millwall they docked £5, probably on the basis that
I should have been glad to play for Ireland while I was at the Den.
Then, when I was playing part-time for Shelbourne I had to take a
week off work to play for Ireland and they wouldn't allow the
expense. That was a sore point for League of Ireland players as they
needed the money more.'

Traditionally, the players had become used to being treated as
second-class citizens. In the hierarchy of football, this was nothing
new, be it in Ireland, England or Europe. The officials and the
administrators who held high office in national football
organisations were treated like the royalty they believed themselves
to be. It was a classic case of the workers being ruled by the bosses,

and it was no surprise to hear stories like those recounted above.

Part of the problem within the system was that while the officials ruled the roost, it was not necessarily the talented officials who rose to those positions of power. Instead, the men who wore the blazers and attended committee meeting after committee meeting, eventually working their way up the ladder of officialdom, were the ones who spent the most time in the committee room, revelling in the minutiae of club rules and points of order. It was they who ascended in the hierarchy of the game. To observers, these men in charge of the clubs, and also in charge of the FAI, were out of touch with the fans and the players, preferring instead to wear their chains of office and look down their noses at those coming through the turnstiles. And so the term 'blazers' came into existence as an insult thrown in the direction of those in charge of the game—men who, literally, wore their badge of honour for all to see.

Complaints about 'the blazers' in the FAI getting priority ahead of the players was nothing new. In 1959, for example, a FAI Council decision decreed that on the very important matter of which officials would travel for away matches, one official would travel per two players. However, a medical officer for the players was not considered due to the cost involved. Perhaps the decision was made with the best intentions, nonetheless it is easy to see how players ended up feeling exploited.

Sportswriter Sean Ryan relates how Shay Brennan described player treatment during his time with the Ireland team:

'The officials were on the trips for the good time. The matches weren't everything for them and this translated to the players. I remember we were playing Italy and it was an early kick-off. We ordered a steak at 12.00, but when two of the selectors came in they were given the steak. They accepted even though the players had to wait another three-quarters of an hour before being served.'

The other problem the officials' behaviour created was in the matter of selection. They chose players based on the League of Ireland club to which they belonged. Dublin clubs were seen to be favoured, with provincial players most affected. 'Players like Dixie

Hale and Cork's Donal Leahy and Austin Noonan would all have been capped had they been with Dublin clubs,' writes Ryan. 'In fact, Sam Prole, Chairman of the Selection Committee, promised Leahy his first cap if he would sign for Prole's club, Drumcondra!'

Player Tommy Dunne recalls a similar incident:

> 'We were having our shower after the game against the Scottish League. Joe Cunningham came in and said, "Well done lads, it will be the same half-back line against Denmark." Once Joe said it we knew we did not even have to look in the papers for the team.'

This despite the fact that Cunningham, the Rovers chairman, was not even a selector.

The truth was that League of Ireland club officials were the main power-brokers in Irish soccer and enjoyed clout and influence that reached well beyond their actual stations. Running and owning soccer clubs meant a strong link with local communities, a strong hold over players and, more importantly, a ticket to international recognition through the FAI and the national team. Suddenly, with a bit of success and a promotion or two up the ladder, officials could be looking at trips abroad and a glamorous lifestyle of power and junkets. In the end though, the old adage about power and corruption comes to mind when reviewing the path of the League. They took their eye off the ball to focus on other things, and what was lost was the strong sense of identity that had once existed between club and community and, especially, between club owners and local supporters.

> 'The soccer clubs never changed, we didn't have the infrastructure in our clubs to deal with that,' admits Ollie Byrne. 'We didn't have social clubs, we didn't have an organisation-wide basis of supporters clubs strategically placed around the city or around the country. People didn't change when television came in and they got the luxuries of life. They didn't put in bars, they didn't try and create a community involvement. They just soldiered on and they never saw the day when they weren't going to get the crowds.'

We keep returning to this question, but it's necessary: Why?

Why did it all pan out this way? And why did 'the blazers' feel this was the right approach? Perhaps it makes sense in the social context of the time. The arrival of Lemass, succeeding de Valera as Taoiseach in 1957, signalled a break away from the old, isolationist ideals and the country began to try to embrace a broader, more Westernised ethos. The government's First Programme for Economic Expansion produced a growth rate double that forecast, national income rose by nearly a quarter, public investment achieved a total of £78.5 million, the number of cars on Irish roads doubled, unemployment dropped by 30%, emigration decreased significantly from 14 per 1,000 to 5 per 1,000—44,000 emigrated in 1961, while just two years later this had dropped to 12,000. The early 1960s showed all the signs of ditching the stagnant, dreary 1950s. Irish society was beginning to revel in a new-found wealth and a new-found world that introduced them to American-style luxuries, such as TV. As early as 1960, ITGWU President John Conroy was already condemning the trappings of wealth:

'Extra millions of pounds have been paid this year to many thousands of people in the higher income group, to dividend drawers, commission agents, profit-takers, gamblers and others. Much of this unearned and unneeded higher income would be spent in pleasure trips abroad and luxury imports.'

Ireland was fast becoming a new, brave and vibrant country that was looking to the outside world for ideas. In economic and social terms, the 1960s marked the start of Ireland's bid to stand confidently on her own two feet. It wasn't just the higher earners who were riding the wave of prosperity either. The working-classes were experiencing these changes too. Travel was the new past-time, both at home and to destinations abroad. The working classes were turning up in places heretofore the reserve of the middle classes. The classes were merging, in some respects—most notably in relation to Irish culture and heritage.

Previous notions of pure gaeldom were being hastily abandoned for a world of sitcoms, rock 'n' roll and motorcars. On 7 January 1965 the old gave way to the new in a very symbolic way: impresario Jimmy O'Dea died, but across the city from the Gaiety

Theatre where O'Dea had made his name the Rolling Stones were playing their first ever concert in Ireland. Irish people raced to ditch the old ways because they reminded them of emigration and stagnancy. The past was an embarrassment.

Sean de Freine writing in his book, *The Great Silence*, in 1965 attempted to explain the decline of the indigenous Irish culture:

'English cultural influence is reflected in the interest aroused in Ireland in any matter which is topical in England. Practically all the issues of post-war life in Britain, such as the welfare state, the death penalty, the ombudsman, have become subjects for the Irish debating societies. England's domestic affairs—the big law cases and murder trials, her political doings, financial affairs and sports events—are extensively reported in Ireland; far more so than similar events on the continent . . . English influence is reflected in many ways, from the introduction of prize bonds, PAYE, zebra crossings and "honest face loans", to football pools, bingo and the adaptation of the slogan "drinka pinta milka day".'

While modernising is a potent force and brings many benefits, it also exacts a price. In this instance, it was the unthinking embrace of middle-class materialism and affection. Alan Bestic, who returned to Ireland in the late 1960s after fifteen years abroad, was scathing about the wealth and affectations that now existed in the country:

'The scampi belt, the Bacardi brigade. They own a house in Foxrock and have a Mercedes on the firm. The wife has a Mini for shopping and a swimming pool for the garden is on order. There is a cottage in Connemara—"I can really think down there" . . . wine name-droppers, BA (pass), top convent wife with *Ulysses* in her handbag. Oyster festival but not Galway races. Hard tennis court, yacht in the front garden during winter . . . unhappy people with easy laughs and eyes that are always moving, looking for Murphy, wondering whether he is watching and whether he has a mohair suit too . . . blurred carbons of English suburbans from the mock stockbroker belt.'

The 1960s may have been marked by the new trappings of wealth and enjoyed by the Bacardi Brigade, but that was in stark contrast to the League of Ireland, where poverty-stricken clubs like Dundalk were a typical example of the state of play. In his *History of Dundalk* Jim Murphy described Oriel Park at the end of the 1964–65 season:

'Even basic maintenance had slipped and the continuous financial problems of the 1950s had prevented necessary repairs and renewals, beyond the periodic purchase of a few railway sleepers ... the terracing had deteriorated, timber palings and the wooden stands had long breached their sell-by dates and the public toilets were to be avoided. A Newry supporter enquired if the committee had heard about cement.'

One fan also recalls these dismal times:

'There were absolutely no facilities and it was so awful there were no women at the football matches. Occasionally you might see a woman in the stand, but girls never went to football matches in any numbers because there were no facilities. If a girl went and wanted to go to the ladies, there was no ladies to go to. There was nothing to eat, you couldn't buy a hamburger and you couldn't buy a sandwich at a football match because that sort of facility never existed. Someone once described a League of Ireland match as sitting in front of acres of wet, empty concrete. The concrete wasn't so much empty in those days, but it was certainly wet and bleak.'

Finances, of course, were still a major problem, particularly now that gate receipts were on a downward spiral—down £1,100 to £4,800 from £5,900 the previous season for the Co. Louth club:

'Dependent on annual membership fees of £1 per member and the efforts of the Supporters Club,' writes Murphy, 'annual gate receipts in most years were not sufficient to cover overheads and player wages. Break-even was the best to be expected, with a good Cup run throwing up the odd surplus—and that would be required to pay off some of the past debts and reduce the club's liabilities.'

Were the officials part of the Bacardi Brigade set, unwilling to spend money in order to make it? One official gives a different

point of view, explaining that the fortunes of football were greatly
damaged when the players maximised their rights and gained
freedom of contracts and the maximum wage was abolished:

'In the old days, in the rules of the game, once you signed to a team
you were nearly there for life—that was the legal and the moral
way,' recollects Shelbourne's Chief Executive Ollie Byrne wistfully,
'Jimmy Hill, that era and the formation of unions for players and
then you had the formation of unions for referees, so any slimy little
difficulty that arises the next thing is, instead of just having an
individual fighting your corner, you had an organised force fighting
your corner. And while that was necessary to a degree, it was too
extreme in its implementation for sport. And so it changed the
whole structure of sport completely and had the downside effect on
soccer, professional soccer, and part-time whatever. Particularly in
this country.'

Whatever the reason, the money wasn't there to shore up the
clubs, improve the facilities and keep the spectators happy. The
situation was both amusing and appalling to the English players
who came over to play in the League of Ireland.

Johnny Matthews came over from Coventry City in 1966 as a
fresh-faced nineteen-year-old on a loan spell and he liked it so
much that he still hasn't gone home. For the next fourteen years
the left-winger notched up a remarkable 147 goals for Waterford
plus another nine for Limerick Utd and along the way he also won
six League medals with Waterford and another on Shannonside, as
well as three FAI Cup runners-up medals (1968, 1972, 1979) and he
made sixteen European Cup appearances plus scored against
Glasgow Celtic and Manchester Utd. Not bad for a six-week loan
spell.

'I had actually never been on a plane at that stage,' recounts
Matthews of his first trip over, 'it was funny because when I got on
the plane I was sitting next to a nun. I am sort of left-legged as they
say—I would be Protestant Church of Ireland—and I really didn't
know how to address this lady. I didn't know whether she was a
mother or a sister or what and I think it must have been her first go
on a plane because she was asking me how did you tie the seatbelt

and she was a bit worried. So I said, "Ah you will be all right" sort of thing, "I go across here now and again." Me being the brave man at nineteen.'

Relocation was to be an eye-opener and a sea-change for him. Jimmy Hill may have just got rid of the maximum wage, but in terms of the way facilities were developing, the League of Ireland was slipping further and further back.

'It was strange getting to know some of the grounds alright. At first I thought, Christ, what have I come to here? In fact, the first goal I ever scored we won 1-0 up in Sligo. But the joke of the trip there was when we actually got to the pitch they had to move about six cows and twelve sheep off the bottom half of the pitch and then this guy came in with a big spade lifting off the cow shit. Oh honestly yeah, and in the dressing rooms I think there was only one shower unit per dressing room. I think there was only one big ceiling hose of a shower unit and the referee was changing in the lime shed. That is actually what it was like.'

VI. Manchester United come to town
On the upside, the biggest night for the League came in September 1968 when Manchester Utd—who had just won the European Cup for the first time, the first English club to do so—were drawn to play Waterford Utd in the first round of the European Cup. Best, Charlton and Law were coming to town! There was only one way to satisfy demand, however, and that was to play the game at Lansdowne Road. This would be the first time soccer had been played at the rugby venue since 1927, when Ireland played their first ever home international as an independent nation against an Italy B team.

The visit of the stars of Manchester Utd guaranteed a 48,000 sell-out: a record crowd for a League of Ireland club and a signal of the shifting taste of the Irish soccer public. Whereas before the interest in the likes of Manchester Utd was more distant, now thousands upon thousands of Irish supporters wanted to see *their* team, 'Man' Utd. They had grown used to English soccer on the TV and now supporting an English club seemed as ordinary as supporting Shamrock Rovers once did. The difference this time was the fans weren't going back to the League of Ireland.

Demand for tickets was unprecedented, but of the 48,000 in attendance, one wonders just how many were there to see Manchester Utd? Even by this stage, the glamour and allure of the Old Trafford club was etched in the Irish consciousness. The arrival of Matt Busby's team was greeted like the arrival of a rock group and the build-up to the Wednesday game continued all week in the papers. The team was fêted wherever they went and anticipation was at fever pitch.

For some of the Waterford players, however, the day of the match meant finishing their night shifts in the local paper mills and going home to pick up their gear before meeting the team bus that would take them to Dublin to meet the Champions of Europe that evening. About 20,000 from Waterford made their way up to the game on buses, six special trains and a mile-long queue of cars. Waterford shut down early in the afternoon, with industry coming to a halt and barely a shop open after kick-off time, at six o'clock. Such was the demand for tickets, they were sold out weeks in advance (resulting in a gate of £22,000—the equivalent today of over €1 million), with touts asking 50/- for 4/- tickets and £10 for a seat in the stand. But still, on the day of the match, hundreds of fans were not to be stopped as they scaled over the walls of Lansdowne for free, determined that nothing would stop them from seeing their heroes—Manchester Utd, that is.

Then disaster struck as the match nearly never went ahead. It was one hour before kick-off and the players hadn't even started to get changed because they were still fighting over the bonus.

'The manager at the time, Vinnie Maguire, had been dealing with the club directors for a considerable number of weeks,' recollects Matthews, 'and they wanted to give us £50 for the two games whereas the players wanted £50 for each game. It was only when one of the directors, Pete Davis—who was a players' man—came in and said he would cover what they were asking for did the players agree to play.'

Having guaranteed themselves a gate of £22,000, the club were still looking to save a few bob on the players. Remarkably, when facing the chance to play against such illustrious opposition, the players were steadfast in their demands until the eleventh hour. Finally, in the nick of time, a deal was brokered and the game could go ahead.

Not surprisingly, Man Utd won 3-1, thanks to a Denis Law hat-trick, but it wasn't quite the drubbing people were expecting. Such was the enthusiasm for the game—and the United players—that Waterford's goal saw a surge of hundreds onto the pitch, at which point they were asking Bobby Charlton and George Best for their autographs. For the ninety minutes, stewards and gardaí struggled to contain the crowds, and the referee even threatened to abandon the game after yet another stoppage when a pitchside spectator stuck his leg out and managed to kick the ball while it was in play. According to Johnny Matthews, Waterford's scorer on the night ('I just skipped inside Tony Dunne and cracked it from an angle outside the box at 25 yards and it flew across and just went into the top corner on the far side'), the great thing about playing against their glamorous counterparts was the respect shown towards them by Sir Matt Busby's men:

> 'We had met them beforehand and they were very good when they came over here. There was no mickey-taking or any sort of thing and I think they just appreciated the way we tried to play football and not kick them. There was a funny incident in the game though with Tony Dunne and our Al Casey, who got crunched by him—he was down on the floor and Tony put a hand down to him. And he said, "Come on, Al, you can't be that tired". And Al looked up and said, "F**k off, Tony." He said, "It's alright for you, you don't have to get up for the six to twelve shift in the morning!"'

(It stands in stark contrast, it must be said, to some of the attitudes shown by young up-and-coming Premiership stars while playing for their clubs against League of Ireland clubs in recent pre-season friendlies. They have been known to slag old pros about the state of their boots and how little money they earn.)

The papers lauded Waterford's efforts, but in the main this was all about Man Utd. They were who the people had come to see:

Denis Law scoring his hat-trick and George Best with his box of tricks. This was a sporting spectacle that Irish fans were prepared to come out in force to see. They had begun to turn their backs on the domestic game, and now they were announcing that they were only willing to come out for the big games. This was, after all, the biggest crowd ever to attend a soccer match in Ireland.

'The game was truly one of the big sports occasions,' wrote Mitchell Cogley in the *Irish Independent* the day after, 'with all the colour and trappings . . . All the stars indeed paraded their stellar class in blistering spells—the masterly generalship of Nobby Stiles and Bobby Charlton, the speed and acceleration of Brian Kidd . . . All round it was a game worthy of the occasion, and the teams fully deserved the ovation accorded them at the interval and at the end.'

For the Waterford players, the second leg, in Old Trafford, was to prove more entertaining, despite the fact that they were hammered 7-1. By this stage they were on first-name terms with Best *et al.* Johnny Matthews remembers Denis Law picking him up after a tackle and enquiring, 'Alright, Johnny, how you getting on?' "Ah, not too bad, Den," I remember saying,' says Matthews.

After the game they were treated to the lights of Manchester and the lifestyle of George Best; he brought a few of the players out on the town, to a variety of hotspots in his new E-type Jaguar.

'It was the first time I'd been to a place where they had peephole keyholes in the doors for security,' remembers Matthews, 'but George brought us around to about three or four clubs and of course the guy peeped through the keyhole. "Oh, Mr Best, Mr Best, come on in, Mr Best", there was us, we all trotted in behind, treated like superstars and free entrance in everywhere.'

The following day, though, it was back to work, and the following Sunday afternoon it was back to League of Ireland pitches, with a man and his spade shovelling cow shit off it before kick-off.

The contrast to the glamour of Manchester Utd could not have been any greater, and domestically the League really wasn't doing itself any favours by doing little to improve the facilities, or the football on offer. Noel Dunne, writing in the *Independent* in 1967 about a 0-0 bore between Bohemians and Dundalk, cried out for the state of the game:

> 'It will be the fervent wish of yesterday's patient spectators that the teams will atone for yesterday's boring production . . . I cannot remember when I recorded so few notes on a game, particularly one which was extended for twenty minutes beyond the normal time. On the whole, the flashes of good football which punctuated the affair were not nearly enough to dispel the general atmosphere of waning interest. Goals and goalmouth incidents really get a crowd going, but on this occasion these were so few in number that long before the end the spirits of the fans were as depressed by the lack of thrills as their clothes were dampened by the rain.'

Only English football, it seemed, could lift the Irish fans' spirits anymore—as proved by Man Utd's visit. No longer was a Drums–Rovers rivalry sufficient to grab people's attention. The world had changed, society had changed with it and people's horizons were being broadened all the time. But while all this was happening, the League of Ireland seemed happy to reminisce about the good old days that would come back someday soon. But 1950s Ireland was a place no one wanted to go back to. Especially not now that they had seen the 1966 World Cup, witnessed George Best swaggering his hips, listened to The Beatles and The Rolling Stones and read about the rest of the real world that was out there. No longer was the sporting axis revolving around Milltown or Tolka down the road—and nothing, it seemed, could change that.

That didn't mean the clubs had given up the ghost. Their passion for the game still held true. On the pitch, Rovers were again to dominate the domestic game by winning an unprecedented six Cups in a row from 1964 to 1969, with Liam Tuohy, Paddy Ambrose, Mick Leech and Frank O'Neill amongst the leading figures. Drums, Shels, Rovers, Dundalk and Cork were all to win League titles before Waterford began their feat of winning six in eight years from 1965 onwards and, although they weren't to realise it at the time, Drums League victory in 1964–65 was to be their last

—although Drums fans will always take great pride in the fact that it was Rovers they pipped by just one point to win the League for the final time.

Waterford's domination of the League from 1965 onwards and for the best part of a decade was to mark the end of the Dublin dominance of the game and a return to provincial sides leading the charge. Why the Dublin clubs declined is hard to gauge, but it did signal a downturn of soccer in the city. Whereas before, the city and the League thrived on the likes of the Rovers–Drums rivalries as well as the legendary Rovers dominance in the 1950s and of the Cup in the 1960s, Waterford's emergence coincided with a discernible drift away from the game in Dublin. Between Drums' title in 1965 and the start of Rovers' four-in-a-row in 1984, Bohemians were the only Dublin club to capture the League in that intervening period.

Soccer was finding its feet in unlikely corners around the country, and often it was around the old garrison towns that it thrived. For Waterford, their reign consisted of a remarkable six Leagues in eight years as well as European nights against the likes of Manchester Utd and Celtic. Packed grounds and a buzz of excitement followed the team each week; it was a good time to be involved with Waterford Utd. The decline of the Dublin teams may have taken fans away from the game in the capital, but in Waterford their rise to the top was attended by huge crowd support and delighted pride in the county. It was a heartening example of how soccer could be, if only all the pieces were slotted into place.

VII. The international team struggles

The international team wasn't faring too well at this time. From attracting a record crowd of 48,000-plus for the game against England in 1957, just ten years later it saw the smallest crowd ever for an Irish international when just 8,500 bothered turning up to see Ireland lose 2-0 to Czechoslovakia.

'There is an old saying,' wrote Seamus Devlin for *The Irish Times*, 'that if one doesn't expect something, one is seldom disappointed

. . . Dalymount Park patrons are pretty well accustomed to defeat and will accept it in the proper spirit; but defeat without honour is a different kettle of fish.'

It was becoming increasingly clear that Irish football was getting left far behind on the international stage. This was largely down to the fact that the League still clung to the old selector system, so the blazers picked the team and ran affairs on the pitch. Plus, the lack of funding and resources for training and coaching further hampered the international effort.

There were two occasions that will be long remembered: one reflected the financial realities of the game in Ireland, the other the playing realities for Irish players; curiously, both involved Spain in the World Cup play-off—one of Ireland's nearest misses in terms of World Cup qualification.

On 5 May 1965, Ireland faced European Champions Spain in a two-legged affair, with the winner securing a place in the 1966 World Cup in England. The Irish line-up included John Giles, Charlie Hurley and Noel Cantwell alongside Ireland's first ever second-generation player, Shay Brennan. Born in Manchester of Carlow parents, Brennan had made his Manchester Utd debut in 1958, just weeks after the Munich Air Disaster, and was to go on to win 350 caps for United and nineteen for Ireland, mainly as right-fullback.

Ireland beat Spain 1-0, but in the return leg, five months later, were beaten comprehensively in Seville, on a scoreline of 4-1. FIFA didn't use aggregate scores then, so the only way to decide which team was going through to the World Cup was with a winner-takes-all play-off the following month.

Where to play the game, though? A neutral venue was necessary: Ireland wanted Wembley; Spain wanted Paris. Soccer writer Peter Byrne suggests there is evidence that FIFA was leaning towards Wembley as its preferred choice, but then Spain threw a cat among the pigeons by offering to pay the FAI's team-travelling expenses if the match were played in Paris. What to do now? Should the FAI stick to its guns and hope it would get Wembley, where the majority of support would be Irish fans? Or should it accept

Spain's offer and hold the game in Paris, where the vast majority of support in the stadium would be Spanish fans? Wembley would offer Ireland the best chance of qualifying for the World Cup, which would bring substantial financial rewards; Paris shortened the odds of qualifying, but guaranteed a nice little earner for the Association. The FAI's finances were in a parlous situation at this time, a fact of which Spain must have been aware, so the choice really boiled down to: finance or football? In the end, the FAI chose the short-term money offer by the Spanish in what has gone down in football folk memory as one of the darkest days in Irish football.

Ireland's best hope yet of playing in a World Cup—one being held in England where there were so many Irish and which was so accessible from Ireland, the chance to further cement the popularity of the game at home, plus the financial windfall that would have accrued all fell by the wayside in favour of saving a few bob on the travelling expenses. To this day fans still talk about the Paris play-off bung as the FAI selling Ireland's footballing hopes down the Swanee, and cite it as just one example, in a long list, of the FAI's cavalier attitude towards Irish football. The FAI countered that a football association in financial dire straits is of no use to anyone and they had to take this into account, but it seems all too possible that the FAI simply didn't believe that Ireland had it in them to beat Spain for a second time—especially after losing so comprehensively in Seville.

In the end, the trip to Paris meant only 5,000 of the 35,000-strong crowd were Irish supporters; for Spain, it was like a home game. Eamon Dunphy made his debut for Ireland that night in the Colombes stadium, where 1-0 was the close scoreline in favour of Spain. The tightness of the result has always led fans to wonder what might have been if the FAI had not succumbed so easily to the thirty pieces of silver, so to speak.

After coming so close, the Irish team went into decline soon after and won only another three internationals over the next seven years; slowly the crowds began to drift away. From highs of 40,000-plus, it was down to 20,000 for the visit of Turkey in 1966, while in 1965 a paltry 8,500 diehards saw Ireland lose to the Czechs.

The inclusion of Shay Brennan in the Irish team that faced

Spain was very interesting as it marked the beginning of the end of League of Ireland representation on the national team—a process taken to its peak during the Charlton years when the FAI came to stand for Find Any Irishman—and at the same time was also a tacit recognition that the standard of the domestic game was no longer good enough for players to be competing at the highest level. Whereas nine years earlier seven League of Ireland players had conspired to beat the World Champions, West Germany, now, in the mid-1960s, it seemed to be accepted that the League just wasn't up to it anymore and that, in future, second-generation players playing in England were a better alternative than locally based candidates.

Soccer writer Peter Byrne summed it up in his history of the FAI:

'As the exodus to Britain grew in the 1930s so the names of cross channel clubs became to appear more frequently in Ireland match programmes. By the fifties that trend had intensified and yet invariably at least one League of Ireland player was nominated, to provide a tangible link between the national team and the local game . . . It was against that background that the FAI changed tack in the mid sixties and embarked on a policy which would on occasions involve it in conflict with those who believed that the domestic game was being disadvantaged in the process . . . The arrival of Shay Brennan was significant then on two counts.

On the one hand it heralded the input into the system of second generation Irish players from Britain thus providing a vital extra layer to what had always been a shallow reserve of talent. Against that it deprived local players of the valid aspiration of representing their country and taken in conjunction with the powerful counter attraction of televised football from abroad it would have a depressing effect on the League of Ireland.'

The link had been broken, and a youngster's aspiration of playing for Shamrock Rovers invariably meant he wouldn't get a chance to play for Ireland. If you wanted to represent your country, you had go beyond the League of Ireland and play for English clubs. No longer was the League of Ireland a point to aim for: players had to seek farther and go higher and, in the process, the nails were hammered into the coffin of the League. The more it was allowed to slip into shoddiness, the more it was derided, the more the fans the looked down their noses at it, the less chance of kids dreaming of playing League football and the less chance of fans going to the games. The League of Ireland was now out on its own and effectively out of the equation when it came to Irish football: where before there had been a connection between the FAI, League of Ireland and the international team, now the link was directly from English soccer to international team.

Second-generation players had not grown up in Ireland, didn't know the local clubs and communities and were unknown to the fans. By removing the local and the identity, the FAI unwittingly removed the last vestiges of connection between the players and the fans, in football terms. In the chase for 'betterment', the short-term fix was to look to second-generationers. While some argue this was merely healing the emigration scar by reuniting the country with its émigrés (an argument thrashed out during the Charlton years), the reality is that this was a quick-fix solution that was only ever going to lead to the League of Ireland becoming more and more of a backwater, with less and less support.

The problem, as Brian Kerr describes, was that while the rest of Europe was busy developing its standards and structures, there was little interaction with or learning from European models. Instead of taking stock of where football was heading, the FAI took the easy, short-term option of drafting in second-generationers from abroad. Fans, journalists and officials were all lamenting the dropping standards and the resultant declining crowds, but the FAI never sought to remedy the problem through a root-and-branch change. Instead, they used the likes of Shay Brennan as the band-aid solution for a much deeper malaise.

'The problem has been that football elsewhere had developed while we stayed still,' explains Kerr. 'Don't forget, football in Holland was still amateur up to the 1960s and we would have expected to be beating the likes of the Dutch league teams when we were both amateur. I even remember Shamrock Rovers only losing 3-2 to Bayern Munich in 1965 when Bayern had the likes of Beckenbauer and Muller on their team.

But we stayed still and didn't develop our football coaching and learning, we were trying to survive day to day and with our island mentality we had little interest in what was going on in the outside world—look at the likes of Malta, Cyprus and Iceland and see how they have struggled. I remember being at an under-18 tournament in the Czech Republic a few years ago and realising then that we were the only ones who had flown in as the rest were just able to drive to the tournament. The world is a smaller place nowadays, but we did fall behind with our knowledge base.'

By the end of the decade, Ireland had reached its lowest point on the international stage, with players blaming the FAI, the FAI blaming the players and the fans blaming both. Finally, after another poor showing to Hungary, in November 1969, when the Irish team lost 4-0 in front of just 17,000, the FAI gave in and decided to scrap the selector system and follow the rest of the football world by appointing a manager. Such was the agonising over the decision, it was remarkable it was ever achieved, but it was only when the situation was so hopeless and the players were exerting huge pressure that the FAI eventually acceded to the requests and the reality.

The prevarication and the reluctance to cede power meant it was enacted only as a last-ditch measure, and yet again the decision was left too late. The fans had already turned their backs on the League of Ireland, and now they had turned away from the international team as well. The blazers were confronted by changes and developments they were unable to deal with. It was only because the international side was in its death throes and the finances were fast depleting due to poor crowds that the FAI handed over the reins to Mick Meagan.

The decision was late, but at least *something* was being done. On the other hand, the League of Ireland was allowed to drift. As the 1970s approached, it was apparent the League of Ireland was at a crossroads and facing bleaker years ahead—unless action was taken, and taken soon.

Part Three

The 1970s: Highs, lows, peaks and troughs

THE FAN

'*I loved the atmosphere of a football match and I loved seeing Shels playing. I quickly realised that I wasn't so much a football fan, more a Shels fan, because Shels were putting me in a deep depression for the best part of a week.*'

I. Changing of the guard

The 1970s was the changing of the guard as the two teams that had come to represent so much of the golden days—Shamrock Rovers and Drumcondra—were put in the hands of new owners, ending family associations going back decades. It was the end of one era and the ushering in of a new one. The Cunninghams and the Proles owned Rovers and Drums, respectively, but had seen the writing on the wall and now decided that enough was enough: the time was right to step back from the League of Ireland. They had done their best, now they wanted to hand over the reins to younger, fresher blood who it was hoped could reverse the fortunes of the two clubs.

For the Prole family, who had owned Drumcondra since 1953 when Sam Prole came down from Dundalk to take over the club, it had been the family business for the best part of twenty years. Sons Royden and Robert Prole had played for and helped run the club with their father, and because the family lived down the road from Tolka, the Proles were closely identified with the Tolka Park venue. Under their guidance the club had taken the title in 1957–58 and 1960–61 and 1964–65, as well as winning the Cup in 1954 and 1957. Remarkably for football club owners, the Proles were held in high regard by those who came into contact with them and they were generally seen as putting football before finances.

'The Proles were very good people,' says Eamon Dunphy, who grew up around the corner from them, 'they weren't in it for money, they were very decent people, they loved football and they put in money and built up Tolka, they did an awful lot for soccer on the Northside and they did it until the very end, until they couldn't sustain it any longer. But there was never any sense of nurturing a community the way the GAA does.'

By the 1960s it was obvious that money was going to play a central role in the future of the club: the more money the club lost, the more uncertain the Proles' involvement with Drums was going to be. For two years in succession (1969–70 and 1970–71) the club finished bottom of the League, and by the end of the 1972 season it was languishing in the bottom three. At the same time the club's debt had grown to £6,000. Sam Prole knew that his family's involvement with the club was drawing to a close. His son, Robert, says the only other option open to them was to allow the bank to use the deeds to their family house as collateral, but this was a step too far for the family:

'The debt had built up over the years alright. My father was losing money more and more and it was obvious that we just couldn't go on. At this time they were also looking to put up the lease of Tolka from £100 to £1,000 and we knew it just wasn't feasible anymore. The last straw then was when the only choice to keep going was if our home was taken as collateral by the bank. And that my father could never do. For all our love for the club and for football, we could never mortgage our home to the fortunes of what happened on the pitch. That was when we knew it was finally over.'

The Proles brought the Drums era to a close in May 1972 when they handed over the club to Home Farm. Home Farm was, and is, the most famous schoolboy soccer club in Ireland. At the time Brendan Menton Snr and Don Seery hoped to take the club on to League of Ireland level by using the conveyor belt of talent coming up through the ranks—all while maintaining the amateur ethos. It was agreed to keep the Drumcondra name by calling the team

Earlier days and packed grounds. Drums v Cork, 1961.   (Lensmen & Associates)

Shels v Cork, 1963.   (Lensmen & Associates)

'Drums': Drumcondra FC, 1960. A northside Dublin institution, their rivalry with the southside Shamrock Rovers was to prove a high point for the League of Ireland in the 1950s and 1960s. (Courtesy of Tommy Emerson)

The great Shamrock Rovers six-in-a-row team, 1965. The club won an unprecedented six FAI Cups in a row from 1964 to 1969. (Lensmen & Associates)

Shamrock Rovers v Rapid Vienna, European Cup, 1964. European nights were a constant struggle for League of Ireland clubs. (Lensmen & Associates)

Cash before football: Spain beat Ireland in Paris in the World Cup play-off in 1965. The FAI accepted Spain's offer of cash to play the match in Paris instead of England. (Hulton Archive/Getty)

Shay Brennan, Manchester United and Ireland. Brennan made his international debut in 1965 and it was to signal the influx of second-generation players onto the Irish team. As a result, League of Ireland representation on the international team declined drastically. (Hulton Archive/Getty)

First signs. The crowds are beginning to stay away, Milltown, 1971.

(Derek Speirs)

Heffo's Dubs, 1975: the great Dublin team of the 1970s which engaged the city in Gaelic football like never before. (Lensmen & Associates)

The dream for Rovers. After an illustrious career in England, John Giles returned to take over Shamrock Rovers in 1977. Both he and Eamon Dunphy wanted to see League of Ireland teams competing at the highest level once more.   (Empics)

'They didn't want us to rise because they knew that they couldn't rise ... I had utter contempt for them. I have never been back to a League of Ireland ground since.' After just one year of the Rovers experiment, Eamon Dunphy had had enough and quit; he remains one of the League's fiercest critics.

(Hulton Archive/Getty)

Good to be back: Derry City returns to football and the League of Ireland in 1985.
(Derek Speirs)

Ghosts of football's past: Milltown lies derelict and overgrown in 1989.
(Derek Speirs)

Home Farm-Drumcondra, but within a season the name of Drumcondra had been dropped; in the 1973–74 season there was no Drumcondra team taking part for the first time since 1928. The old days of 'Drums' were now well and truly history, and one half of the famous Dublin rivalry was gone forever.

'That went against our wishes,' says Robert Prole. 'Part of the agreement was that the name of Drumcondra would live on and Home Farm were to keep that name for their team in the League of Ireland. However, they obviously thought differently after they got control of the club and soon after the name of Drumcondra FC was dropped and left to the history books—and there was nothing we could do about it. There was anger and bitterness at what they had done.'

The Drums transfer was the biggest financial deal in the history of Irish soccer up to that point, with all Drumcondra shares transferred to Home Farm trustees Brendan Menton and Don Seery. The hopes for the future of the club were soon proved unfounded when Menton and Seery declared they would be not taking the club professional, but rather would remain amateur. 'We are not interested in professionals,' declared Menton at the takeover, but as one FAI official noted at the time, 'Bohemians saw the light—they turned professional'. Indeed, Bohemians' decision to change their status from amateur to professional highlighted the difficulties of competing with amateur players, and also suggested an increased bargaining strength on the part of the players. The folly of Home Farm's decision to remain amateur was obvious in the following years: the club never finished higher than tenth for the next fifteen years. At that time the League was split into two divisions and the club was relegated into the First Division in 1987.

Even though Shelbourne are the home team at Tolka Park these days and despite their recent successes, the crowds have never returned to Tolka. When Drums went, so too, it seems, did their fans. It bears testament to the fact that Drums and Tolka meant far more than just football to the northsiders of Dublin—it was tribal. If you were Bertie Ahern growing up in the suburb of Drumcondra, it meant picking gooseberries to buy a season ticket.

If you were his brother, Maurice, it meant marching to the house of the owners with a gang of schoolfriends to let them know they couldn't sell one of your favourite players and you'd be protesting by not turning up for games anymore. If you were one of the thousands who supported Drums, your heart just wasn't in it after Home Farm took over. The good times were gone, now just memories to be held onto and stored and retold to kids and grandkids. The Drums fans are a unique clan; thirty years on they still call themselves and identify themselves as Drums fans. In all likelihood they have seen the current League of Ireland offerings and refuse to follow any other team. Remaining a Drums fan is a way to stick with the past and the golden days, and also a refusal to be associated with the modern norm of half-empty stadia and half-empty hearts.

Shamrock Rovers watched as their great rivals changed hands and the Rovers' ruling family, the Cunninghams, also started to look to get out of the game. As speculation mounted about the future of the club in 1972, Joe Cunningham Jnr was explaining that they had probably taken things as far as they could:

> 'I feel we have gone off the boil at board level. What is needed is an injection of new blood. New ideas and new enthusiasm could steer the club in a different direction.'

The Cunninghams' deep involvement with Rovers was unique and stretched back to the 1920s, when Joe Cunningham, a local bookmaker, took an interest in the club in 1925; he had virtual control of it by 1936. With Joe as Chairman and wife Mary Jane as Director, as well as sons and daughters involved in later years, the Cunninghams' link to Rovers stretched across family generations. The decision to sever this link must have been a heavy one to bear. It was the sign of the times, however. Ireland—and Irish football—had changed and the old guard knew it; it was out with the old, and in with the new.

Enter the Kilcoynes to take their place in the annals of Irish football. For the next twenty years, for better or worse, the Kilcoynes were to have a determining influence on the game in this country. Opinions on that influence differ: to this day the Kilcoyne name is still dirt to many Shamrock Rovers fans because of the family's decision to sell the football ground at Milltown in 1987. Back in 1972, however, the Kilcoynes saw only a bright opportunity to enter the football scene and bring some entertainment back to the game.

The Kilcoynes were building developers, while their younger brother, Louis, worked in the hotel business. He was assistant manager at the Gresham Hotel in the city centre, and dreamed of running his own hotel one day. But then he experienced an unexpected change of heart:

'I was twenty-nine and realised I didn't want to do it anymore. I knew I wanted to be involved in football and to be a sports promoter, so just like that I quit my job and career prospects at the Gresham to be a football promoter.

I managed to get Pelé and Santos to come over to Dublin in 1972 and later on, through John Giles, managed to get Don Revie to bring Leeds here. Through the Santos connection I managed to get an invitation for the FAI to go to Brazil in between the World Cups in 1972 to play in a Mini Cup, as it was called. In doing all that I remember talking to my brothers and they said, "What are you after?" and I think I said something to the effect that there is a niche in here where you can make [it]—you can change football.

You could liven it up … we seemed to be forever playing Poland and very occasionally someone like Spain in what was becoming the FIFA Cup qualifiers. We very seldom got a decent glamorous side and I saw that niche in bringing those teams over and I thought I could make changes. The realisation then was to make a real impression, you want to be involved with the game on the inside. That resulted in my brothers looking at getting into football and an easy way was to acquire a club because it gave you automatic membership of a council or of a management committee, so simplistically that was the thinking.'

Although the Kilcoynes are synonymous with Rovers, it nearly wasn't Shamrock Rovers that they got involved with, as Louis Kilcoyne explains:

'Ironically, we thought to buy Drumcondra initially. The Proles
were looking to move on, they were fed up. We knew it at the time,
but we didn't realise the extent of their desire to finish. And we
actually made an agreement with old Sam Prole [but] he backed
out of it and sold it to Home Farm instead, on the same day as he
was to come and sign an agreement with us.'

The revelation that the Kilcoynes might have taken control of
Drums leaves one of those tantalising *what-if* scenarios. How
different might football in Ireland have been if Sam Prole had not
reneged on the deal and had sold the club to the Kilcoynes? Would
Milltown still be standing and Rovers still playing there? What if
they had kept the name of Drumcondra and remained
professional? What if the Drums–Rovers rivalry had lived on?
What if Eamon Dunphy had returned to his boyhood club along
with John Giles? What if the faithful tribe of Drums supporters
had never drifted at all? Would the game have been very different
if the Kilcoynes took Drums? It's a question that could be debated
over many a pint. The true story, however, is that the Kilcoynes
took over at Shamrock Rovers:

'... then I met Des Cunningham by fluke and there were rumblings
that one of his players had refused to come out at half-time over
two and sixpence, or a win bonus, or whatever. And he was
confirming that and saying that he would do anything to get out of
it. So, in a matter of two to three weeks we had bought and taken
over Shamrock Rovers.

The Cunninghams were keen to get out as they were all
exasperated because the crowds had stopped coming. The
Cunninghams really knew that in the 1960s, whilst they won a few
Cups, they weren't winning any leagues. They may have won a
League in the 1960s, but they weren't beating all and sundry and the
crowds had diminished and the Cup would give a false sense of
"here we go again". But, and I hate using clichés, we took the club
over thinking we could awaken the sleeping giant. However, in
hindsight, there was a bit of naivety there.'

Naivety there may have been, but that unfettered enthusiasm for
the game saw Louis Kilcoyne bring Pelé to Dalymount Park,

organise an Irish team to play Brazil in the Maracana and help with the first All-Ireland XI team to play in Lansdowne in 1973. If such talent could be brought to bear on a League of Ireland team, then perhaps Rovers fans could dare to harbour hopes that the good times would come around again.

So that's how things stood at the opening of the decade, in 1972: the old families of the Cunninghams and the Proles were gone; Rovers had taken a step forward with the Kilcoynes now in charge, who had money to spend; while Drums took a step backward by becoming amateur under Home Farm's control. Neither approach, as it turned out, would bring success.

II. The administrators

As well as new faces at club level, a new breed of power broker was also rising through the ranks in the FAI at this time, men who were to become powerful not just in Irish football but also eventually in European terms. They were breaking away from the old family power bases in the League and emerging with a fresh impetus and fresh ideas on how to change things for the better. But, as ever, the system ensured that change would come slowly, and too late. To attain any position of influence or power, one had to work up from local club level onto the FAI Council where, after a few years of meeting after meeting, committee after committee, politicking after politicking, one could eventually hope to rise to a position of influence. As with any organisation whose structures had remained the same for over fifty years, the wheels of change spun slowly and rarely smoothly.

Pat Quigley is what they call a 'lifer'. He gave his life to the cause of Irish football, working his way up from junior football in Mayo to eventually become FAI President. Over a career that spanned thirty years, he saw at first-hand the culture of officialdom that ensured the cobwebs were never swept out:

'I was with the Mayo League for a number of years and then I got onto the Connacht Football Association and at that particular time the FAI Senior Council had written to us to say that the representative—we were allowed one seat from Connacht—and that the representative from Connacht wasn't really turning up to meetings and that wasn't really acceptable. So they asked us to nominate somebody that would be available to go on the Senior Council. I was elected because I had the best car at the time. I was a medical rep. and had to drive around the country, you see, in my Avenger, so it was decided I would be the best man for the job.

I remember going to Dublin to my very first meeting. I arrived at 80 Merrion Square and the meetings were always on a Friday night at about 7.30pm. I arrived and said that I was the new representative from Connacht. Now, the post hadn't arrived or the fax hadn't arrived to say that I was taking over the new position. I told Charlie Walsh, who was President at the time, who I was and so on and someone said to me, "Look it, we don't have any official notification in writing so therefore you cannot come to the meeting." I was being told this after I had travelled 150 miles and I was a bit disappointed to say the least! But in fairness to Charlie Walsh he said, "We have to let Mr Quigley in, he would be doing a round trip of 300 miles and can't he come into the meeting? He can just listen, observe, make no comment and won't he get the feel of the thing and the next time everything would be all right." So thankfully that is how I got into my first meeting in Merrion Square and little did I think that on that particular night that eventually it would lead to me becoming President of the Football Association and Chairman of the UEFA Youths.

The meetings though were tedious and very political. That was the time of Peadar O'Driscoll who was the long-serving secretary, and that was the time when we would go through all the correspondence and letters. Peadar would take an envelope out of his pockets and he would say, "Here, lads, I have a good one, and God knows who it would be from—some other association and so on. There would only ever be two or three letters for correspondence and it was whatever Peadar decided which it would be at the time. He was unique in his own way, but extremely well-known throughout Europe and respected throughout. I suppose it was the age of not bringing out much correspondence, of letting things go along and if things were going all right, well don't do anything to upset them. It was a culture of don't look much to the future at all, things were going grand so let's not upset them, just keep playing the football, that is what it is all about.'

Quigley's background in junior football—he had rarely gone to a League of Ireland game—and the growing strength of junior football within the FAI together gave rise to a power struggle that would plague the League for the next thirty years. In short, the League of Ireland and the Junior Football factions sought to create their own power-bases, and came to resent more and more each other's influence on Irish football. This led to a stand-off, with little or no interaction between them in a footballing sense and both sides looking down their nose at the other's role in the game.

Ollie Byrne, Shelbourne's Chief Executive, believes that the advancement and development of the junior game detracted immensely from the League and affected its future:

'People wanted power and realised that there was power and there was strength from being in power in football. There were a group of people that manipulated and got together for power. There was Des Casey, there was Joe Delaney, there was Fran Fields, there was The Doc, Tony O'Neill, there was Louis Kilcoyne—they all got together within the League and the FAI and it was all about power.

Now don't get me wrong, there were all people in the old days who were also prominent powerful people and they too had power behind them. But these legislators were far better. They go in like a politician does, "I vote with you on this, you vote with me on that and then I tell you what I will support you on that motion, etc." And you had three or four groups who were manipulating and controlling everything for power and that destroyed the game. There was the football side of it, but they then realised that there were benefits to being in power. Now, I am not saying anybody— and I want to clarify this—had their hands in the till or anything like that—but it was all about how they could utilise their positions in a self-centred way.

The power brokers that got into the League, they lost control of themselves, they lost sight of what their purpose was. The League's job is to manage that League and develop that League. To develop association football within that League. It is not to develop association football *per se*. Now I have no disrespect to anybody, but they felt they should bring the League to every quarter of Ireland, or as many quarters [as possible]. But there were two agendas. They publicly put that agenda out, but the second part, which was the real part, was what they were really after was more votes; the more clubs they got into the League, the more votes they got around the table.

And that was brought in to counteract the strength of the Junior game. So what was happening was the infighting and the internal structures of the game destroyed it. I am not saying that anybody deviously, maliciously, or purposely set out to do it, but that is what happened. Now think about it, I am not going to name clubs because they are genuine, great football people. But there are certain clubs in the League today that shouldn't be there. But people moved and changed things and diminished the strength and appeal of the game in the way they did it.'

Ollie Byrne is a unique man. Ask anybody who has met him and they will the say the same: he bleeds Shelbourne Football Club; it is his consuming passion. For better or worse, Byrne sees life through Shelbourne FC and, as a result, can annoy and frustrate some people with his single-mindedness and brash honesty. He is also a man who chooses to see himself as being on the outside, fighting the forces conspiring against him and his beloved club. He has never been one to curry favour with anyone, or to work with others in a 'power-broking' sense, as he refers to the approach of those administrators who began to emerge in the 1970s.

Two leading administrators were 'The Doc' Tony O'Neill and Des Casey. The Doc was one of this country's leading football brains and was probably the single biggest loss to the game when he died at the age of just fifty-four in 1999, leaving behind a powerful legacy at UCD, the FAI and UEFA. Along with The Doc there came Des Casey, who became UEFA's vice-president, where he oversaw the beginnings of the Champions League. Casey rose all the way up to UEFA by working up through the ranks of Irish football in the 1970s:

'I worked in CIÉ as a clerical officer but was always involved with Dundalk football club—my father was involved in the establishment of the club and also became treasurer of the League. I was chairman of the social club for a number of years and got the bar licence there and then in 1968 I took over as secretary of the club. Then in 1972 there was some financial difficulties in the

League and I was approached by two or three club reps to take over as treasurer on an acting basis. The first thing I had to do when I went in was I had to levy the clubs an amount of money and that was just to pay the secretary's wages The following year I was elected Treasurer on a permanent basis and that was when I started to devote my time to the League; at the same time I left CIÉ to take up a job as a trade union official in Dublin and as I was commuting between Dundalk and Dublin it suited me fine.

At that time though, the clubs were seriously struggling for money. With the agreement of clubs I introduced a system whereby we introduced a collective insurance scheme for all the clubs for the players when they would be off sick or out injured. And in conjunction with that we also introduced a system that they paid their affiliation fees along with their insurance on a standing order over a period of eight months during the season to try and alleviate the hardship on them.

Further to that then we did a number of things, we integrated the travelling expenses of referees to lessen the disparity between the Dublin clubs and the provincial clubs. The majority of referees being based in Dublin meant that the provincial clubs were faced with higher expenses and travelling costs for the matches. So we changed that. What we did was we introduced a system whereby the clubs would just pay the referee's fee for the match and we then introduced a system whereby the travelling expenses would be paid by the League. But the clubs would contribute equally to the cost of that, it could be maybe £15,000, £20,000 and they would start off and the League would pay it and all the clubs would contribute the same. I suppose I started a cooperative—with equality.

I have often said that from a position of when, taking up the position and having to levy the clubs that paid a secretary's salary in 1972, to when I left in 1994, the League's finances were in a very healthy state and were certainly one of the most financially viable of any of the affiliates. They had about £150,000 in a building society; they had about £170,000–£180,000 altogether, which was good and the League was financially sound.'

New sponsorship money for the League arrived in 1974 thanks to a deal with Bass. The prize money was increased, but it was still very small relative to what the clubs needed to survive. It always seemed as if the League was grateful for any kind of sponsorship and prize money rather than seeking a partner in sponsorship and arguing its case. In 1976 the prize money was just £2,500—barely enough to cover a club's overheads for a month. It wasn't until 2005 that meaningful prize funds were being offered, when eircom's sponsorship deal with the FAI resulted in a prize fund of over €400,000, with €100,000 going to the League winners: a massive increase of €82,000.

The League may have been improving financially under Des Casey in the 1970s, but for the clubs the financial burdens were getting heavier as the League's popularity continued to deteriorate. Of course, no one wanted to admit that the League's popularity was waning, but the signs were there. Peter Thomas, Waterford Utd's legendary goalkeeper during their heyday in the 1960s and 1970s, remembers when he first realised that the rot had set in:

> 'I remember in one game standing in the goal and looking at the crowd and there was certain areas of the stadium that if you had a good crowd in there, there they would be banked up on the left-hand side. But as the years went by the numbers were declining and there was nobody there. You could clearly hear the mimicking from the wags in the crowd whereas when you got a good crowd you could never hear it. It struck me then, standing in my goal, that people just weren't interested anymore.'

Over at Shamrock Rovers, Louis Kilcoyne had been at the helm for nearly five years. In that time the team had drifted from fifth place to bottom of the League and the fans simply weren't interested in a struggling team. The Kilcoynes' initial enthusiasm had faltered, given the harsh realities of club management, but Louis Kilcoyne still had one more trick up his sleeve—and if this didn't work, then surely nothing would.

III. John Giles and the Shamrock Rovers dream

> 'I want to see Irish football standing on its own feet, to set standards to be followed by others rather than for us to be led. We should not worry about England but set our own standards at League and international level. We must entice young boys to stay at home and create something worthwhile here.'

That was John Giles stating his case and his ambition after the announcement, in June 1977, that he was taking charge of Shamrock Rovers. In an interview with Vincent Browne for *Magill* magazine in December 1977, Giles stated boldly:

'Ultimately, I want to win the European Cup with Shamrock Rovers. This may sound fantastic, but when you consider the amount of football talent there is, it isn't all that outrageous an ambition.'

So here it was, at last. This was the greatest opportunity for Irish football to get back on track and regain its place of honour. John Giles, Ireland's greatest ever player and one of Europe's best midfielders, a man who was central to Leeds Utd's revival and subsequent dominance of English and European football, was coming home after twenty-one years. And he had a plan of action.

Giles was a green youngster when he left Dublin, but even then he was a superstar amongst schoolboy footballers. He joined Man Utd under Matt Busby and broke into its stellar first team at the age of seventeen. However, Giles' single-minded determination, which was to mark him out throughout his career, led to his departure from Old Trafford after a disagreement with Busby. United's loss was Leeds' gain; Busby would come to rue his decision to let Giles go. Two English League titles, two FA Cups, two Fairs Cups and one League cup later, Giles had done it all and won it all in the game.

By 1977 he had enough of English soccer. A successful first season as manager at West Brom had taught him that club owners were always going to be in charge. For a man who was a perfectionist and who wanted full control of footballing matters, this state of affairs was never going to work out. He had been managing the Irish team for the past four years and had built up a relatively successful team. Now, however, one more challenge lay before him and he was eager to grasp the opportunity to tackle it:

'I never liked management and that is the reason I came home. After we got promotion at West Brom the first board meeting with the directors didn't sound good. I thought they would say, "Okay,

well done, what do you want?" They were sort of a bit cribby and I
got the attitude that no matter how well you did as manager, you
are an employee. That was it, you are an employee, they were going
to do as they liked. I said to the chairman I wasn't happy about it
and he said that wherever you go in football, you get the same
problems. In other words, you just have to put up with that. But at
that time Louis Kilcoyne was married to my sister and Louis asked
me to come back to Rovers and put an option on 50%. I thought at
the time the only way to do the job and to have control of what you
are doing is to be a part-owner, like a lot of people do in their own
business, and so I decided to come home.'

Giles was returning home for good and he wanted to instil the
highest of standards, have the best coaching and the finest facilities
to bring the League of Ireland up off its knees. It presented the
League with a golden opportunity to shake off its mediocrity of
the past twenty years and actively look to a better future; a chance
to restore some pride; a plan to bring the crowds back; and, most
importantly, the possibility of proving to Irish lads that England
wasn't necessarily the Holy Grail of their ambitions. It was nothing
short of a revolution:

'John and I would talk about it because we were brothers-in-law,'
explains Louis Kilcoyne, 'and we would talk about it regularly.
Mutually it seemed like a good idea for John to come back and
invest in the dream of what Rovers might achieve. I think the
attraction for him was similar to ours in that we might be able to
upgrade football in Ireland and particularly at Rovers and we
agreed to establish a full-time policy and the concept was obviously
very exciting.
    The dream was to develop Glenmalure Park and make it a 12,000
seater, but the financing of that was serious and it was going to take
some time. It wasn't going to be built or redeveloped in a year—it
would have to take its course.'

Giles was clear on what he wanted to achieve, and what he
needed to achieve it. Louis Kilcoyne recalls his determination:

'… Even Glenmalure was a jaded old shithole, which we attempted to upgrade, and one of John's first demands was that we had better have a good playing pitch. And his quote at the time was, "It is hard enough to play football, but at a minimum let's have a decent surface." Because when he came over here we were probably guilty of not having the pitch up to standard. And he was the spur to reinvigorate and reinvent us.'

Eamon Dunphy was one of Giles' first appointments and he helped coach the youth team and contributed to the vision of what they could do:

'We thought we would be a big club. We said to ourselves, if we can lay down the standards at Milltown and build on it over a five- to ten-year period, which was the project, then grand, it can work.'

Fran Gavin, now General-Secretary of the Professional Footballers Association of Ireland (PFAI), played in the League of Ireland for over fifteen years. At this time, however, in the late 1970s, he was a promising young centre-half at Derby County—but he wanted to come home.

'I remember sitting in the office with John Giles and Eamon Dunphy and Ray Treacy. They explained to me what their plans were and there would be a European League and there would be representatives from Dublin in it and it was going to be Shamrock Rovers. That is what they were going to do and their intentions were right. We had a full-time professional set-up, we had a lot of young players there. At the time it was the only full-time professional set-up. Rovers was geared to absolute professionalism with John Giles and that is the way he worked.

The facilities were very good, we trained in Belfield, and you know Eamon Dunphy was an excellent coach, there is no doubt about it; and you had John Giles who was highly regarded on the international scene from his days at Leeds and West Brom. It was good as a purist of football, I would have been eighteen or nineteen and it was ideal. They tried to teach you the right things to do that they considered this is what you did when you got the ball; you passed the ball and built up slowly and it was patient and it was good football. It was away from this kick-and-rush stuff all the time. And that was good if you felt comfortable with the ball at your feet—John Giles went for those sort of players—but if you didn't, you were lost.

They even sent us to college once a week. We went to Sundrive and that was an idea they had to get a more rounded player. We did all sorts of stuff, we actually did cooking, we did a bit of French, some Civics. It was once a week and they had the idea that they wanted to have a more rounded player and to educate the young players. It was compulsory at Rovers to go, whereas in England they said to you if you wanted to go, you could go. It was not an issue of forcing you to go, or even encouraging you. But it was compulsory with Rovers for all the full-time players, the younger lads particularly. It was an afternoon a week—three hours a week. We would all go out and do whatever was on at that time and it was very interesting that they could see that you had to work not only on the physical fitness but on this overall approach. It was more of a wholesome approach. They were more interested in the rounded footballer.'

After all the hype and preparation, the opening game of the 1977–78 season was surrounded by high expectations and hopes for Rovers. The game was away to the Cup holders, Dundalk, up in Oriel Park. The crowds came to Oriel that day curious to see what this Rovers team would be like. They duly won 1-0, but to many the manner of their victory was unconvincing. The *Independent* went straight to the point:

'The eagerly awaited meeting of the new-look Shamrock Rovers and FAI Cup winners Dundalk brought the expected big attendance which paid £2,000 at the stiles to Oriel Park last night, but Rovers did not show enough to justify the widely held belief that they will sweep the decks this year.'

The knives were out already for Giles and his Rovers dream.

First to go was Eamon Dunphy, who, within that first year, had seen enough to convince him that the League and other clubs weren't interested in what they were trying to do.

'I thought about it for twelve months, but then I got out. I ran away from it because I was not going to involve myself any longer. I mean there were fellas robbing clubs, there were players robbing us, putting in for overtime they never had to do playing matches. And it was awful stuff, they were totally ripped-off. Giles had to put up with awful stuff by players, by other people, by other clubs; there was jealousy, the press was hostile and the schoolboy leagues were hostile—they wouldn't even let us in to play in their top league. It was hopeless.

They wanted to keep it down at their level, at the Athlone/Finn Harps/Drogheda Utd level. They didn't want us to rise because they knew that they couldn't rise and they didn't want a professional club dominating the League, as they put it. These were small-minded people with their own parochial interests. It took me six months to realise that this was happening. I had given up as a player then and I made the decision to come home. I had massive opportunities in England—huge opportunities—Fleet Street and all sorts of things and I committed to the League of Ireland because I really thought I could change and modernise it, blah, blah, blah . . . Boy was that a mistake.

I even gave my FAI Cup winner's medal away after we won the FAI Cup in our first season. I gave it to the guy that got me my NUJ card, Sean Kinsella, and I didn't think nothing of it. He was a Sligo fan and I said, "Here it is, you got a medal and thanks for getting me my card." I had utter contempt for them. I have never been back to a League of Ireland ground since.'

So where, and how, did it all go wrong? Fran Gavin espouses one theory:

'I think the rest of the league weren't ready for Shamrock Rovers; the FAI weren't ready for them and they were ahead of their time. They won the Cup in the first year, they didn't win anything the next year, and then I think there was problems then.'

Some of those problems definitely involved the weight of expectation and good old Irish begrudgery. The new-look Rovers arrived with great fanfare and people sat back and dared them to to sweep the boards. Instead of allowing them the breathing space to build up to achieve their ambitions, the footballing world was ready to sneer if they fell at the first hurdle. On top of that, much was made of a comment John Giles allegedly made, declaring that Rovers would win the European Cup within five years. To this day he claims he never made that remark:

'It is amazing what journalists write in their papers, saying I had a five-year plan to win the European Cup and this sort of thing. I had no plan. I always made sure that I never put a time limit on everything. I knew even in those days that it was deadly to do that. But of course the papers have to put a story in and suddenly there is a five-year plan to win the European Cup, which is madness. I would never say anything like that. I wasn't a fool. I wasn't stupid enough to think that we were going to get as good as Real Madrid, but it could have eventually have been possible to win in Europe. I would say it was perfectly possible. But what I was trying to do was to stop some of the good young lads going to England and build up a team that could play in the League of Ireland and put up a good show in Europe.'

The pressure to achieve everything at once eventually undermined the team. Although they did win the Cup in the first season, they finished fourth overall in the League, which meant they wouldn't play in Europe until the following season. Inevitably, the gibes started: 'How are you going to win the European Cup if you're not even in it?' Once the floodgates were opened, all the old football grudges against Shamrock Rovers, Giles and Louis Kilcoyne came pouring out in a tide of insult and derision. Anyone who had an axe to grind took the opportunity to do so now; they queued up to dance on the grave of Rovers' dream.

Louis Kilcoyne remembers it well:

'There was great jealousy out there and you either love or hate Rovers, and most clubs didn't love us because we had that great tradition, well before my time, of winning Leagues and Cups. There was enmity and bitterness there. There was a suspicion that we were too uppity and too big for our boots and that we would steal a margin. I say perceived because we didn't have a bottomless pit, you know. But our motivation was just to make Rovers great again. And nothing else.'

Fran Gavin agrees:

'There was a lot of jealousy when they saw Rovers coming back. Rovers being successful meant that someone else wasn't going to be successful so as a result they weren't encouraged amongst the clubs. My way of looking at it was, there was a bit of envy around the place and Rovers had this huge set-up you know, but that is only natural.'

Gavin also feels that men like Giles and Dunphy were ahead of their time, and ultimately pulled back by the narrow-mindedness of their peers:

'I think the problem there was the type of football John Giles wanted to play, you could play it in Milltown because the pitch was absolutely fantastic and he saw it that way and he made sure that it was a big priority. I mean if the surface was right, you could play football on it. But when you went outside of there and you went to some of the country clubs and some of the other clubs in Dublin, you just couldn't play football on them. It was very, very difficult and in the middle of winter it was even worse. You were brought down to their level. That is the way he worked: he brought in the international set-up, he brought it into Shamrock Rovers and, unfortunately, we weren't ready for that. It was kick-and-rush stuff here, people were impatient and you'd be playing against big strong lads, you know.

I just think that they didn't have the wherewithal to do it basically, you have to realise that John and Eamon came from full-time professional backgrounds and a long time in football, but professional football. People here didn't have that, it was a part-time set-up and most of them had other things to do; most of the boards were voluntary, the people that ran the clubs were business men maybe and with the exception of maybe one or two clubs. So they didn't have the wherewithal to do it. It wasn't a case of they didn't know how to do it, they wouldn't know how to invest; they didn't have the people to invest that sort of money and they were doing okay as they were at the time, so why put themselves into huge debt to do it? What was the return for it? You might get into Europe and in the first round get knocked out. That was the way it was—very short-term thinking.'

Giles had a very definite vision of what he wanted to achieve, but he was hampered by the reality of football in Ireland. Perhaps he could have modified his vision in order to be successful within that reality, but then, modification just wasn't his style. A story recalled by Johnny Byrne, former coach at Rovers, is very telling:

'I remember once when we went down to play Thurles town. We walked the pitch before the match and there was a greyhound track and the pitch was in the middle of it. The grass wasn't cut, it was probably the worst pitch ever—there were some bad ones, but this was bad. I went and spoke to John [Giles] about this and I said, "John, far from me to tell you what to do, but I would be telling the lads today to hoof the ball up and pick up bits and pieces and go from there." And this is exactly what he said to me: "I know you are right JB, but in my heart I cannot do it—it is not what I believe in." And still to this day I haven't mentioned that to him because he had a way, he had a dream of the way he wanted football played and there was no way you could achieve that on a pitch in Thurles town.'

Dunphy is still unforgiving about the fact that their biggest enemies were from within their own footballing community. That really was the rub:

'It is the kind of people that are in the League of Ireland. There is a breed of person in it that is small town, county councillor, freebie, who contribute nothing and take as much as they can. They have always held the power in Irish soccer and still do to this day. They have never contributed to anything and don't like big ideas and they don't like independent-minded people around because they upset the little cosy apple cart and they will show up the other clubs. They don't want a club rising that will show up their own; look at Pat's at the moment, they have been up and down and Derry too have been up and down. The worst thing that happened to Derry in terms of money was getting into the League of Ireland and winning. Dundalk, Drogheda, Finn Harps, belly up all over the place.

Nothing good is ever allowed develop here because they won't allow anyone to do it. We tried it when we were here, but they didn't want it. They said, no thanks, because it will interfere with our club.

They want what is best for the lowest common denominator. And that will always be the case.

They don't like talented people. They hate talented people—they are repelled by talented people. They vilified Giles when he came over, vilification beyond belief. This was a guy that was making a massive sacrifice and he was making one to do this thing and he was vilified. That is it. That is the story. It keeps happening and it keeps happening. I don't see any sign of change. There is an awful lot of chancers out there with coaching badges now.

And the Kilcoynes came along at Rovers with a vision and tried to implement it. First of all there were greedy players and they were exploited. Secondly they were mocked, thirdly people, other people in the League, feared them and tried to do them down. And fourthly they packed their bags and left and sold the ground and although that it is a very controversial thing and it is very sad to see houses there, but I thought they were right. This was no place for people with aspirations or ambitions because we were going to Athlone and changing in a hut.'

And that, in a nutshell, was that.

IV. The GAA revival

In stark contrast to the tale of woe that was Irish soccer in the 1970s, the GAA was embarking on the course that would see it come to prominence in the coming decades. John Giles and Eamon Dunphy may have been back in Dublin with great plans for Irish soccer, but it was Kevin Heffernan's Dubs and their titanic struggles with Kerry that were really transfixing the city. Under the stewardship of Heffernan, led by Tony Hanahoe and including such colourful characters as Jimmy Keaveney and Brian Mullins, the new Dublin team that emerged in 1974 set about winning hearts and minds by bagging Leinster and All-Ireland titles for the capital. The fact that the Jackeens were duelling for supremacy with the culchies from Kerry only made it all the more enthralling. Gaelic football was suddenly sexy and everyone, soccer fans included, wanted a piece of it.

Fran Gavin, a diehard soccer man, recalls that time with envy:

'When Dublin became successful in the 1970s, it was the equivalent to Ireland doing well in Germany in Euro '88 for the first time. That buzz that was around Dublin—people were painting their cars the Dubs' colours, people had the flags all out—it was exactly the same feeling in the community that you had when Ireland played for the first time in Europe, so you could not help as a young impressionable teenager but to be involved in it. I remember my mother knitted me a scarf even in the Dubs' colour and going down to the games and it was a huge thing. It was the nearest we were going to get to an FA Cup final. Going with 80,000 people and standing in Croke Park to cheer on the Dubs.'

It wasn't a given, though. At the opening of the 1970s, no one could have predicted what lay in store for the GAA and Dublin. Back then, it was still a quiet, depressed time for sport in the city: the League of Ireland was declining and the GAA had not yet gained a foothold in Dublin. Looking back now, soccer writer Peter Byrne poses an interesting question: with things so quiet and depressed, and with the city just waiting for someone to come along and grab it by the lapel, what if John Giles had arrived to take over at Rovers in 1973, a year *before* the success of the Dublin GAA team?

'When Heffernan came back to take over the team again in 1974 the amount of spectators at a Dublin match would have been 200 or 300. In 1974, Dublin played Kilkenny and they were in the Second Division and there were forty-eight watching them and that included subs. There was a club match before it you see, between two teams in Kilkenny and there had been something like 10,000 people in the ground and when the match was over Paddy Grace the county secretary was so embarrassed that he came up afterwards and said that a legend in hurling in Kilkenny had died and was getting buried that day, which wasn't true at all, but he was trying to make up a thing. The whole thing was dying in Dublin, you see. Now, John Giles came back to Rovers in 1977, but what if Giles had come back four years earlier when he ought to have come back? If he had come back in 1973 and done what he had said he would do, Heffo's army would have been aborted and it never would have happened.

Giles' arrival would have pre-empted Heffernan's Army. The same public were going—there has always been that floating public. There were diehards who would go to the GAA and there were diehards that would go to the football, but in between the vast majority of people would go where the best value was. So they then aligned themselves with the rise of St Vincent's in the GAA as it was significant and because it gave Dublin people something. It is an interesting point that the demise or the lowering of standards in the 1970s in the League of Ireland helped the GAA. There was nothing else there, and Heffo's Army filled the void.'

How it managed to fill that void provided a master class in what could be achieved with the right attitude, a lot of hard work and some good luck. Until Kevin Heffernan came along Dublin hadn't exactly shone in the GAA: they last reached an All-Ireland final in 1963, which they won by beating Galway by two points, but then nothing, for a whole decade. Arriving onto this barren landscape in 1973, Heffernan was aware he had a big task ahead of him, but as with so many of sport's legends, he had it all clearly mapped out. First up was fitness:

'We were down so low. When we started we wanted to get fitter than the others. So we did a thing that was quite unusual, believe me, in the 1970s: we began to train in the winter quite a lot. Now there might be a genuflection made towards winter training, but nobody really trained [then]. We started to really train from October right through and nobody—that was the theory—nobody played football on a Saturday before a Sunday match because there was a view that came out of the Ark: you should be hungry for the ball. As if suddenly you saw it and you were going to eat it! So we trained two nights a week, heavy stuff in the winter, and we played football on a Saturday. We had a match as well for club or county on a Sunday. Now the idea was to get as fit so that you are eventually going to be running when these other fellas are feeling the drag.'

Winning in sport is 90% belief, but that was going to be difficult to instil in a team whose heads had been bowed for so long:

'The players we had weren't actually bad players; they were good players and once we started to win—we had been so long without winning the confidence was at a very low ebb—so as soon as we started to win, fellas got really interested. They began to listen and began to observe and began to take on board the messages. Once we started to win, it was then possible to start putting some sort of tactical plan together. We were now fit and we were now starting to play with a tactical plan, which in turn was seen to be working, which in turn was increasing confidence and optimism. And which in turn was giving us the results.'

Simple in hindsight really, but then Heffernan was ahead of his time. Quite literally, Heffo's Army helped save the existence of Gaelic games in the capital. The GAA following that he helped to create was nothing that the Association had ever seen before:

'None of the soccer teams, like Rovers, were doing very well at the time. The rugby team was doing nothing at the time and it was in that vacuum that we suddenly arrived. I think there are a couple of things that appealed; first of all, we came out of the blue—nobody expected it; secondly, we started to play a decent type of football; and the guys on the Hill were looking for something to do on a Sunday afternoon. Remember there is a place down there called Croker waiting. And they started to arrive again and then it was an amazing surge of enthusiasm. If you were to go back and see some of the pictures of the slogans and the banners, they were terrific, they really were. It was reminiscent of Shankly's Army and all that, you know. But it was a huge thing and it was only subsequent to that it was curtailed because the gardaí got worried because there was so many people coming; there were so many banners and there were so many poles and they stopped them bringing the banners. And they were wonderful. I remember the first time I saw a banner that read: Kerry for the holidays, Dublin for the Sam. When you see that for the first time, it is something different.'

While Heffernan and Giles shared a sense of vision and purpose, a marked professionalism and a determination to change things for the better, there was one thing that made them very, very different: Heffernan had the support of his organisation behind him. The GAA was open to new ideas and looking for its path into the future:

> 'Up to that there was the traditional county board selection committee. Nobody had ever heard of a manager, there was a selection committee and they were usually five guys. And it was the usual inter-club rivalries and who you know and all this shite. Bitterness and rancour and old scores being settled. It was depressing now. But fortunately, Jimmy Grey came in, took the bulls by the horns then and said we are not going to have this. The county board used to nominate and select these five guys at a meeting, with people proposing other people. So Jimmy said, "I am going to appoint you and I want your approval," so he appointed myself and Donal Colfer and Lorcan Redmond. I didn't actually know Donal or Lorcan and then we were all twelve years together and we never had an argument and we never had a vote on what team we would pick. We would debate it and discuss it and we would start afresh and start from a different point of view and we continued until we were agreed. But we never, not once, had an argument.
>
> It was a remarkable association. We would start off from different points of view, but there was never an acrimonious point of view, it was always one that clearly recognised the value of each other's view and the fact that there was a legitimacy about it. I remember we started off late one night and said there is no way we can win on Sunday because we can't win centrefield. And that was the opening comment, and then we spent hours and hours talking about it and eventually we came up with a combination that would upset the opposition and change our structures and our set-up.'

Adding spice and colour to the Dubs' renaissance was a resurgent Kerry team under the care of Mick O'Dwyer. For the next five years Dublin v Kerry, City v Country, became the focal point for the GAA. It was a remarkable time, as Micheál O'Hehir recalled in his memoirs:

> 'Dublin's remarkable comeback in 1974 was extraordinary and it brought support for the county's teams to a new level of interest and fanaticism . . . It was, I believe, helped by the more widespread access to television . . . soon Dublin people who hadn't been in

Croke Park for years, if ever, were flocking to the national headquarters and to venues all over the country in support of their new idols.'

Leinster Champions six years in a row, from 1974 to 1979, and All-Ireland Champions in 1974, 1976 and 1977, as well as finalists in 1975, 1978 and 1979, the city's sports fans finally had something to cheer about and a team to rally around. In simple terms, GAA became the new soccer. But it was also about the need for a tribe, the need to feel a sense of belonging and a sense of pride. The fans could hold their heads high again—it was great to be a Dub in the late 1970s.

'With the GAA you just had Dublin against the Culchies, that was basically it,' Fran Gavin recalls, 'and you wanted to beat them. They were all coming up and taking our jobs and we could get them all in Croke Park and beat the shit out of them on the pitch— metaphorically speaking. That is why you could feel an affinity in that you wanted to be a part of something good happening. You have to remember that Ireland at the time was a depressing place to live. We didn't have a huge lot of things to cheer about, particularly in soccer and our international team was being hammered almost every week; we weren't doing well in the Olympics, we had never had any sporting icons, but now you had Jimmy Keaveney, Brian Mullins, Kevin Moran and all these guys were people living in the community, doing their business within the community and you could talk to them and they were all there available and that was a huge plus to us.

It was the height of the Troubles as well, it was a very tense time in Ireland, so people felt that this was their game and they felt a loyalty to it. Dublin never did [before] because it was a Culchies' game and soccer was always Dublin—it just was a very strong base for soccer. But now we had a very strong Dublin GAA team and the soccer fans had a reason to follow the Gaelic team and to be a bit more Republican and support the Troubles. And it was the success. Everybody wants success. But we also had this little Republican thing going in the background and those soccer fans who didn't like GAA, and personally I didn't, but it gave me an excuse to say, but it is the Dubs, it is not really GAA, it is the Dubs.'

Perhaps the finest moment was the 1976 final against Kerry. Bettered in the 1975 final by the Kerrymen, Heffo's Dubs were determined to get one over them in the final this time round, and duly did so with a not-unflattering score of 3-08 to 0-10. For the second time in three years the Dubs were All-Ireland Champions, and this time they had wreaked their revenge on the Culchies and dethroned them by a margin of seven points. It was a victory to be savoured, and the *Irish Independent's* post-match analysis summed it up well:

'The Dublin players did not forget what the support of the Hill has meant to them over the past three years. In the late September sunshine Captain Tony Hanahoe and his men did a victory lap across to Hill 16. This was what the Hill had been waiting for and this was for me the finest memory that will remain as they cheered their heroes, something deep and personal between the ordinary Dubliners and the team.'

While the GAA was reeling from its new-found success, there was also some reservation. The audience for Dublin games wasn't a traditional GAA audience, and it brought with it some very non-traditional habits and practices. Fintan O'Toole explains:

'The people who were up in Croke Park supporting the Dubs and queuing for the tickets were exactly the sort of people who were going over to Anfield and going over to Old Trafford. I remember at the time it was very disturbing for the GAA people that you had the chance of the atmosphere at the games changing when you had the Dubs involved. They were quite hysterical about it, the fact they were singing 'You'll Never Walk Alone' and all these foreign imported songs, but the reason they were doing that is because they were soccer people actually. And the GAA were very aware of this and again you can't forget the hysteria that was around the stuff. I remember Dublin played Cork in 1977 or 1978 in Cork and the hysteria around the Dubs coming to Cork. I mean the place was practically closed down. It was like England are going to play in Cork or something. And at the end of the day there was no trouble at all and it was great *craic* and Dublin slaughtered them because they were freaked out, I mean they were actually freaked out. Cork couldn't deal with the idea of all these Dubs coming down.'

The Dubs went on to compete in two more All-Irelands, beating Armagh in 1977 before losing heavily to Kerry in 1979, by eleven points. The high of Dublin GAA was over, to be revived only briefly in 1983 and 1995. As with any team, once the success dried up so too did the support and Heffo's Army began drifting away. Nonetheless, they left an indelible mark on the history of Gaelic games, putting Dublin on the map in a way no one had expected.

V. The GAA looks to the future

Flux and change are necessary in every society, but in the sports arena they can be destructive unless clubs are well established and have deep roots—as the League of Ireland was to learn. While there was an awareness of the ongoing changes in Irish society, the League's efforts to keep abreast of them never quite hit the mark.

In the 1970s the great white hope was the introduction of new clubs into the League, which it was hoped would help spread the gospel of soccer. This didn't quite work out as planned. A sixteen-team League was created for the first time in the League's history upon the accession of Thurles Town and Galway Rovers to the serried ranks in 1977. However, while soccer was becoming more popular throughout the country, teams like Thurles Town simply could not sustain it at senior level (increasingly, the junior ranks picked up the debris from the League of Ireland levels when it didn't work out). As a result, Thurles Town lasted just four seasons before resigning from the League. In Cork, meanwhile, things went from bad to farcical as the famous Cork Hibs were disbanded and replaced by Albert Rovers, from the same county, who then became Cork Albert, who then became Cork Alberts, and then Cork United, until finally dissolved in 1982. Is it any wonder that League of Ireland fans often wondered which team they would be following that season—and what their team's name would be.

The League was trying to be innovative and to secure the role of soccer in Ireland, but these sorts of shenanigans—uncertainties, name changes, dissolutions and disbandments—gave the League and its clubs even less credibility than before and played into the hands of their detractors.

Their failed efforts were thrown into sharp relief by the strides being made by the GAA. The legacy of Paddy O'Keeffe was a robust understanding of the direction in which Irish society was heading, and an awareness of and plan of action for the continuing urbanisation of the country. Just as the GAA began to act on O'Keeffe's advice, Alf O'Muiri came to the fore as the Association's new President. A native of Milltown, County Down, O'Muiri was more closely associated with Armagh GAA, and it was the Lurgan club that gave him the model for the profile and development of local GAA clubs as social centres within their communities. The Lurgan club had achieved this status in unique circumstances, where the Troubles had heightened the community's sense of heritage and belonging. Nonetheless, O'Muiri's first-hand experience of the club as social centre in Lurgan allowed him to pursue this vision across the country. This approach was, in fact, the saving grace for the Association in the volatile years of the 1970s.

In 1968 the GAA introduced a new system of grants, allowing for up to 20% of the cost to clubs for providing premises suitable for centres. The following year the Council appointed a Community Centre Committee, which was tasked with advising clubs regarding the types of centre suitable for particular areas and providing assistance and information, such as plans of existing centres. Following this, the Club Development Scheme was established in 1970 to help provide finance for new social centres by considering club's loan applications and raising the necessary capital. Its initial target of £250,000 was met within one year.

The most important development was still to come, however. In the 1960s a Commission on the GAA had been established to carry out an indepth study into the organisation and make proposals for its future. It published its report in December 1971, and it was hailed as being more important than any other document drawn up by the organisation.

The nineteen-member Committee, comprising both members and non-members, investigated every aspect of the GAA, their work representing 'the most exhaustive self analysis by a voluntary organisation ever undertaken in this country' according to Marcus de Burca, the eminent GAA historian. That analysis was divided under eight previously agreed headings: Structure, Finance, Youth, Grounds, Communications, Hurling, Discipline and Sponsorship.

The 60,000-word, 140-page Commission report was the blueprint for the development of the GAA in the 1970s and 1980s. In its overhaul of the administration, it helped streamline and restructure the expanding organisation, making it better able to meet the challenges that lay ahead. It made wide-sweeping recommendations, such as: the Central Councils should meet quarterly; the Management Committee should handle the Association's affairs and be answerable to Council; the Central Development Committee should be responsible for the development of the GAA; the General Secretary was to be known as the Director General and should be supported by an accountant, activities officer, central development officer and a public relations officer (a position the FAI would not appoint for another twenty-five years). Significantly, its largest chapter was that on Communications, and it went into great detail on the issues of improving press relations, improving television coverage and publishing annuals and magazines. By contrast, Sponsorship was just three pages long and pitted with reservations.

It truly was an astonishing document and showed an admirable willingness to honestly assess and constructively criticise the organisation and its structures. The GAA had recognised that its very future and place in Irish society was at stake, and it produced a document that not only sought to deal with that in the rocky early years of the 1970s but to put in place structures that would see the Association through the next two decades. The organisation had done its homework, and done it well enough to ensure that the GAA would become a vital and exciting part of modern Irish society.

It goes without saying that all this was light years ahead of the League of Ireland. In traditional form, the League rushed to initiate a quick-fix solution, bringing in Des Casey to sort out the financial mess. Casey was forced to resort to levying the clubs a stipend just to pay the League Secretary's wages. It's like trying to compare chalk and cheese: while nobody knew exactly how Irish society would turn out by the end of the decade, at the beginning it was painfully obvious just who was going to survive between the League of Ireland and GAA.

To be fair, however, one of the most significant factors in the GAA's development and survival was the role played by the Church and the Christian Brothers, in particular. In this the organisation had a huge advantage over the League of Ireland. The League was trying to create loyalty out of nothing, whereas the GAA had a legion of young people who had been force-fed its ethos and its games. If the League had had that kind of support, things might have been very different indeed. Fintan O'Toole explains the extent of the Church's impact on the GAA:

'They were able to actually link in with the most forward-thinking movement, in terms of strategic planning and organisation in Ireland, which was the Church. If you look at the way the Church operated in terms of the suburbs, the cement was hardly dry before there was a new Church in—and the Church actually went into very substantial debt in the 1970s due to its building programme. Dermot Ryan, who was the Archbishop at the time, borrowed huge amounts of money for it on the basis that if you looked at it in business terms, it was an investment. It was a double threat for them, you see. If these suburbs … grew up without the Church, it could be really dangerous, but also the opportunity was fantastic because there was nothing. They recognised there was so little in terms of infrastructure or entertainment or anything else. You build your church, the church becomes the centre of the community and the way in which people define themselves. The GAA was kind of drawing on this mentality you see.

Schools were also being built at a great pace and with schools it was a great base for connecting in with the GAA. The fact that soccer was kept out of the schools was a huge disadvantage to them, but it was a disadvantage which could have been turned into an advantage in that there was a huge cachet around the unofficial nature of soccer. Certainly when I was in Crumlin we played GAA in school, but on the road we played soccer. If you went up to the local park at any time when the schools were off, it was 99 per cent of the kids who were playing soccer. They had only put the jerseys down and all that sort of stuff. It was simple stuff like that in a way.'

Soccer, then, could provide an alternative to the prevailing authority and be seen as a quiet rebellion against the Church and the Christian Brothers. It did not exploit this opportunity fully, however, and failed in its attempts to provide an alternative to the authority, as writer John Waters describes:

> 'We did not look to Merrion Square. The attitude at the amateur level towards home-grown professional soccer and its administrative organisations was ambivalent, a little suspicious perhaps on account of the hierarchical structure of both Irish professional and semi-professional soccer being in some way analogous to the GAA hierarchy, but also a strange kind of contempt arising from a sense that the game as played at local level plugged directly into the international level—that it was to Manchester Utd rather than Athlone Town you looked for inspiration . . . Every boy who ever kicked a ball dreamed of playing at the highest level, so ending up at Sligo Rovers would be, by definition, a defeat . . . In a sense, then, the FAI has always seemed to be a kind of interloper in the dream that soccer offered. Like virtually every other level of institutional Ireland, it failed to interpret or nurture the dreams of the people in a way that might be termed remotely useful.'

VI. Derry City and the Troubles

The GAA benefited from Alf O'Muiri's adoption of the Lurgan club model, as we have seen. The League of Ireland, too, had a similar blueprint for sport as community focus, but it just didn't seem to recognise it at the time: Derry City FC.

Throughout the 1970s the situation in Northern Ireland got steadily worse. Sectarian tensions became more entrenched as the violence spiralled out of control. It was a bleak time, with no hope, no light at the end of the tunnel to counter the wanton bombings, killings and maimings. For those living with the daily terror of the Troubles, it was a time of suspicion, fear and intense tribal loyalties. Incredibly, amidst all this, sport retained its place at the heart of the community.

When you think of Derry and the Troubles, you immediately picture the Bogside, the scenes of riot in the aftermath of Bloody Sunday—and the Brandywell, the home of Derry City FC. A truly great club belongs to its people, and Derry's particular place in the North and the Bogside's particular place in Derry lends the

Brandywell and its supporters a belonging quite unlike that found at any other League of Ireland venue, indeed, at any venue anywhere else in the world for that matter. Surprisingly, perhaps, it is soccer, not GAA, that has always been the first sport of Derry. Inevitably, though, in the 1970s the sport was steeped in the political and social upheavals going on all around. Nowhere have Derry City supporters had to endure more than on and at their soccer pitch, where sectarianism and violence attended nearly every encounter.

One of Derry City's most famous fans, and most prominent commentators, is Eamon McCann. A journalist and social activist, McCann is a lifelong Candystripes fan, as well as being a lifelong civil rights campaigner: his activism and his football support go hand in hand.

'There was a lot of sectarianism in those days and certainly in games against Linfield, in particular, it would have been there. Their fans would have been all packed at Windsor Park and we kept going there and it was good. There was considerable nervousness going to Windsor Park because it was not only that you felt you were entering into a hostile environment but you also had the perception that if trouble did break out the police force, far from protecting you, might even be on the other side. So this gave way to a certain nervousness.

Certainly there would be trouble after matches at the Brandywell and so on. I do remember the bus coming down Rossville Street after a match and the Linfield fans were leaving and holding up a herring and shouting "Cured at Lourdes". There was a certain wit to that. I think people threw stones at them with a smile on their face.'

Of course, the Troubles changed all that and the Bogside, and by extension the Brandywell, became synomous with the struggles of Derry's Catholic population:

'The civil rights march which was seen as triggering the Troubles [took place on] 5 October 1968 and was a Saturday,' continues McCann. 'I remember we sent someone out from a meeting we were planning at to check that Derry City were playing away so we wouldn't have a rival distraction in the city. A person called Fergal came back and said it was okay, they are playing away, maybe Crusaders or something like that, so we went ahead with our plans for the march but it turned out to be completely wrong.

I don't know how much difference we would have made to history if that information had been right—we might have had a bigger crowd or something—but that was just a little minor indiscretion to the extent that it was relevant and we were aware of it. But when the Troubles started there was always going to be trouble for Derry City and eventually, of course, the ground was banned and other teams refused to come there after the Ballymena Utd bus was burned.

The people in the Bogside burned the bus because it was there really, they could have burned any bus. It just so happened that it was the Ballymena Utd bus. They weren't targeted specifically, there were lots of vehicles being attacked for no reason. But nevertheless I could see why the other team would be saying, "This is too dangerous a place for us to go" and a lot of other teams had just been waiting for the opportunity to able to say, "We are not going to go to the Brandywell, it is alien territory inside a Catholic working-class area." It became inevitable that there was was going to be a bust-up between Derry and the Irish League structure.

There were attitudes on all sides of course, but the Derry City fans weren't paranoid that they were treated in a sectarian way. When Derry qualified for Europe in the 1950s and 1960s a few times, the IFA leaders in the North refused to support Derry City in wanting to play their matches at the Brandywell. They were saying, "This is unsuitable and the ground isn't fit for it" and so on. And that was perceived as sectarian—there was a lot of sectarianism in it. It was sort of understandable that the way Derry City was treated seemed to fit into a pattern. Although the way Derry City generally was treated by the authorities in the North and the IFA was seen almost as the sporting wing of the Stormont Government. You didn't have to be too paranoid to be able to imagine it like that and that shaped the perception of fans.'

Time and again Derry City FC pleaded with the IFA management to allow them play their home games at the Brandywell, but even though the security forces gave it the green light, the IFA continued to disallow it. Portadown were scheduled to play City on Saturday 14 October, but it was not to be. The day before, Friday 13 October, Derry City FC withdrew from Irish League football because they were not permitted to play their games at the Brandywell. After forty-three years, Derry was without a senior soccer team; City would remain in the wilderness for another thirteen years before being accepted into the League of Ireland.

'Don't forget, it was the year of Bloody Sunday in Derry,' says McCann, 'when the whole place went haywire here and then leading up to between Bloody Sunday to the Hunger Strikes, Derry City was out of football. Looking back on it it is difficult to see how regular football could have been played in the Brandywell at that time. There was a lot of violence, a lot of turmoil and it may simply be the case that it wasn't possible. Football fans certainly missed having a senior soccer team to support and to relate to. And there were a number of activists who kept the club going. The social club kept going and the structure was still there and there was annual elections and a chairman of the club and all that kept going, but there was just no team.'

While the fans in the South were ignoring the tasty treat of revival of soccer at Shamrock Rovers and instead feasting on English football, Derry City fans were deprived altogether, bereft of a team and distracted by the other, more important battles that had to be fought. For once, though, soccer retained its foothold, against all the odds. Thirteen years in the wilderness wasn't enough to drive the Bogside into the hands of the Gaelic Athletic Association; Derry was soccer to the core.

'One of the facts about Derry in the city itself,' explains McCann, 'is that it has always [had] a very well-structured junior soccer framework … This goes right back to the nineteenth century with local teams on the Bogside and all over the place. When I was growing up in Derry some of the big teams would have been Wellington Rovers, Foyle Harps, Rosemount and so on, who played to crowds of 2,000 or 3,000 in local competitions. And for all the kids on the streets your aspirations at [age] ten, eleven, twelve was to play for Bohemians, which was a local team run by Paddy McGlinchey, who was a coalman. Whereas that whole layer of activists of people who usually ran the local GAA and kept it going in parishes were predominant elsewhere, in Derry these people were soccer people. Once people get into it, it is very difficult to shift.

Derry had been captured by soccer at a very young age. It was an urban thing, but in terms of work and everything else it would also be because of the constitutional position. People would candidly look towards Britain as they would to people in the South obviously. And with that whole urban thing it just came naturally to people, I suppose. The GAA seemed almost as repressive and rural in its way when I was in St Columb's College. You weren't allowed to play soccer, they only played Gaelic and that was resented. It was run by the people who came from the borders and rural areas and most of the staff, the clerical staff and the priests, the vast majority of them were from rural areas. They were big into the GAA and us lot from the Bogside were into soccer. There was a feeling of being treated like a second-class citizen. We felt that we were regarded as less than wholly Irish and there was a real resentment towards the GAA.'

The North may have been in turmoil and the hunger strikes around the corner, but the Republic had its own problems to contend with heading into the 1980s. The boom years quickly became a distant memory as the economy went into a nose-dive and the old national wound of emigration was re-opened. The bleak 1980s would hit the country hard and none more so than the League of Ireland, now on the back of a twenty-year slide. Despite the arrival, in 1986, of the most successul Irish international manager ever in the form of Jack Charlton, the domestic game was on the verge of petering out entirely. The same old pattern was being repeated: empty terraces, clubs in debt and Mickey Mouse administration. People might have been glad to leave the old decade behind, but if they had known what they would face in the years ahead, they might well have decided to stick with the peaks and troughs of the 1970s instead.

Part Four

The 1980s: No worse there was none

THE FAN (IN A LETTER TO THE *EVENING PRESS*)

'I was out at Milltown last Sunday. There were a lot of old faces at Milltown that day. Quite a few of the old Rovers fans were in tears leaving the ground. Soccer in this country is going to fade away.'

I. The Rovers dream dies

'There was this beautiful photograph of a graduate class from UCD done for an IDA campaign, and they all looked very bright and hopeful, it was "employ us before we employ you" sort of stuff. A year after the photograph had been taken, the *Sunday Tribune* went through each and every single person in the class to find out what they were doing and every one was gone. Just gone. They were all working in America or England, there wasn't one of them who was still here. I actually remember walking down Grafton Street once and meeting somebody who asked me, "Are you still here? What the f**k is wrong with you? Are you just totally lazy?" It was like there was a sense that it was particularly profound because it didn't feel like it was a once-off. It didn't feel like there is a bit of a crisis going on. It felt like we were right back to where we started.'

So remembers one graduate of the early 1980s, giving some inkling of the doom and gloom of one of the most miserable decades in Ireland's history. The country had taken several steps backwards and was now back to where it was before—worse still, it was sliding even lower than people thought possible. It was a society on the brink of disaster. The 1979 oil crisis had plunged the world into its worst economic crisis since World War II and the Irish government's heavy dependence on foreign borrowing exacerbated the situation in Ireland still further. The statistics said it all: between 1979 and 1982 unemployment rose by 77% (although, interestingly enough, public service employment rose 13% from 1977 to 1981); by 1984 unemployment stood at 208,000, or 16% of the population—the EEC average was 10%; 25% of those in employment were public servants; 33% of the unemployed were under twenty-five years of age; 130,000 left the country in a five-year stretch between 1983 and 1988, with 1985 alone seeing 30,000 people emigrate. If you were young, ambitious and talented, Ireland was no place to be. The one difference from earlier emigration was that the emigrants were no longer looking for work as brickies or labourers, now they were the NIPPLES: New Irish Professional People Living in England.

Those who stayed behind had to witness the slow death of the Irish economy and society. The lingering image of Ireland in the 1980s was, as Paddy O'Gorman told us, of people queuing for a living. Dole queues were a regular part of people's lives; there were queues for job applications; job opportunities in the local chip shop saw lines of hundreds of people, all queuing for a chance, any kind of chance to earn money. It was a return to the fears of old: fear of unemployment, fear of losing one's job, fear of not being able to pay the bills, fear of losing one's house and fear of not providing for your family. The country was at its lowest ebb in every way.

Little wonder, then, that the League of Ireland also suffered in these years. Unlike the GAA, it had no contingency plan, no worst-case scenario handbook and no foundations in place to deal with the terrible effect of the recession-hit 1980s. Sports commentators were writing that:

> 'The past League campaign has been one long financial struggle with most of the teams playing before sparse attendances and the survival of the clubs, especially those filling the bottom eight places, has been in question right through the season . . . there is no way a club can survive a season of League of Ireland football from the turnstile receipts at home games.'

These were the bad tidings that greeted the League of Ireland in 1980, at the end of their first season and the start of a new decade.

Of all the sporting organisations, the League of Ireland felt the effects of recession most keenly, its lack of forward planning leading to week-to-week financial planning and internal rivalries and petty jealousies. The League needed new momentum badly— some would have said it needed nothing short of a miracle. So, what of John Giles' attempts to reinvigorate the sport and the system?

In three seasons, Shamrock Rovers had only managed to win a single FAI Cup and grandiose dreams of European domination were looking to be farther and farther away. What was worse, however, was how rival football people took great pleasure in seeing them fail. Here was somebody taking the initiative, trying to drag the League up by its coattails, but now that it was failing the short-sighted response from many within football was to crow over its demise. Giles remembers those days only too clearly:

'When I arrived back there would have been an attitude of, "Who does he think he is?" Big shot from Dublin and all that. In those days it was, and still is to a large extent, a lot of players did not do so well out of the game and they would be down on their luck and that was the culture. I was probably seen as too big for my boots. The papers would pick it up as well and the papers would go with the flow. Supposedly I was coming back to sell players and make a fortune. And even from the clubs there was a negative response to our plans. I thought the clubs would get on and we would work together. But instead they would try and bring you down. There was no feeling of goodwill. I didn't feel any goodwill at all.

I was surprised at it. I thought this was an opportunity and I couldn't see the sense, I couldn't see the logic in it; anybody with a bit of sense would look at it and say, "Well, where was the money in it for me?" There was nobody going along with it. I was always complaining about the state of the pitches. People got a pain in their arse listening to me. But the fact is that very few people did anything about it. It just wasn't there. The mindset just wasn't there. It was a case of, "We have always done it this way, this is the way we will still do it." I think it was too small-minded, "F**k Rovers, we will show them, what are they trying to do?" it was just petty. It wasn't like, "This is Rovers and they are trying to do something and if we go along with it, everybody will benefit." That wasn't the case.

I don't know if it is the case today even, I don't know. From what I can see, they are still bickering.'

By 1981 the writing was on the wall for Giles. Vancouver Whitecaps had come calling, and Giles took up the offer to move to Canada full-time:

'It wasn't going any further, I had a family to look after—by now I had six kids. We decided that it wasn't happening, so we toned it down then, the full-time lads had to come in part-time and we phased the thing out.'

Rovers weren't the only casualty of the League's attitude. Surely the writing was on the wall now for the League itself? A last-ditch chance had fallen into its lap, a chance to make change, rethink its position and plan for the future, but it had failed, and why? For observers it was the creeping disease of small-mindedness, petty jealousies and a lack of interest on the part of the fans, who had already been disenfranchised by a decade's worth of decline.

'We were very disappointed when we split,' says Louis Kilcoyne, Shamrock Rovers chairman. 'It was a serious investment in the club and we had very little to show for it, and we were down-hearted to such an extent that we went through the whole summer without even thinking of replacing John. And then we got Jim McLaughlin in, who, almost overnight, took on what John had, but he somehow understood the League of Ireland part-time mindset better than John did and had terrific success. But it was all still without any support from the great public.

Football wasn't your regular business project where you could budget and plan and put down strategies easily. The crowds didn't really respond. They had gone, period, and to get them back was more than difficult. I think the biggest attendance we ever had in Milltown in those four years was the year of the Cup the first year when we had something short of 4,000 to play Bohs. Less than 4,000 was the actual gate.'

The failure hurt Giles financially and personally, but he remained philosophical about it all.

'You only do what you can do. A lot of people said to me, Giles failed in doing what he did and I tried to do what I did. It was a case of climbing a small mountain and getting there or else going for Everest and not getting there. You have a much better chance of failing, but nobody else had done it or tried to do it.'

Rovers did go on to achieve notable successes, as Kilcoyne pointed out. They took a famous four League titles and three FAI Cups in a row from 1984 to 1987. Once again, Rovers were dominating the League in historic and thrilling fashion, but whereas in the 1950s and 1960s their wins had garnered fans and support, now the success of Jim McLaughlin's men was noticed by only a minority of fans. The simple fact was that fans had turned their backs on League of Ireland for good: it was too late.

John Byrne has been a lifelong and fanatical Rovers fan. As he sees it, in those early years in the 1980s the League was lost, with only a dedicated few interested enough to attend the funeral:

'One of the problems was that the sort of football that Giles played was too possessive. I remember the away games in particular, it was a case of, the game started nil all, so, why change it, you know? And especially then because all people knew was the thrust of English football. I think now people appreciate other styles of football. Unfortunately, Giles just tried to plant something there without understanding: he needed to be League of Ireland first and then develop it. It was too much, too soon, too suddenly and it was unbelievably at the wrong time. That was the worst decade because it got completely crap. You would go down to a match in Cork and there were daisies on the pitch. They hadn't even cut the grass.

The League had sunk so low that by the time Rovers got the four-in-a-row together, people had given up; there was only 9,000 in Lansdowne Road to see them winning the Cup. People had switched off; the greater mass of people had switched off, it didn't exist for them anymore. Rovers were like the Metropole and Nelsons Pillar. There was something like ring-a-ring-a-rosie about it, it just didn't exist for them anymore. People were turning their backs on them and I remember Louis Kilcoyne's attitude at the time was, if you've got a Rolls Royce in the garage, you don't have to show it off—it wasn't marketed at all. Stupid, you know. People didn't know it was a fantastic team, [but] it must have been one of the best part-time teams ever, anywhere. It actually got boring, they were too dominant, they were too good.'

For Robert Goggins, another lifelong Rovers fans and author of the club's official history, the failings reflected the club's inability to respond to change:

'The opening game of the 1984–85 season coincided with the first live match on ITV and our attendance was cut in half. This was on a Sunday afternoon. Even though they had installed floodlights two years earlier, they were still playing on Sunday afternoons and going up against live English soccer on TV. It was a different mindset, you see, and I don't think clubs really knew what to be doing. And I suppose it is like if you take the fan base we have now and you moved the matches to Saturday nights, I suppose you would have the majority of people saying, no, leave them there because we prefer Fridays. Whereas at that stage, you know, people were used to going on Sundays. That was the thinking behind it.'

Despite the apparent inertia, there were efforts at change. But, sadly, all imagination and creativity seemed to have left the country with the latest batch of emigrants because any attempts at dragging the League out of its doldrums only added up to papering over cracks, when what was required was much deeper thinking.

The pattern of disbanding and dissolution continued. In the late 1970s and early 1980s a number of clubs disappeared, folded or changed names. They would go out of business and then reform, leading to a confusing situation in many clubs: Cork Alberts became Cork United, Limerick AFC became Limerick United, Galway Rovers became Galway United, Waterford AFC became Waterford United, Cork United was expelled and then dissolved, Thurles Town resigned from the League, and some members of Limerick United broke away to form Limerick City, which then led to a high court case in which City were elected to the League in place of United, which was subsequently disbanded and then dissolved. How could a club build loyalty and identity when nothing stood still long enough for people to relate to it?

If that wasn't bad enough, desperation for sponsorship money saw the League take on the moniker: Pat Grace Kentucky Fried Chicken League. The points system was also changed: four points for an away win, three for a home win, two for an away draw and one for a home draw. By the end of the weekend, fans, journalists and officials would all have their calculators out trying to figure out just who was now going to be in first place in the Pat Grace Kentucky Fried Chicken League.

For the clubs, then, this was a time of constant struggle. At least there was some comfort to be taken from the fact that fairytale stories were being played out on the pitch, with the likes of Limerick Utd and Athlone making significant breakthroughs in winning League titles. Limerick, under the guidance of Eoin Hand, captured only their second ever League title in 1980, while Athlone Town won their first ever one in 1981 and followed that up with another in 1983.They were slowly coming out of the shadows of their larger Dublin rivals, and these smaller, more local clubs were better able to harness local imaginations and support. Like any of these sudden and short-lived successes, however, the initial burst of support couldn't be sustained and would trickle away when the team's glory years were gone.

Welcome though they were, even League titles couldn't hide the real problems for clubs. Athlone Town director, Seamus O'Brien, in an article for the *Sunday Press* at the end of November 1980, gave some impression of what life was like on the inside:

> 'It costs us £50,000 a year to keep the club going and we're relatively close to Dublin, where five of our away games are played. What depresses me is the amount of work we know has to go into the running of a club and the headaches of other clubs who are not in such a favourable location must be worse, so I wonder what's going to happen to football. If we got £3,000 on each of the home gates we would still have to make up some thousands to keep the game going in Athlone. How much worse it must be for other clubs I can only imagine.'

If it was tough being a club official, spare a thought for the lowly club manager. Even though he was International Team Manager,

Eoin Hand was still getting a raw deal from both the League of Ireland and Merrion Square. He was fighting it on both fronts: his Limerick side was fined by the FAI in 1980 for failing to fulfil a fixture, despite the fact that the previous year Rovers had escaped a penalty under similar circumstances, and he was also meeting opposition from the FAI and attempts to undermine his role as International Manager. Most famously, he tells the story of having to enlist his wife to act as chef on a trip to Moscow because the FAI was unwilling to fork out the money for a chef to accompany them, despite horror stories about Russian food. Then there was the time spent travelling in the baggage compartment of a train in Poland, or the time when Chris Hughton, on his way to join up with the squad in South America, received a phone call from an FAI official telling him to go back home because the Association was trying to save a few pennies. It might raise a laugh now, but such incidents were part of daily life in dealing with the FAI and made everything so much more difficult.

Working with the League of Ireland and the International side in the early 1980s was hard enough, but to be doing it while fighting against those same officials who were supposed to be on your side made it impossible. In later years, Hand himself made it clear just what the goings-on in Merrion Square were like at this time. The depressing thing is, if his criticisms were read aloud to a group of soccer fans or journalists, they really wouldn't be able to say which decade he was talking about—it was the same problems, again and again and again.

Hand describes the FAI in the 1980s as

'collectively ... inclined to lose sight of the overall objectives of the FAI when local and sectional interests are at stake ... setting the tone for disharmony ... As in every other walk of life, often the silent majority stand idly by while the negative-thinking and destructive minority make hay ... football politics abound and very often the position of manager is used as a bargaining ploy by certain factions seeking support for their own candidates in the upcoming Presidential election ... I often felt it was a case of them and I rather than it being, as it should have been, a matter of us.'

Since much of their attention was taken up with 'penny-pinching', as Eoin Hand called it, it should be no surprise to learn that any efforts to lift the game out of the doldrums proved to be monumental disasters, always failing to address in any meaningful way the underlying problems.

In 1985, for example, the League decided to extend to two divisions—a Premier and First Division—in an attempt to generate interest and excitement through relegation/promotion play-off battles. The League was thus extended from sixteen to twenty-two teams. This ploy didn't seem to take account of the fact that teams like Thurles Town had dropped out of the League altogether, unable to sustain the resources needed to compete at this level. So the decision to bring in an extra six clubs to make up two of the divisions seemed questionable, at best.

That said, it should be noted that there was a positive result from this decision. The six clubs elected to the League were Bray Wanderers, Cobh Ramblers, Derry City, EMFA (Kilkenny), Monaghan Utd and Newcastle Utd. Derry's return to competitive football after thirteen years in the wilderness was welcome news for Irish soccer and for the club. Derry City brought with them a colourful and passionate support that was sorely lacking, especially at this dire time—hosting teams were guaranteed a raucous and exuberant Derry following when the team came visiting.

II. Football heritage for sale

In the manner of these things, just when nobody thought it could get any worse… As far as the fans were concerned, at least, 1987 marked the nadir in the League of Ireland. This was the year the Kilcoynes decided to sell Glenmalure Park, the hallowed ground of Rovers.

While Dalymount Park was synonymous with the international team, there was something special about Milltown to the League of Ireland, and to Rovers fans especially. That 'something' was intangible—like the atmosphere that defines Anfield, or Old Trafford. Milltown's extraordinary history stretched back to 1922, and it truly was the place where dreams came true and legends were born. From the 1920s when Rovers won titles and Cups with

Bob Fullam, to the 1930s and Charlie Moore winning doubles and Cups, to Paddy Coad and the unforgettable team of the 1940s and 1950s, the thrilling tussles with Drumcondra, to the rampant 1960s Cup team who took it home six years in a row and on to the 1980s and the four-in-a-row team, Milltown had seen it all. It was the best pitch in the country, the most hallowed turf and the place where countless stories had been told about the ninety minutes of action seen there. There were hundreds of special moments, of victories and defeats, that would be remembered forever. Glenmalure Park's glory days were sepia-toned by now, but that just added to its allure: it was the direct link to the past. Standing on the terrace, you were standing in the footsteps of the fans who had seen Paddy Coad in his prime, marvelled at Liam Tuohy and wondered at Paddy Ambrose. It held a kind of magic, and it was the place fans chose to remember when thinking back to halcyon days. And they line up now to tell their stories:

Brendan McKenna, former *Evening Press* man and Rovers fan:

'The stories about Milltown are legendary. I remember I used to get up on my bicycle in Killester and cycle to Milltown. We used to park our bikes on Milltown Road and go up past the Jesuits; there was a petrol station where there was a big wall and maybe up to 500 bicycles would be there and your man would give you a cloakroom ticket and he would write the number of the ticket on your saddle—there were about 500 bikes there as I remember it. And there was such a crowd in there one day that the boundary wall around the pitch collapsed because of the crush of people around it and against it. I always remember we had a picture in the Press one year taken from behind the goal. There was only one entrance to Milltown and you could only get in at one end. So it took you a lot of time to get out of the ground if there were a lot of people there; if there were 16,000 or 17,000 at the game it took you ages to get out. But I will always remember there was a picture taken at Milltown from behind the goal at the road end. I remember it was Maurice Swan who was playing for Drumcondra at the time and he went out to save a ball at the post and the photographer caught him as he grabbed the ball at the post. But the shot contained the crowd underneath the stand on the unreserved terrace at that time and also on the roof of the stand. And the roof was caving in with the number of people that were up on top of it. It was a smashing shot and it outlined the crowd that Milltown had that particular Sunday.'

Robert Goggins, fan and club historian:

'January 1980 was my first game to actually go there. I was involved with a team in my job and they were cousins and they were mad Rovers fans and they were saying, you will have to come along, and all that. I had only ever seen Milltown from upstairs on a bus, but the ground did actually impress me and I suppose after the 1978 Cup final, which they won, I did start taking a bit of an interest. But then two years later when I got my own car I was a bit more mobile and I decided to go along one Sunday to a match and I came up to the turnstiles and I came in through the turnstiles. When I got inside the ground all I can say is something just enveloped me basically. I cannot explain it. It just caught me immediately.'

John Byrne:

'My own son, Stephen, is mad into it. I didn't force it on him because if you force it on him he will resist, but he is a kid for God's sake. So I just sort of bring him to the odd game. I remember the moment when it just clicked. It was a semi-final against Bohs in 2002. It was a great day, obviously beating those guys and getting into the Cup final and in the second half the atmosphere was fantastic. Then, he just got it, he is big into the Dubs and all that, but it just clicked with him. He said, "Dad, this is better than anything else".'

The problem was, of course, that magic doesn't conjure up finances, and for the Kilcoynes it was becoming increasingly clear that the sums just weren't adding up anymore. They had tried an ambitious plan with the biggest man in Irish football, and that failed; they had brought in a League of Ireland man and won all before them, and that still failed. Nothing they could do, it seemed, would bring the crowds back and with it the big paydays for the club. Louis Kilcoyne remembers the clock ticking down to the decision to close:

'As we grew over four years our crowds diminished, from 1,600–2,000 [spectators] they had reduced to 800–1,000. The game was a beaten docket. It was still a poor product and there was to be no rising boats after John Giles' best efforts. It was in the fourth year of success when we were unbeatable and getting to Europe—and not with any success in Europe, I might add—that my brother, Paddy Kilcoyne, who was our financial controller said, "I'm out of here, I'm not propping this up anymore and I am certainly not going to look at these meagre lodgments for the bank and cry to the bank manager. We have other things to do and we are throwing money, we are wasting money here." You weren't talking £100,000 now, but you were talking serious thousands and everything is relevant. So there was serious money being lost down the drain. It was our company, Healy Homes, that was propping up Shamrock Rovers for seventeen years.

At the height of our success, we were plodding along not enjoying it. I was running a disco bar and doing parties and bloody weddings in Hoops, as it was called, the Hoops club, and trying to make ends meet. We were running raffles and whatever you did in those days, horse racing nights and quiz shows and the like. But it was bad old times. We had a patrons' club and we were always going back to the same guys for a few quid to try and convince them to do it for next season and get a few pounds in. Then towards the end we were talked into getting floodlights by the Supporters Club who undertook to fundraise for that and it was fine. But our view was once they started fundraising for the floodlights, we would lose any other monies that we were in receipt of. It was always modest but that wasn't their fault. We didn't want to invest. They cost us £80,000 at the time—a stupid amount of money.

So one day Paddy put it to the three of us. We could keep going, but he was not going to. And you know he was talking realistically. But my much maligned brother Barton, who is the principal at Healy Homes, wasn't going with him, despite the fact that he knew we were having trouble. But then reality began to set in and at the same meeting we all agreed it was time. I argued that we would stay on for one more year and would give notice because in PR terms we knew we weren't going to be popular. Then we began to talk to Home Farm, Brendan Menton Jnr particularly, about sharing with them at Tolka and he was delighted because we would make a contribution to the upkeep of Tolka basically. When it was established that we could go there the decision was not one year's notice, we'll just get up and do it. We did that with about two or three matches to go. When word got out, by way of the beginnings of the protest, we got 1,200 at our next game whereas before we were getting 300.

We had bought Glenmalure from the Jesuits a few years previously and we bought it on the premise that the rent they were getting from us was a pittance in relative terms, whereas if we gave them x thousand pounds to purchase it they were far better off. And they agreed with that. It was a good business decision as well, though.'

Once they had bought the ground outright from the Jesuits, the Kilcoynes were now in a position to do as they wished with it. What they had was a prime property development site in South Dublin that was leaking money every week: it was pretty obvious to the Kilcoynes what the clever business decision was going to be. Within weeks, Glenmalure was up for tender.

The thought of moving grounds—and to the Northside as well—was bad enough, but for Rovers fans the fact that Milltown was going to be sold off and houses would be built on it only added salt to their wounds. On top of this, anger towards the Kilcoynes for their decision turned to suspicion about their motives, and soon the conspiracy theories were doing the rounds concerning who owned what, who sold what to whom and for how much. The fans responded by setting up the Keep Rovers at Milltown (KRAM) campaign, which for the next few years was a boisterous and sometimes violent campaign to prevent Glenmalure being turned into a housing development for a multi-million-pound profit.

The League of Ireland, and the Kilcoynes, may have been caught offguard by the level of resistance to the decision to sell Milltown. Irish society was fairly downtrodden at this point, so protests and passions were very slow to ignite. Up to this point, the plight of soccer in Ireland hadn't provoked a strong response from the fans—no one was picketing or protesting. Now, however, Milltown was being sold and suddenly Rovers and League of Ireland fans were speaking out. Never before had the League received so much attention and media space. These may have been depressed times, but the selling off of a dream was one step too far.

Liam Christie, a Rovers fan, became chairman of KRAM when it was formed in 1987 and over the next two years he was central in keeping the campaign front-page news, involving everyone from ordinary people to politicians to pop stars, even the Pope, in the desperate bid to save Milltown. As he regales you with his tales— some taller than others—of those hectic years, he does so with a laughter in his voice. Despite ultimately losing the war, along the way Christie has accumulated a bank of stories to last a lifetime, and memories that will go on even longer. All the while that he's talking you can't help but think that if it hadn't been the League of Ireland, the despair in losing would never have been so momentous—and there would never have been so many characters and so many stories to be told.

'KRAM was made up mostly of sponsors and patrons but they wanted a link with the supporters,' explains Christie, 'because it was mainly the ordinary supporter who was going to be instrumental in trying to get them back. I was linked with the supporters club and I was co-opted onto the KRAM board. I was just the ordinary supporter, everyone else had money. They were supporters but they were the higher echelon supporter. When there didn't seem to be any getting the Kilcoynes to change their mind, the main aim was for KRAM to get enough money and buy the club from Rovers. But the Kilcoynes, for some reason or another best known to themselves, were very anti-KRAM. I don't know why. All we were doing was trying to keep the club in the Milltown ground. And if they got their money they were looking for, what did it matter who it went to? But whatever happened, once any of the Kilcoynes got word that KRAM were involved in negotiations they just dropped it like a hot potato. So if somebody went up to Kilcoyne and said, "Listen, I am interested in buying the ground", the first thing they would want to know was what involvement he had with KRAM. The Kilcoynes just wouldn't have any association with KRAM at all.

Why? I think they were totally taken aback by the response from the supporters. They thought it would just be a matter of taking the club out of Milltown, moving into Tolka Park with Home Farm and everything would be just fine. They were taken aback when there was such an upheaval against them and what they didn't like was people on the KRAM board were people who were patrons, who had membership cards and some of them were sponsors.

The campaign took off very quickly and we were getting money in as quick as possible from everybody. Supporters on the ground, supporters away in America and England; they even got a publicity firm involved very much like, say, a politician would do and the whole campaign was to get as much publicity as they could in the newspapers, on the television and on the radio, to get it everywhere. Then they started bringing everybody they could think of on board and soon a piece was put in one of the Sunday papers saying that Bono supported the KRAM campaign. Now whether Bono was even a Rovers supporter, well, I don't know the answer to that, but to tell you the truth, the rumours that were going around at the time, Idi Amin would have been a Shamrock Rovers supporter, or even Saddam Hussein could have been. I even remember one incident when they decided that they would try and go over and meet the Pope. There was a piece in the paper about it because we had a few media people on board who were quite friendly towards us and they put as much as they could into the papers.

Everyone says it was Charlie Stuart who got the scoop in the *Press* about Milltown being sold, but it wasn't, it was Karl McGinty who put a little piece in the *Indo* saying it was Milltown for sale. I know this for a fact because Karl used to come up to me, as I used to be involved in the club programme, and he used to come up to me and ask me for any scoops. I used to be always having him on saying, "Yeah, I have a scoop for you, Karl". But he came up to me this day before a match and he says, "Is there any truth in the rumour that Rovers are leaving Milltown?" and of course I laughed at him, I said, "Karl, your scoops are getting worse by the minute!" —little realising that it was true. I remember Louis Kilcoyne was passing me by at that very moment and I said, "What is this that Karl McGinty is going on about Rovers leaving Milltown?" and Louis just smiled and he said, "Well, you know what reporters are like".

But then sometime later somebody rang me at eight o'clock in the morning. I was working for myself at the time, so it wasn't the time I used to get out of bed at. One of the newspapers rang me anyway and asked me had I seen the report that Rovers were leaving Milltown and I couldn't believe it. Again I thought it was a joke about, but then about half an hour later Louis Kilcoyne rang me. He wanted to know how I felt and all I said to him was, "Well, Louis, if it is really financially imperative that you leave Milltown, well what can we do?" I thought, well, if the finances of the club are that bad, then you have to share a ground.'

Suddenly, after taking things for granted for so long and being so complacent about their club, the alarm bells were ringing for the fans, and ringing loudly. Everyone was agreed that something had to be done to prevent the ground being sold. Christie describes the reaction:

'Everyone was running around like headless chickens trying to think of things they could do. At the Sligo Rovers match the fans all got onto the pitch with a "F**k Tolka" banner, but the KRAM board wanted to try and stop bad publicity like that happening. There were KRAM guys with big jobs and they didn't want to touch any controversy with a pole so they were kind of embarrassed, they didn't want to be associated with anything like that. It was up to me then to try and rein in the fans and say, "Just leave it until we get a meeting going, let's have a huge meeting and see what we can do". Then we had loads of meetings and we were getting as many big meetings as we could. The first big meeting we had was in the Clarence Hotel when Con Houlihan famously pledged £1,000, which he said was back underneath his pillow in Portobello, but that was Con—his mouth was in gear before his brain was.

There were 700 in the Clarence Hotel that evening and the room packed to capacity with people. It was unbelievable, there were people coming out of the woodwork who I didn't even know were Rovers fans, like your man out of 'Star Trek', Colm Meaney, we met him a few times. And then of course Maureen O'Hara came out and she said she used to be brought to Milltown by her father when she was only a toddler. Everyone was coming out and declaring they were Shamrock Rovers supporters. The only person really that I know that didn't come out and say he was a Rovers fan was the Pope.'

Kilcoyne, on the other hand, dismisses the notion that the people suddenly supporting KRAM were Rovers fans at all:

'All these fellas came out of the woodwork who claim they were there all those barren years but they were not. But they mustered together and got publicity. I think it was a great shock for so-called Rovers diehards. It was a wake-up call, but it was too late. There was a lot of passion out there and a lot of waffle too. There was an attempt to raise funds by KRAM and I think the most they ever had in their bank account was about £30,000, and let's just say that Glenmalure was sold for a lot more than £30,000.'

Although Kilcoyne wouldn't divulge the final figure, he did admit that it ran to six figures; Rovers fans claim that the Milltown ground went for as much as £5 million.

'That is not bad when you consider how much they got it for,' claims Christie. 'We had several meetings with Fr O'Donoghue, who was from the Jesuit order who leased out the ground to the Kilcoynes. They got it for something like £5,000 a year; it's mad, isn't it, when you think of what a ground would cost now. You wouldn't even get a house for that. They had a nine-year lease and the Jesuits sold out the lease to them. We had several meetings with Fr O'Donoghue; he was a very nice guy and we were pleading with him, asking him was there any way he could renege on the deal, saying that Kilcoyne never told him that they were going to sell up for a housing development; but they said they didn't realise. We had several meetings with them, but it didn't get us anywhere. People used to say that they knew what the bottomline was and they didn't care once they were getting the money. Having said that, Fr O'Donoghue was always there for us to have a meeting with and he seemed very amenable, but there was so much politics involved and they didn't really want to be involved, piggy-in-the-middle between Shamrock Rovers and the supporters and the club owners.'

Real fans or not, the outpouring of support for the Milltown ground revealed the love of the game hadn't gone away. The fans may not have been going to games anymore, but that didn't mean they didn't appreciate the clubs and the grounds and the sense of history. Of course, that was no use to cash-strapped club owners. If anything, the support for the KRAM campaign revealed the level of nostalgia for the League and just how dear it was to people's hearts. It was as if their old train set, which had for years lain dusty, cobwebbed and ignored in the attic, was now being thrown out and they were kicking up a fuss over it. Did the fact that they ignored it mean they loved it any less? Maybe. Maybe not. Either way, it was decades since they had paid the League any attention, and in 1987 players' wages had to be paid, grounds had to be maintained and overheads kept to a minimum, and all this had to be achieved when nobody was interested in supporting the club anymore.

Regardless of motive, the KRAM campaign gathered support and momentum later that year. Christie recalls:

'I don't know what it was that saw it took off. It seemed to be just one of those things. But it was organised very well. We had a public relations machine and I never knew anything about these things, I was just an ordinary Joe Soap, but the politics of things amazed me. If you can get this over an ordinary football ground, imagine what was going on over a motorway? But they sat around and basically they would have meetings and they would try to think up the next mad thing they could get into the newspapers, anything like Bono, for example. I think it was Brian Murphy who knew somebody who knew Bono—Brian had plenty of great contacts over in America and all that—and apparently Bono came out and said, "Oh yes, I am a Rovers fan now". You can take that with a grain of salt, you know.

Then the Pope idea came up. I wasn't at that meeting, but somebody mentioned something about if you could go over to the Vatican and get something signed. Before you knew it, it was in the *Evening Herald* and they had a headline with "The Famous Shamrock Rovers went to Rome to see the Pope", borrowing it from the football chants. I remember it because at matches for a long while after this we would be playing Bohs and they would be chanting this.'

The KRAM publicity machine was now in full swing, with leaflets being printed and badges being sold, while the Tallaght Marching Band supposedly came into existence at this time, stemming out of KRAM's vigils and protests. The experiences of those years ranged from the surreal to the sublime. They probably never truly believed that they could buy the Kilcoynes out, but they weren't going to give up without a fight, and Christie's tales tell quite a story.

At one of their all-night vigils, Terry Byrne, a supporter and businessman based in England, turned up at their vigil at midnight. There was sixty of them there that night, with their tents pitched, ready for the long-haul through the cold of the night. They were huddled around a fire that had been lit outside the ground, trying to keep their spirits and their body temperatures up. Terry Byrne went down to the local chip shop and bought every fish and every chip in the place—so much, in fact, that the chipper had to close down after he left. The night of the free supper stuck in people's minds for another reason: it was the day Stephen Roche triumphantly crossed the finish line to win the Tour de France.

Then there was just the madcap:

'One of the guys that we had on the campaign,' explains Christie, 'he was a little bit slow for want of a better word. When Louis [Kilcoyne] used to come out of the ground, there was always a surge forward towards him; now, people never meant anything, but there was always a surge forward as if they were going to do something. And of course, there was always a big Garda presence. But this particular evening Louis came out of the ground with his son and this guy who was a little bit slow—he was kind of well-known amongst Rovers supporters, he would say silly things from time to time. So as a kind of a gesture, he kicked out; now Louis was about the far side of the road from him, so he could never have made contact, but what happened was his shoe came off and it hit Louis' son and with that a Ban Garda came over and grabbed this guy to arrest him. We turned around and we said to the guard to leave him go as he was a little bit . . . how did we put it . . . simple. And the guy, "Brian" was his name, he turned around to myself and Dick and he says, "Thanks very much lads". I had never heard anyone thanking anyone for being called simple in my life! But we had got him off the hook. There were so many funny incidents that happened. All the balls used to come out over during the match and the lads would hide them and the club members would come out looking for them and . . . you could go on and on with all the different stories . . .

Then there were the Rovers families that were split down the middle over it. Some supporters would refer to it as the Civil War because I know there was one household who had four or five of them that went to all the Rovers matches, but two of them decided to pass the picket and go into the matches and the others wouldn't and there was a civil war in their house. They weren't speaking to each other. There was loads of incidents like that and best friends falling out over it because they passed the picket. It was crazy.'

In spite of all the efforts, all the arguments and all the love, Milltown was lost. We shall leave the last word to Con Houlihan, one of this country's finest sportswriters, who wrote a moving and eloquent obituary to Milltown in his *Evening Press* column:

'And so Glenmalure Park is to be developed. It is a symptom of our times that this word is employed to give respectability to vandalism. Seemingly faceless men have sold it to other faceless men who will wipe out the loveliest football stadium in the island to placate their greed. And silly people who imagine themselves to be pillars of wisdom will nod sagely and say "it had to happen". Their judgement will be based on the word "money" a term which they invoke in such a way that it seems man's master rather his servant. And Dublin Corporation will no doubt do nothing to frustrate what they deem progress, the massive own goal perpetrated on Wood Quay is their trademark. "People need offices"—that was the Corporation's theme during the debate "People need houses" will be the new pearl of wisdom. And of course people need offices and houses—they also need green spaces, if only to look at them.

. . . The news about the demise of Glenmalure Park caused me to laugh at my own innocence: a few weeks ago when Craven Cottage was under threat I said to myself, "Thank heaven that Milltown is safe" . . . Whether this is a link between their financial state and the end of Glenmalure Park I do not know. It has been suggested that they cannot afford to stay there—perhaps this is true. That shouldn't, however, excuse the Corporation if they allow the developers to have their way. It is all very well to talk about the rights of the individuals to sell their property but it isn't as simple as that. Thomas Aquinas had something to say about this: "The farmer doesn't own the land—he holds it in stewardship for the common good."

. . . And I suppose the League's continued existence is something of a miracle. I would be very sad if it died. It is hardly the most glamorous competition in the football world but it has aspects that are peculiarly its own, including the scent of Bovril at Tolka Park and the pigeons in Dalymount and the intrepid wellingtoned men who fish the ball out of the river at Emmet Road. Shamrock Rovers incidentally weren't always in Glenmalure Park as far as I know they played originally in Ringsend. And I suspect that they have sufficient prestige and goodwill to survive the exodus. And yet the loss will be enormous: for me Milltown without Rovers will be like the bed of a river that has dried up forever.'

IV. The Charlton years

To some, the selling of Milltown represented an ignominious end to Irish football: selling out on a dream for financial gain. To others, it was merely an incomprehensible schoolboy argument between rowing nutters over a ground, a club and a League that nobody cared for anymore. And now that Ireland had qualified for Euro '88, there were bigger things to worry about. This was the first time *ever* that the Irish soccer team had qualified for a major soccer tournament. Forget that parochial Milltown–Shamrock Rovers stuff, thanks very much—people were dreaming of trips to Germany, status, acclaim, and all on the international stage. In the end, it took an Englishman to get us there.

Just two years into his job as Ireland manager, Jack Charlton, World Cup winner in 1966, a stereotypical blunt English centre-half, inherited a talented squad and moulded it into his ways. His drive to win, plus a little bit of luck along the way, helped forge some of the most memorable occasions in recent Irish history. Few men have had as big an impact and effect on Irish society and culture. For the next ten years, Charlton dominated the popular, cultural and economic scene; according to some devotees he was even responsible for the Celtic Tiger! Just one year on from the sale of Glenmalure Park, the Irish soccer bandwagon was about to get into gear and the whole nation was eager to clamber onto it.

In true FAI fashion, it nearly never happened. Eoin Hand's tenure as International Manager was coming to an inevitable end, and fans were drifting away from the team in greater numbers than ever before. On 9 August 1984 the smallest ever crowd for an Irish international—barely 5,000—witnessed Ireland and Mexico play out a drab 0-0 draw; by the end of the match, less than half the 5,000 remained in the ground. The pundits shook their heads in disbelief: Irish football was in dire straits, and only a remarkable change in fortune would swing things around.

Initially, the appointment of Jack Charlton to succeed Hand didn't look like a remarkable change in fortune. His appointment was more an amalgam of grudges and votes against other candidates than a vote for the future of Irish soccer. In the end, the gruff Englishman slipped in by two votes on a third count in the FAI Council. The story of how he got the job bears witness to how things were being done in the FAI, and how sometimes enough haplessness can engender luck. Des Casey was FAI President in 1986, and he describes the Charlton saga in detail:

'Eoin Hand was manager of the team when I came in as President. We had beaten Russia in the first match in Dublin and I remember we got beaten by Norway who were an amateur team then. For that game Eoin brought Frank Stapleton back when he wasn't fit and really 100% and there was a misunderstanding between David O'Leary and Mark Lawrenson in defence and they beat us 1-0. But anyway we went on and the crucial match was when we played Russia in Moscow in October 1985 and we lost 2-0 and were out of it then. I knew then that there had to be a change. Notwithstanding, I had a great deal of sympathy for Eoin Hand who was an honest broker, but the team had simply not performed collectively to its collective potential.

I was impressed by the fact that Billy Bingham, living in Southport, had brought Northern Ireland to the World Cup in '82 and they were going again in '86. I knew then we needed an experienced outside manager, someone based in England. So I rang Liverpool—Bob Paisley had stepped down—and asked Peter Robinson to enquire would he be available. He said he was not available nor would he be and in the meantime we lost the last match against Denmark 4-1. So we went to the [FAI] Council and I had a chat with The Doc [Tony O'Neill] and said, "Look we need to go for something different." So we put the idea about Billy Bingham to see if we could get somebody similar to him in the UK where all the players were. The Council agreed to give us the mandate to go, so Tony and I embarked for England to scour for prospective candidates. It was the first weekend in December and I will never forget it. We headed off to Manchester and the first man we met was Jack Charlton in the old Excelsior. He knew all the players off and "Bloody 'ell," he says, "great players" and he obviously knew what he was talking about. We then embarked on this odyssey of interviewing managers; we went and met Pat Crerand in the Midland Hotel in Manchester and he would have taken the two arms off us to get the job.

We then drove up the M6 in the torrential rain to the Knutsford Service Station where we met Gordon Lee and he was a Born Again Christian and he would exert discipline and all that. Then down to London and we met Terry Neill—he used to manage Arsenal. Then the following day we went out to see Theo Foley. Next Sunday we drove up to Peterborough and we met Noel Cantwell and from that to Birmingham and we met Billy McNeill and Johnny Giles was the last one. I would have been in favour of Johnny if you had asked me, but McNeill was mad for the job and he had a big profile at the time as he was managing Manchester City. So we went back home and we narrowed it and we interviewed Paddy Mulligan in Dublin, Jim McLaughlin, Liam Tuohy . . .

The interviews in England were all conducted in a weekend. We went from Friday to Sunday criss-crossing across England and meeting all these managers and we had a great time, Tony and myself. So we went into the Council meeting in January and there was a shortlist of Charlton, McNeill and Giles, I think it was the three of them. And McNeill was the favourite, but then City, they wanted us to pay a hefty slice of his wages in Manchester. I said, "You must be joking,' so effectively then we couldn't do it. It transpired then that it had become very political with the media. The media seemed to be totally opposed to a non-national or a non-resident. They had Eoin Hand who was resident in Dublin and he was available to them all day everyday. So it went to the vote and another person who shall be nameless, and it wasn't Louis Kilcoyne, brought in Bob Paisley from nowhere.

I thought this is strange because when I rang Liverpool in October we didn't even get to interview him and he wasn't available or interested, but he had obviously been persuaded to be interested. I think because either Jack was there or whatever it was, but it went

to the meeting anyway and there were now four candidates—
Paisley, Jack, Johnny Giles and Tuohy was also there. Paisley got
nine votes on the first count and there was obviously politicking
going on—people's tails were wagged to vote for Paisley. I was mad
now because there was an individual who I cannot name who had
brought him in who taken the mandate away from The Doc and me
at the last minute. So it went to the vote and I was asked was I
recommending Paisley and I said, "Under no circumstances, he
wasn't interviewed and he wasn't on the shortlist". At the end of the
day Jack got the vote by two when somebody switched their vote—
he got the vote by ten to eight. As things turned out, he was the right
man, in the right place, at the right time.

When Charlton took over he immediately changed things
around and let the players know who was boss. When Eoin [Hand]
was in charge there was a degree of player power creeping in. Jack
arrived for the first match against Wales in February 1986. It wasn't
a big crowd now, but it was a start. And there was an arrangement
whereby Hertz left six or seven courtesy cars at the hotel. It was a
sponsorship thing and the players could take the cars off and visit
their homes and all the rest of it. When I told Jack, he said, "Get
them the f**k out of here, we are all going to the pictures tonight,
there is none of this lot leaving this hotel unless of a family
bereavement." That was a sign of how things were to change.'

Just how much things were to change nobody—least of all not
the FAI—yet realised. Over the next ten years Charlton would have
an unprecedented impact on soccer and society. The day that Gary
Mackay put the ball in the net to give Scotland an unlikely away
win over Bulgaria, and by doing so sent Ireland on its way to the
European Championships in 1988, was a moment that quite
literally changed Irish football forever. Ireland's appearance on the
international soccer stage—with credible performances, including
a narrow defeat to the Dutch, a draw against the Russians and a
memorable, memorable win over the English—came just as Irish
society was emerging from the cold grip of the 1980s, and the
country was ready to proclaim herself proudly on the international
stage. Nothing represented the scattered diaspora of the Irish
nation better than the team that took to the field in Irish jerseys,
representing the first, second and third generations of the migrant

Irish, those forced to leave their own country because of economic hardship and poverty: here, now, was the chance for them to shine and to bring it all back home once again. It truly was a special time for anyone who lived through it. In his one-man play, 'In High Germany', Dermot Bolger poignantly summed up what it felt like to be Irish and part of 'Jackie's Army' after being knocked out by Holland in the final game:

> 'And when they were gone, we turned, solid to a man and a woman, thirteen thousand of us, cheering, applauding, chanting out the players' names, letting them know how proud we felt. I thought of my father's battered travel-light bag, of Molloy drilling us behind that 1798 pike, the wasters who came after him hammering *Peig* into us, the masked men blowing limbs of passers-by off in my name. You know, all my life it seems that somebody, somewhere has always been trying to tell me what Ireland I belong to. But I only belonged *there*. I raised my hands and applauded, having finally, in my last moments with Shane and Mick, found the only Ireland whose name I can sing, given to me by eleven men dressed in green. And the only Ireland I can pass on to the son who will carry my name and features in a foreign land . . . All thirteen thousand of us stood on the terrace, for fifteen, twenty minutes after the last player had vanished, after Houghton had returned, forlornly waving a tricolour in salute, after Jack had come back out to stand and stare in wonder at us. Coffin ships, the decks of cattle boats, the departure lounges of airports. We were not a chosen generation, the realisation of a dream any longer. We were just a hiccup, a brief stutter in the system. Thirteen thousand of us stood as one on that German terrace, before scattering back towards Ireland and out like a river bursting its banks across a vast continent.'

Coffin ships, the decks of cattle boats, the departure lounges of airports. We were not a chosen generation, the realisation of a dream any longer. We were just a hiccup, a brief stutter in the system. This was what it meant to be an Irishman, and this was what it meant to see the realisation of a dream come true on a football field. But then, in just ten short years, the country would take a huge step forward: not only would it stand proudly for the migrant generations, Ireland would be a place others looked to, others would migrate to. The circle would come full circle for the first time: instead of sending out her people across the world, Ireland would become a destination for the migrant hopefuls from Europe, Asia and Africa.

Ireland had experienced boom years before, of course, most notably with the 'Bacardi brigade' of the 1960s. This time, however, change was going to be more radical, more permanent, and somehow less Irish and more global. This would truly be 'New Ireland'.

> 'I remember the day it changed,' says Rovers fan John Byrne. 'The last of the Old Ireland crowd was there and they beat Spain 1-0. That was in 1989 and after that it changed. It just changed. The atmosphere wasn't the same anymore. Suddenly Ireland was successful and a team to be followed. It was like something to do. Some people wear Gucci shoes or they go to certain pubs. Now you went to Ireland games—it became a thing to do.'

As the New Ireland was celebrating success on the international stage and presenting a modern image to the world, one part of the Old Ireland was still alive, just about, dragging its dying corpse about. Unfortunately, the League of Ireland was still stuck in Old Ireland—the elephant in the sitting room that people didn't want to be reminded of. It was a place where facilities stank, where things weren't done right and where customer care was getting a cup of hot Bovril at half-time. While the rest of Ireland started to believe in itself, the League of Ireland was dogged by the old fears and resentments and jealousies. It seemed almost embarrassed of itself, like it wanted to crawl under a rock and hide away from the rest of changing society.

Peter Byrne describes how the League got left out in the cold—yet again:

> 'The reality was there was never any tangible connection between the international team and League of Ireland football. I wrote at the time in the 1980s that it didn't matter whether we went to the World Cup, it would do nothing for League of Ireland football. I remember someone in the FAI having a go at me over it and I said

well, you don't know what you are talking about and I was right, he didn't know what he was talking about. The thing was that there was no connection. The time in the 1950s when you had two or three League of Ireland club players onto a team was [gone]. That time at least gave a sense of belonging to the fella who went to League of Ireland football. He felt involved in some way with the state of the international team his players were involved in, but as things went on and Giles' players and League of Ireland players dropped off the radar, the international team became more and more removed. The League of Ireland didn't develop in the 1980s as it should have, and more and more football in this country was perceived as being about the Irish team and Jack Charlton and Charlton's Army as a result.'

Worse was yet to come. Italia '90 and USA '94 brought ever greater achievements for the Irish soccer team, while the arrival of the Premiership and Sky Sports further glamourised English soccer for an adoring Irish public. New Ireland—especially as represented by its football team—was being embraced warmly by her people, and any last vestiges of the old ways were not going to last long. Soccer—without the League of Ireland—was about to become popular to an incredible extent and in a way that transcended class, religion and even politics. But the League of Ireland was not part of this equation. 'Here Come the Good Times' went the song heralding qualification for the World Cup, while at the same time the old corrugated stands and concrete terraces of Glenmalure Park were being demolished to make way for a housing development. It was the cusp of another new decade: Ireland's most famous soccer club was homeless, the international team was in vogue and property was going to become the obsession of the nation.

Part Five

The 1990s: World Cups, long knives and Celtic Tigers

THE MANAGER

'You see the joy that you bring to people when their club wins and if you ask them was the heartbreak worth it for that feeling at that moment they say, of course. I've neglected things in my life to make it happen—especially when I was manager—to make sure we won the League and I'm sure the fans felt the same feelings I did after all the struggles to go through to get there.'

I. Dark nights of glory

Italia '90. Some memories:

'We went down O'Connell Street. Every car horn in the city was being leaned on. We went to Beshoff's, got cod and chips, sat at a window seat and watched. The pool around the Anna Livia statue was full; people were queuing up to climb in and get drenched. Every van that went by had people hanging off it and sitting on it. Lads stood on the street, waiting to grab a car and cling onto it. Every tree and monument along the street was occupied. One guy sat by himself in a tree wearing only tricolour shorts; he seemed to be lost.'

Roddy Doyle, writer.

'I remember being in Palermo for the Ireland v Holland draw and was sitting there amongst the FAI blazers in my T-shirt and shorts and there were officials crying around me at the thoughts of going through to the next round, but I remember thinking, that's what I have every week with Pat's and it's sad that they had to wait so long to experience that feeling.'

Brian Kerr, former Irish manager.

'I was down in Doolin in Clare—I used to go down when there was nothing there, not even a bed and breakfast—and I was going down there one particular week for a musical session and I was getting petrol in the car. The petrol shop was a little grocery shop and the

bloke had kids who had pictures of the Irish players who were going
to play in the World Cup in the window. That is the first time I had
seen that in Doolin. You would see that in Dublin alright, but in
Doolin, Co. Clare? Certainly the Charlton thing awakened people
around the country, there is no question about that.'

Noel O'Reilly, former assistant to Brian Kerr.

If you were one of the 17,000 standing in Lansdowne watching
Liam Brady score a sublime goal against Brazil in 1987, would you
have believed the person next to you if he had told you what the
next ten years would bring? That by 1997 Ireland would have gone
to two World Cups, including one quarter-final loss to Italy and
one second-round exit to Holland; that a nation would get behind
its footballing heroes and the whole country would come to a
stand-still when World Cup matches were on; that families would
empty savings accounts and credit unions would be tapped up just
to get the chance to walk a few steps of the way along the football
team's journey?

Or would it perhaps have been even more unbelievable to hear
that Ireland would become a wealthy nation, with property prices
hitting unprecedented levels, unemployment almost eradicated
and the country becoming the preferred destination for
immigrants from around the world, that an all-white society
would become multi-coloured and multi-cultural for the very first
time, that Moore Street's traders would set up stalls next to Afro-
Caribbean and Asian traders? Would you have believed this would
be Ireland in the 1990s?

Ireland, the brand, was on the way, and it was kick-started into
existence by a football team that broke the mould. Two World
Cups breathed life back into the country and reinvigorated our
pride and, of course, made instant heroes of Charlton and his
players. Italia '90 and USA '94 would be the pinnacles for Irish
soccer in the 1990s, but the decade wasn't an entirely smooth
ride—it was marred by scandal, off-pitch battles, corruption,
resignations and shaftings: and that was just from one FAI AGM!
While the game took off and never looked back, the boardrooms
and clubhouses were struggling to come to terms with this new-
found status and would soon be found wanting in all the usual

places: empty League of Ireland grounds, insolvent clubs, poor management structures. The problem was that although Irish football was suddenly flying high, it had nothing to anchor it to the ground because its success was built on the shaky foundations laid by the League of Ireland management. If they couldn't run their own clubs, how could they run an organisation that could compete on the international stage?

For now, though, in 1990, it was all good. Italia '90 was arguably the precursor to the new self-confident Ireland that would emerge so strongly later in the decade. Fintan O'Toole has tried to put some understanding on the madness of those years:

'You had this reality which everyone recognised deep in their bones, which had been silent. Silent in terms of art, in terms of literature, in terms of representations of the place, but particularly in terms of official representations so the idea that you now had, this is Ireland you know. It is Ray Houghton and it is Kevin Sheedy and it is all of that. That was very, very powerful because it articulated something that people wanted to articulate. The second thing was that it was the very first time that, if you like, the cultural centre of gravity was suddenly working-class Dublin. That the images that you associate with all of that period, '88, '90 and all of that, are the flats covered in tricolours.

The Van, the Roddy Doyles, it was all that stuff very much around it. But again there has never been a time really when the sort of centre of gravity of Irish culture, the self-representation was working-class Dublin and again that gave it a huge impetus because again there was a huge desire in a way, certainly on the parts of those people, to be seen as representatives of their own culture and their own society. So it started to work quite perfectly from that point of view. Jack's Army became a sort of compensation for failure, it was more feeding into the horrors of the 1980s.

If you compare it to the last World Cup [in 2002], I know people were hugely enthusiastic about it, but it was nothing like the same hunger. There wasn't the same desperation, that sense that what you really wanted in those tournaments. People didn't care about the football and it was embarrassing in some cases. But that didn't matter because it wasn't about the football in a sense, it was about having this event continue as long as possible. And people were prepared to sacrifice almost anything to just keep it going, because we just needed something that took us out of the reality. And the sense of disappointment when it was over it was like, we have to go back to real life now.'

It was sport, more than anything, that allowed people forget the miseries of the 1980s and feel good in the present. They desperately wanted, needed really, the sense of celebration and exuberance the football successes gave them—and they didn't want to be distracted from that. As a result, attempts at hard-hitting, truthful analysis were met with resistance and derision. There was no appetite for criticism or questioning, but that didn't deter the outspoken Eamon Dunphy. He continued to speak openly and honestly about the problems in Irish football, and he was vilified for doing so, as historian Diarmaid Ferriter remembers:

'Every time Dunphy came on the screen there was just this barrage of missiles. None of us ever listened to a bloody word he said and it was only afterwards when I went back and began to actually read what he had been saying that it seemed entirely reasonable and intelligent to be saying what he was. It struck me as being very contradictory that probably now most of us would acknowledge that the level of informed comment on Irish soccer and soccer generally in Ireland is vastly superior to anything that you will get in the home of the beautiful game. And at the same time we would pride ourselves in being sophisticated analysts of sport. None of us had f**king notions—we were along for the ride, like—and of course there wasn't that same critique developed of soccer that there had been of GAA. You could argue that it wasn't there in the GAA either, that it is more of a tribal thing, but it is only ten years afterwards when you look back, and particularly when Charlton is on his way out and McCarthy is on his way in, and people are actually saying, but what kind of football are we going to play? As opposed to it being a question of, if we get through another campaign without a series of scoreless draws, well, we really have won kind of thing.'

The questioning, the re-opening of old wounds was to become a defining theme of the 1990s as Ireland struggled to come to terms with the sins it had committed against itself. By the mid-1990s the whole edifice had come tumbling down and society was faced with the reality of what had been going on behind those closed doors:

'All fixed points collapsed,' argues O'Toole, 'and that is liberating in a way because they were not nice fixed points. I suppose it was also terrifying, like, what the f**k is going on? There is no sense of control. The rapidity with which the Church collapsed as a moral authority was astonishing if you consider that this goes back thousands of years and was so deeply ingrained and identity was so tied up with it and then it just kind of goes in a matter of four or five years. The Bishop Casey affair was obviously the big moment—the sense of astonishment around the Casey thing was just staggering.

It was cathartic, but it was also experienced by a lot of people as being traumatic. It is very easy to forget how deeply huge numbers of Irish people believed the Church and how important it was to them. And how the sense of shock and betrayal and hurt was really strong. I suppose what it all contributed to—and I hate this notion—but, this idea of identity, that people's identity was wrapped up in nationalism, in Catholicism, and perhaps there was a lot of Irish people in the land—that was kind of the classic markers, you know, that we were agricultural Catholic nationalist, you know, all those sorts of things were gone by the mid-1990s—that we had become an urban society. Catholicism certainly in terms of its public identity was just wiped out and nationalism became at least very complicated and difficult because of the Provos and the things that were associated with it had become sort of untouchable.

In terms of sport there is again a kind of hunger for something else to identify it with. And it happens to be Jack's Army became the thing at that time because it was safe. And apart from anything else in simple nationalist terms, it was the first time for a long time that you could actually wave the tricolour without feeling, Oh f**k, what is this saying? Am I going to be accused of all kinds of stuff? And the fact that people would actually identify with it in an uncomplicated, simple way—it is not the flag of the nation so much as the flag of the team.'

It may have been the flag of the team, but was this a team people could really identify with? Would it have mattered if eleven green

Pelés from Mars came down and accidentally put on Irish soccer jerseys? Probably not—especially if they knew the words to 'Amhrán na bhFiann'. For Irish soccer people, however, the point was that this was a team with little relevance to what they knew, to their everyday lives or to their culture. The connectedness to diasporas is a complex issue, but for most of those celebrating the good times, it was black and white: Ireland team at World Cup, therefore all is well. On the other hand, for those in soccer circles, especially those involved in the League of Ireland, they very much felt left out in the cold—the party was raging, but their invite had got lost in the post.

> 'It was great to see the international team get some sort of success,' says Fran Gavin, then a player at Galway Utd. 'You felt that we would all benefit, that all boats would rise with that tide. Now that you had finance coming into the game, it would be pumped back into Irish football and into the League of Ireland at the time. Facilities would improve, generally the whole thing would be on the up and up. But that didn't happen. Questions must be asked about where did all that money go? It certainly didn't go into the League of Ireland. So at the time, while there was an affiliation to the international team, there wasn't a huge affiliation because you really didn't feel any connection to them. Only that they wore the Irish jersey, but you couldn't really relate to that the way you could relate to say a Dublin team much closer. Because they were all Dublin people, they were all people that lived in your locality. The Irish team were a lot of second- and third-generation English, while that is not a bad thing, there was just no connection. There was no League of Ireland players considered in the 1990s. They just wouldn't even think about it. They would rather go down to the Fourth Division in England than look at some of the players here. Charlton just didn't have an interest in it. He took the approach that: my job is the international team, not Irish football. Irish football and the international team are two different issues.'

Former Ireland manager Brian Kerr, a man who had great success in the 1990s with St Patrick's Athletic and Irish youth teams, agrees about Charlton's legacy to Irish football:

'The Charlton era had a positive impact in that there was more people interested in the game, more following it and more playing it, but it had a negative impact in his dismissive attitude to the League of Ireland. People weren't encouraged to go to the League of Ireland because of his [Charlton's] and Maurice Setters' attitude to the game here.'

Just a month before Ireland's World Cup exploits in 1990, St Francis provided a backdrop of fairytale proportions when they became the first non-League side to reach the FAI Cup final. The team from the Liberties in Dublin, which came from humble beginnings in 1958, had risen through the ranks to reach an FAI Senior Cup final. Their story gripped local imaginations, and 33,000 turned up at Lansdowne Road on a hot May Sunday to see them in action. The Cup wasn't for the Liberties, though, as Bray Wanderers ran out a 3-0 winner with a hat-trick from John Ryan.

What was the impact of their achievement, however? The streets of Dublin heaved with 200,000 clamouring fans who welcomed the international team on their triumphant return from the World Cup, after losing 1-0 to Italy in the quarter-finals. But how many of those cheering that day would have known of St Francis' success at reaching the final? More importantly, how many of them would continue their interest in Irish soccer come the start of the next League of Ireland season in September 1990? Hopes were raised when over 20,000 turned up to see Shamrock Rovers' first game in their new grounds at the RDS at the start of the season, but it turned out to be wishful thinking. The swelled attendance stemmed from the publicity surrounding the KRAM campaign of the previous year. Now it was back to football as normal, and soon the crowds drifted away as quickly as they had arrived. Robert Goggins, football historian, sees it as an important moment in the evolution of the League:

'I think it was just one of those moments where everybody wanted to say they were in the RDS the day that Rovers came back to the southside of the city. I suppose it died a little bit after that because we were rapidly going into the winter period. The matches were starting to kick off at half two because there was no floodlights and then I think that when you have a full programme of junior and schoolboy during the summer it just affects the League. There was one Sunday in the RDS when they were playing Athlone and the place was packed and the game, it meant nothing really and I was looking around me and saying, where did all these people come from? And someone said to me all the junior and schoolboy fixtures had been called off.'

Quite simply, it was going to take more than a World Cup to save the League.

II. Junior soccer v League of Ireland

The disaffection between junior soccer and the League of Ireland is a topic that looms large in the fall of the League. After the euphoria of St Francis' Cup exploits, Ireland's performances at Italia '90 and Shamrock Rovers' first game at the RDS, it is evident, looking back now, that fans were yearning for big-time events. Just as the big European matches of the 1960s had proved and as the big internationals were now proving, sports fans wanted events that grabbed their attention—not just local Dublin derbies five or six times a season.

Irish soccer couldn't fulfil this desire, however. Worse still, it seemed incapable of adapting or changing to allow it to happen. One of the main problems—one which could have been so easily solved—was that matches were still played on Sunday afternoons, thus clashing with English soccer and, increasingly, with junior soccer matches. Between 1986 and 1996 the number of players registered to play football in the country trebled. As more and more people wanted to play the game, there were more and more involved in fixtures that were kicking off at roughly the same time as League of Ireland games. Interest in soccer was hitting explosive proportions, but the irony was that the more popular the game became, the more the League was adversely affected.

The increased participation in soccer opened another can of worms in that it highlighted and widened the divide between the proponents of the League of Ireland and Junior Soccer. Relations between the two major power brokers of Irish soccer had always been fragile and fractious and this only got worse as Junior Soccer became more dominant due to the continuing failures of the League of Ireland. In order to understand the faltering development of the game in this country, it is necessary to examine the pivotal relationship between the two.

Former FAI President Brendan Menton wrote a book about his time with the FAI. In *Beyond the Green Door* he describes the problems between Junior Soccer and League of Ireland:

'Irish football is very much divided between the eircom League [League of Ireland] and the junior game. It is all about the political power. Bernard [O'Byrne] was from the junior game while the opposition to eircom Park was concentrated among the League. Many Council and Board members, who had abandoned him on the Stadium Ireland vote the previous week, would back him politically now to ensure that the junior football camp remained in the ascendancy. It has nothing to do with right or wrong or with overall interests of the Association . . . never-ending petty rows within the FAI that probably still continue. It would have included the attempt by the Schoolboys Football Association to undermine Brian Kerr as manager of Ireland's underage international teams. One league club also did not want Brian because he had once managed St Pat's . . . Success does not bring you support within the FAI, it makes you a target.'

All politics is local, they say, and it is clear that even at local schoolboy level, all football is political. Rightly or wrongly, junior football was vying with others, such as the League of Ireland, at Council level in the FAI, where each vote counted. At these levels the idea of working together for the good of the game didn't seem to have cropped up. Des Casey is very clear on this, describing how the lines of communication often got tangled:

'Football in Ireland is a very political scenario. There was never any harmony with the schoolboys and the clubs. There was never any harmony between the Junior clubs and the League, there was always a them-and-us situation. You have got to look at the GAA's structure if you want a perfect model. And we never did that. I have always said and I do believe it because when I went to UEFA the frustration of what I had felt at home crystallised in that every country you went to, the whole basis or foundation of football was community-based, there were no demarcation lines between the club and players, it was an all-embracing situation.

I can remember in Dundalk when I started away back in 1963, Liam Tuohy had a team there with seven locals on it at one time, but inevitably insofar as the League of Ireland clubs are concerned, they hadn't the patience to develop young players. Every club wanted instant success, they wanted to win the League or they wanted to win the FAI Cup. The structures are pretty much the same as when the Football Association was formed in 1921. Now that is eighty-odd years ago and the structure is the Leinster Football Association, the Munster Football Association, the Connacht and the Ulster associations. Plus the Schoolboys Football Association was there—that has never changed. But there is a resistance to change. A fundamental resistance to real change to bring the Association in line with the social, political and demographic changes that have taken place in the country over that time.

There are rules in the junior game, but they have no avenue or opportunity to advance to the senior game, you know. In one part of the country, for example, there is a very vibrant schoolboys league, but there is a vacuum of a relationship with the local League of Ireland club. It has generally been the same story for numerous other League of Ireland clubs down through the years. You only have to look back at the hundreds of schoolboys who were shipped off to English clubs in recent years to appreciate the extent of the difficulties; and the fact that only 5% actually make the grade to top professional football highlights the problem in this area. The drain is slowing up now as English clubs are cutting back and looking more to Eastern Europe and Africa for young players.'

The absence of a structured relationship between the junior game and the League goes right to the heart of the matter. Structurally, there is no direct link between schoolboy clubs and the League (although the situation is now changing with the likes of Shelbourne, who have their own underage teams). For the junior clubs, the main aspiration is to play in England, bypassing the home League. In some cases there are stronger links between English clubs and schoolboy clubs than with League of Ireland clubs. As a result, the League doesn't get the best players coming through from the underage ranks and it can't call upon the top underage clubs as nurseries for emerging talent. The League's role in all this, says Casey, has been hugely diminished over the years:

'The League has no real clout in terms of numbers now at all. You have a situation where the Schoolboys Football Association is affiliated to the FAI, but many of the clubs have guys, mentors, managers on the one hand running schoolboys teams in their respective leagues and on the other hand they are agents or scouts for x, y and z clubs and they have this constant stream of youngsters going, like a conveyor belt, back and forward to England. I worked hard for over thirty years in the FAI to achieve change, but I was simply unable to break down many of the barriers I have mentioned.'

Pat Quigley, former FAI President, who was involved with junior football in Mayo for over thirty years, believes there are, and have been, bad relations between the two sides of the game:

'You would have to say that there was a kind of "them and us" mentality. The League of Ireland tended to rule the roost, I suppose one would even say that is the case with the under-21 situation at the moment. It is only in the latter years that you begin to realise that there are a good number of junior players—I can even see it locally here in Athlone, Sligo and Galway—and you don't always have to go oversees to get out there. There were fellas that went over and didn't make it fully and came back. There are quite a number of good young fellas and even with them coming through we never got a player looked at outside, or we felt that we never got them looked at outside of Dublin. Now recently we have had Manchester Utd over here, we have had Liverpool over here and you know, that is not the best idea in the world because it is the people from Athlone, Sligo, Shelbourne that should be coming down to have a look at our players.'

Noel O'Reilly, Brian Kerr's former assistant, is another who has much experience of trying to work between the two levels, having been coach and manager at the famous Belvedere schoolboy club in Dublin for twenty-six years:

'I don't know whether the people who run junior football would have a very good opinion of the League [of Ireland]. But that opinion would result in looking at the League's hierarchy, in looking at the structure of the League. Take Limerick, for example, Fairview Rangers were a far better team than Limerick Utd over the last couple of years. People knew that aspiring players weren't aspiring to play for Limerick, they would go to Waterford, they wouldn't go to Limerick because there was no organisation. It was known, for instance, that Limerick to get to away matches there was no bus, so they had to scab lifts and even once at under-21 level they had only nine players going down to play and they had to pick up two bangers along the way to make a team.'

Having seen both sides of the divide, O'Reilly reckons it has changed now, but for a long time the culture of coaching and training just wasn't there:

'I think the people who ran League of Ireland clubs weren't forward-thinking people. They didn't have the development of the future of football at heart. Regularly for years we would run Belevedere teams and we were very successful, so lads would come through the system and they would leave at eighteen—they were finished with Belevedere, they never handled players after eighteen—and they would go into the League of Ireland. I don't mind saying this, but you would see the lads and they would tell you it was terrible, the training was terrible and they had no facilities. The training was better at Belvedere. The culture was better.

I don't think the League of Ireland was run properly. They didn't have the expertise. I am putting my hand down now to have it slapped, but for the people who ran the game there was no such thing as coaching in the League of Ireland. There was no such thing as organised coaching or developing young players. Giles tried to do it and it didn't happen.

I remember even years later, in the early days, when Brian [Kerr] was on the way—and I don't want this to sound big-headed—we would do warm-ups in the League of Ireland grounds and you had the whole team warming up before the match. They were serious about it, but people were like, what is going on? They maybe had a long trip up north or south and the players needed to get out and stretch. But we would actually organise warm-ups that were designed to get the lethargy and the tiredness and stiffness out of you before you played the match. It just wasn't done back then, but there is an awakening now, there is no doubt about it. You had organisers or administrators running the League and you had administrators in clubs who a lot of them, controlled the purse strings. And there was managers who had far-seeing ideas that weren't given the money to invest. The biggest factor was always the lack of training facilities.'

So while some point the finger at Junior Soccer and blame their motives, others point to the League of Ireland and blame their facilities and organisation. It's all part of the cycle of begrudgery, fight your own corner and don't give an inch. These problems are deeply rooted in a long tradition of mismanagement and complacency. The structures are still in place that allow the culture of 'blazers' to predominate.

The career path is straightforward: start out with a local team, rise to the top there, attend enough meetings to get onto local League level, from where you can catapult yourself onto the regional scene, before finally attaining the lofty heights of the FAI. It is a self-serving, narrow culture that encourages administrators and paper-pushers, men who enjoy nothing more than a Friday night discussing the minutes from the last meeting and raising points of order. Their honour and glory comes from knowing that people know they are *someone*, that they can, perhaps, sort you out for tickets, or can see to it that some grant funding makes its way to your club. This type of man likes being in the pub on a Sunday night, wearing the blazer with the crest of the local league sewn into it as a badge of honour, and mingling with the locals on a networking level—'just to keep the contacts up'. They bask in their own self-importance, regaling anyone bothered enough to listen about the crucial meeting last night that centred around a vital rule of underage football and really, in fact, his vote might just change the course of the future of the game. Sure, while he was there didn't he bump into the Leinster official and weren't they all saying what a fine job they were all doing . . .

It might be only a caricature, but anyone who has ever been involved in soccer will recognise some of the traits of 'the Blazer'—

the man who lives life at committee level and dreams of one day getting the chance to attend meetings in Merrion Square. In their methods and motives they are reminiscent of the local county councillor and politician: the man who would schmooze for a living, spend a lifetime in elections and lives to hear his name being mentioned. Yes, this is the power and the glory that is local football and parish-pump politics.

III. Ireland: old and new

This was the decade when those prophecies of GAA dominance finally came to pass, and the GAA witnessed a resurgence that hasn't tailed off yet. It was sparked off by the emergence of the Ulster counties in football, the renaissance of Clare hurling and, most spectacularly of all, by a Dublin–Meath Leinster series in 1991 that was able to find a winner only after *four* scintillating games. Soccer had grabbed the headlines for much of the previous year, leading GAA people to worry about the possibility of losing fans and players to the beautiful game. Their worries were unfounded. The League's inability to manage and build on its success left the door wide open, and the GAA stormed through.

Ever looking forwards, the GAA noticed that, on foot of the World Cup, there were goalposts going up in tiny little villages where they never had been before, and in many of these places the parish teams were drawn from the same players as were staffing the soccer team: people were playing both games. The GAA saw this trend and asked themselves: How do we fight it? Top of the agenda was prioritising coverage through the media and the re-development of Croke Park into a world-class stadium.

The continuity of the officers in the GAA—especially at Director-General level—was to prove a big advantage for the Association in seeing through long-term plans and being able to lay out visions ten, twenty years hence. Liam Mulvihill has been in charge of the GAA since 1979 and has overseen the revolution that has put the Association firmly in the spotlight. However, a glance through the annals shows that the redevelopment of Croke Park has always been a factor for the GAA: as early as 1988, then chairman John Dowling was travelling around the world looking at the top sporting stadia and seeing what influence could be brought to bear on Jones Road.

This long-term planning meant the GAA was on the ball when TV sports hit the big time in the 1990s. Broadcast rights to sporting events were spiralling out of control: 1992 was the year Rupert Murdoch's Sky Sports took over in the Premiership for £305 million, and within a decade broadcast rights to these games had soared to a value over £1 billion. Sports markets were following a trend set in the United States, where the rights to the NFL, NBA and MLB were on an upward scale in the billions, while at events such as the SuperBowl advertisers could be charged as much as $2 million for a thirty-second commercial slot.

This was all a long way from the GAA in the early 1990s, but the process of commercialisation of Gaelic games had begun and media coverage of the sport would radically change the game's popularity and perception. This in turn would entice blue-chip, corporate sponsors into multi-million-pound deals with the GAA.

'They [the GAA] were more astute than the soccer or the rugby people and they came on board,' says Fred Cogley, Head of Sport at RTÉ from 1972 until his retirement in 1999. 'The GAA, even way back in the 1960s, said you can broadcast five matches: St Patrick's Day, the semi-finals and finals were all negotiated. But now, at long last, the senior authorities were recognising the importance of sport in the schedule. BBC have had an awareness of this for a long time. RTÉ had only just come in and consequently, if you look at the various people that they have lost, I mean they shouldn't have lost, and they have a strange attitude not only to sport.

RTÉ have had a strange attitude to success, I think, and the Sports Department became largely sort of a little cocoon and we went ahead and did our own thing and we had a certain freedom, but we didn't have wild support. The biggest thing in the 1970s and 1980s was trying to encourage the GAA to provide more television coverage and it was only in the 1990s when that came about. Twenty years I was trying, but at the time they had a point, I suppose, they decided it would affect the club games and the club championships all over the country.'

Despite the fact that sport was undoubtedly becoming more

mainstream, some of the powers-that-be were slow to recognise it and the change of mindset wasn't to occur for another few years at Montrose:

'In general terms in RTÉ the vast majority of people outside of the sports department didn't really have much interest,' says Ian Corr, Head of Radio Sport from 1990 to 2000. 'They would have seen sport as trivial and of no great consequence and unfortunately that meant that there was a danger that they would be inclined to cover the thing in a trivial fashion, which is a completely different thing. It is a bit like the story about Edward R. Morrow, the great American broadcaster back in the 1940s and 1950s who was working for NBC. He used to do a nine o'clock programme that would go out in the middle of the week. It was a prime-time current affairs programme and he was doing it when suddenly it was moved to a different timeslot. So, Morrow went to see William Paley, who was the head of the network, and asked, "What is going on?" and he said, "We have moved it because we have put a new programme in your slot—the $64,000 Question." And Morrow said, "What are you doing putting a programme of that consequence in instead of my programme?" And Paley said to him, "Well, the difference between your programme and the $64,000 Question is that your programme is done in the public interest but the $64,000 Question is what the public is interested in.' They are two different things and in terms of sport, my experience, although I would be just as interested as the next man in current affairs and a lot of other things outside of sport, I would recognise that at any given time, sport is the one and only thing that has the capacity to bring this country to a standstill.

In the forty years that I worked in RTÉ there were maybe three, four, maybe five events that brought this country to a standstill. One was the Pope, the other was Kennedy, but outside of that there was the Irish thing in Italy and Japan. More in Italy than any other time that brought the country to a standstill and brought people into the area of sport that wouldn't have known a golf ball from a football. There were other things, Sonia [O'Sullivan] running in the 5,000 [metres] in Sydney or a couple of the boxers, in other words it had the ability to grip like none of the other programmes had.

There was a great story told after one of the elections in the 1980s and it was when Charlie Haughey went into coalition with the PDS.

There was great dismay and one of the people who got a ministry in it was Bobby Molloy, who by that stage had joined the PDs and the question was, and everybody inside in RTÉ were talking about it: what is Máire Geoghegan Quinn going to say when Bobby drives down the big main street in Tuam in his big black Mercedes? And somebody said, "Listen, for f**k's sake the election was two weeks ago, people in Galway have moved on, what they are concerned about now is not Bobby Molloy and his Mercedes but is Finnerty going to play in the All-Ireland Final." That's basically what I am saying about sport. It is trivial in a whole lot of ways, but it has an extraordinary ability to grip people and that is something that, generally speaking, is lost on a lot of people on the programming side of RTÉ.'

It wasn't lost on the GAA, though, and the four-part epic series between Dublin and Meath was a perfect televisual spectacle. Over the coming years, the colour, passion and sheer unbridled joy of Ulster's return to football dominance would provide another visual spectacle that seemed to sum up just what Gaelic games meant to the populace.

Aside from the amateur status of the games, the one advantage the GAA has always had is its definitive claim to identity and Irishness. As Ireland began to change and develop, as its culture, society and economy became more global and multi-cultural, many Irish people began to yearn for something to reaffirm their identity. While so much was being lost in the rush to economic boom, some wanted a firm hold of their Irishness and it was the GAA that became, as it had nearly 100 years previously, the marker for people's identity.

It could have been otherwise. After Italia '90, soccer was the dominant sport and, through the international team, it became the identity of Ireland with its connection to the diaspora through the second-generation players. Soccer had moved beyond its traditional urban roots in the likes of Dublin and Belfast and now reflected a larger consciousness. By 1990, even republicans could talk about soccer and not seem unpatriotic. In earlier days people wrote to *An Phoblacht* talking of the 'mongrels or traitors' who played 'foreign games' and heartily approved the ban on these games as a 'bulwark against colonialism'. Attitudes were changing, however, and soccer came more and more to represent the people.

Soccer failed to take up the baton when it could have. The latter half of the 1990s proved the most revolutionary in the history of the State—in economic and cultural terms—and the pendulum began to swing back once again to the GAA as the yardstick of Irish identity.

These were the bloated Celtic Tiger days. Irish consumer spending was £23 billion in 1995, rising to an incredible £34 billion just four years later and then hitting an unbelievable £40 billion the following year, in 2000. House prices sky-rocketed, the price of living shot up, unemployment plummeted, foreign investment reached unprecedented levels and with it came immigration, creating a situation that was quite unique to a country so used to emigration. In his seminal work, *Ireland: A Cultural and Social History*, Terence Brown gave the title 'Revelations and Recovery' to the chapter dealing with the 1990s. Irish society had opened Pandora's Box and what Fintan O'Toole referred to as our 'fixed points' began to collapse beneath the weight of inquiry, confession and public debate:

'All that really happened in the 1990s was that people started saying things that they knew. Take, for example, the child abuse stuff in the institutions, these things were around. The child abuse one was a very interesting thing because for every boy of my age or younger there was always a paedophile in the school. There was always one. I haven't talked to anybody who went to a Catholic school, either working-class or middle-class or in any part of Ireland in those years, in the 1960s and 1970s, that there wasn't at least one. And it was quite sort of open in a way and everybody knew about it. But nobody talked about it at all, everybody just conspired to try and ignore it because usually they just picked on the vulnerable kids and part of the emotion was just, like, I am really glad that is not me. There is that sense that that was all there, so it wasn't a revelation at all, but there was some sort of weird disjunction about what we knew and what we could say. And then when it is said it takes on a whole other meaning, it becomes a fact.'

These may not have been facts the country was willing to take on board, but at least being able to say it aloud meant it was acknowledged. For a country that worked so hard to bury its recent past, that was a start, at least.

Now, however, with the Irish returning from abroad and new immigrants from across Europe and even Africa and Asia coming to these shores for the first time, our sense of identity, as espoused by Mary Robinson, was changing and a deeper soul-searching was taking place. Even our perception of the national soccer team had changed: how much could we really identify with Scottish or English grandchildren of Irish emigrants going back two or three generations? They were Old Ireland. The New Ireland was one that could stand on its own two feet and not rely on hand-outs from the diaspora.

The change from Old to New was only an ongoing process, and in football terms it came to a head in 2002 in Saipan when Roy Keane and Mick McCarthy faced-off over Ireland's World Cup effort. Before that watershed moment, however, the FAI's very public crises and cock-ups revealed a soccer organisation that was lagging well behind the times. The Merriongate ticketing scandal and the Night of the Long Knives were about to prove this beyond doubt.

IV. FAI crises

Jack Charlton's tenure at the international team was coming to an end after nearly ten years. After a decade of success, the fortunes of the team had started to wane: the stalwarts from its heyday were getting older, and Ireland's 'put 'em under pressure' style was easily countered by opponents now well aware of our limited tactics. Ireland's play-off defeat to Holland in 1995 was Charlton's swansong, marked by the fans raising thousands of scarves aloft and delivering a heartfelt rendition of 'You'll Never Walk Alone'. It was a fitting tribute to his remarkable contribution to Irish football. Charlton was leaving, and Irish football's future seemed uncertain. There were few answers and many questions: who would be brought in as 'Big Jack's' successor? Could Ireland keep qualifying for World Cups and European Championships? Were the good times over?

While all eyes were on the changes taking place on the pitch, soon the focus would switch to changes within the FAI off the pitch. Within a few months the Irish people would discover the murky details of FAI incompetencies in relation to ticketing at the 1990 and 1994 World Cups. What was to emerge, via the newspapers, in the first half of 1996 permitted a rare insight into the culture of power at the FAI and brought old internal enmities to a head. A sleazy trail of back-stabbing soon became front-page news across the country as the FAI washed its dirty linen very publicly. It seemed the doomsayers were right all along: the good times were a temporary stroke of luck, but the cracks they had papered over were still there, causing massive structural damage. In the words of soccer writer Peter Byrne:

> 'For all the change in infrastructure, the demarcation lines between the professionals and the voluntary corps had never been fully defined. Now at a time when Irish football had moved into the big league and the pressures on the administrative structures became intense, that flaw was magnified.'

Noel O'Reilly, who has been involved in Irish football from schoolboy level all the way up to the international team, where he was assistant to Brian Kerr, expands on this:

> 'What was going on was that the administrative people in the FAI in Ireland and the League all jumped on that bandwagon. To them— and not them all—but to lots of those people the international team and the cavalcade and trips around it was more. Plus, there was all that money that the FAI had made during the Charlton era. They must have made some—you hear people arguing about the stadium and all that—where did all that money go?'

The year of transition was 1996. Mick McCarthy took over from Jack Charlton and attempted to take Irish football forward into a new era. The FAI, on the other hand, was not yet ready to move into the future. The organisation had been unprepared for and unable to deal with the resources and management skills required at international level, and root-and-branch change was still needed before progress could be made. There was a lot of dead wood that needed to be cut away if the FAI was to survive in the new multi-million-pound business of international soccer. The question was: did it have the men capable of achieving this, or was the old mindset too entrenched and the various cabals still too interested in protecting their own local powers to be able to see the bigger picture? Before the FAI could prove itself one way or another, a crisis hit the organisation that left everyone reeling.

The first hint that all was not rosy in FAI HQ came early in 1996 when Michael Morris quit as the Association's accountant in disputed circumstances, with some saying it was voluntary, others claiming this was not so. Morris was followed by Sean Connolly, who resigned as General Secretary and Chief Executive in February of the same year after run-ins with the honorary officers and pressure from others who wanted him out. It didn't stop there. Next out the door was Joe McGrath, the National Director of Coaching, followed soon after by Shelbourne Chairman Finbarr Flood, who resigned from the Executive Committee. That meant that within just a few weeks there were four high-profile departures, most notably that of the Association's Chief Executive. There was speculation and rumour, of course, but no one guessed what would happen next.

Just two days after Connolly's resignation, on 18 February, the *Sunday Independent*'s Veronica Guerin revealed that in 1994 a London-based ticket agent had absconded with FAI ticket money amounting to £200,000; the shortfall had been met by a FAI official. Slowly it came out that the FAI's strategy over the last two World Cups was to buy non-Irish match tickets and then trade these with agents and other football associations in exchange for Irish match tickets. This practice, the *Sunday Independent* was able to reveal, had resulted in a loss of £154,000 in 1990, and the not inconsiderable figure of £210,000 [the figure was revised upwards after the initial report] in 1994.

The FAI's first response was to deny the allegations and hope the story would disappear. Then suddenly a character popped up who went by the name of 'George the Greek' *aka* Tio Marcos *aka* Theo Saveriades. The FAI claimed it had dealt with him as a known ticket dealer, not realising he was a tout, and that he was the man responsible for running off with the tickets without paying for them. It was a farcical situation, but at the heart of it was £210,000 and suddenly the FAI Honorary Treasurer, Joe Delaney—who was responsible for ticket trading and had been assuring his fellow officers that there were no concerns at all—took centre-stage as the plot thickened. It appeared that not only had the media been misled but so too had the FAI's Executive Committee. It was obvious that heads would roll as the Irish media homed in on the nitty-gritty details of the scandal.

Despite initial denials, Joe Delaney issued a statement confirming it was he who had met a £110,000 shortfall (which later became £210,000 to meet the entire amount) due to dealings with a 'less than trustworthy' ticket agent and that he regretted not informing the FAI of his actions. Of course, what everyone wanted to know was: who knew? Had Joe Delaney really been acting on his own, without telling any of his fellow officers? If so, would any of them stand by him now that the heat was on?

It didn't take long to find out as the political manoeuvrings quickly kicked in. It was the law of the jungle: survival of the fittest. The media and the public were baying for blood, and FAI officials moved quickly to save their hides. Knowing that it was Delaney's head on a plate, three of the five FAI officers tendered their resignations in an effort to distance themselves from the Honorary Treasurer and his actions. Des Casey, the Honorary Secretary, Vice President Pat Quigley and Chairman of the League Michael Hyland all announced they were resigning ahead of the forthcoming FAI Council meeting, and that it would be up to the Council to reinstate them at that time if it believed their sides of the story. Joe Delaney then tendered his resignation, claiming that he also wanted the chance to tell his story to Council. FAI President Louis Kilcoyne was the only officer left, and badly isolated by his decision to remain.

The showdown came on Friday 8 March at the FAI Council meeting, held at the Westbury Hotel in Dublin. Motions of 'no confidence' against the entire officer board were tabled and for ten hours the 51-man council debated and voted on who they wanted back and, more importantly, who they believed.

The media was waiting en masse for developments, and thus began the 'Night of the Long Knives'. One by one the officers of the FAI presented themselves and their case to the Council members, stating their role, knowledge and involvement in the Merriongate ticketing affair, as it was now called. First up was Pat Quigley, and he won the vote of confidence easily. Michael Hyland also survived comfortably, as did Des Casey. Louis Kilcoyne was up next, but he must have known that his involvement in the sale of Milltown in 1987 would count against him and cost him votes from the League of Ireland clubs; it did, and he was duly defeated. For Kilcoyne, this was the end of a colourful and controversial career in Irish football.

Finally, it was Joe Delaney's turn. He had attempted to smooth his path by issuing a press statement ahead of the meeting, claiming that the sole motive behind his actions was to secure tickets for fans, but it had backfired. The statement went on to apologise for misleading his officers, the public and media—but ultimately it failed to impress his Council colleagues. The FAI Council saw Delaney as the man at the centre of the storm, and he would bear the brunt of the responsibility. Delaney was easily defeated in the vote of confidence and it was hoped his sacking would consign Merriongate to the annals of history for good.

It was well after 3.00am when Pat Quigley was elected Acting President and Bernard O'Byrne Honorary Treasurer. The infamous Night of the Long Knives drew to a close. In truth, however, only one battle had been fought that night, and for the next nine years the FAI was troubled by the feuds stemming from that encounter. Factions and divisions were now part and parcel of the Association and 'by any means necessary' became the war cry of those who wanted to control the game and its development in Ireland. One battle was over, but the war had just begun, and those still standing were digging in for trench warfare.

Pat Quigley, former FAI President, has painful memories of the whole affair:

'It was a very difficult time. It was full of all kinds of ups and downs and it was a very difficult time because people weren't agreeing with one another and we were trying to change things . . . As I often said, if you don't like me, please respect my position and I wasn't behind the door in letting people know and a lot of these people have now gone and at that particular time they would hardly bid me the time of day . . . Anything that could be dragged out would be and if you happened to say something today and in five years time somebody says, "Well, you said that five years ago what do you mean by it now?" . . . There was a great deal of uncertainty in the air that night [of the Long Knives]. People couldn't really believe what was being said at the time. Nobody tended to believe anybody. They couldn't trust anybody at that particular time.'

To this day the questions over Merriongate and the ticketing fiasco remain unanswered. Just who was George the Greek? How did he disappear into thin air? Did he, in fact, ever exist? Is there any truth in the allegations of a FAI official divvying out tickets for cash in hotel lobbies at both World Cups? We will probably never know.

In an attempt to salvage the dignity and honour of the Association, Brendan Menton appointed Ray Cass, a management consultant, to look into the workings of the FAI, with particular reference to the handling of World Cup tickets. At the end of May the *Cass Report* was ready to be published and when it was, it provided a window into the workings of one of the biggest sports organisations in the country. It gave details, in the words of Peter Byrne, of 'an administrative structure that had failed to keep pace with the changing times'. It highlighted various key points, including: a loss of £132,000 from Italia '90, compared to a profit of £176,000 for USA '94; that Joe Delaney had paid stg£210,00 to settle a liability to the FAI for World Cup tickets; that £230,000 was due to the FAI on ticket sales going back two years; that there was no audit trail of the ticketing system, with management reporting very poor; that one in fifteen tickets for home internationals was complimentary.

The report's recommendations were, not surprisingly, forthright and far-ranging: authorisation of all expenditure was to be in writing and supporting documentation to be retained; tighter credit control over ticket sales; a review to be conducted of pricing and commission for the Ten Year Ticket Scheme in light of the poor sales (only 1,500 of 5,000 had been sold); preparation of regular management accounts; assessment of capital expenditure proposals, including capital/development grants for clubs and affiliates, should be subject to a documented review and assessment by the FAI financial management, prior to approval.

Cass was highly critical of the FAI's structures, calling them outdated and ineffective, and he gave the clearest view yet of the ruling interests at the heart of the game in Ireland: 'lack of vision, direction and planning, its fragmented and indecisive structures and its marked reluctance to consider necessary change.' There was, he said, the perpetuation of unwieldy, central decision-making bodies, composed of a series of sectionally focused interest groups; there was a concentration of power with neither accountability or a broad democratic mandate; and there was a tendency for the same people to retain power at the centre:

> 'If the Association is to achieve credibility as a competent, imaginative and professional governing body for Irish soccer, it needs to press ahead with a major overhaul of its decision-making structures and administration.'

(It was very telling that in 2002 the *Genesis Report*, commissioned on foot of the Saipan debacle, echoed the criticisms contained in the *Cass Report*.)

While the *Cass Report* was remarkable in its clear-sightedness, the criticisms levied at the structures, decision-making processes and power-brokering were all common knowledge and nothing new to anyone with any understanding of Irish football. The report did bring it all out into the open, however—no longer were we to rely on rumour and conjecture about the FAI's workings, here it all was, laid out in black and white. Now that everyone was happily saying 'I told you so', the FAI became an object of ridicule and scorn (some referred to it as 'F**k-All Intelligence'). That could have been the death of the Association, but miraculously it appeared that a line had been drawn in the sand and lessons would finally, finally be learned.

V. European Champions

Against the backdrop of this continuous feuding, one man was quietly performing miracles on the pitch and marking himself out as a future manager of the Irish international soccer team. Brian Kerr took over St Patrick's Athletic in Inchicore in 1986 and spent almost eleven years at the club, winning two League titles in 1989–90 and 1995–96. But it was his time as Ireland Youths manager for which he is most famous, having guided both the under-16s and under-18s to European Championship titles in 1998.

In his time at St Pat's, the team won the League on two occasions, the last in 1996 as allegations were flying and knives were being drawn. Kerr's style and substance couldn't have been more different from the antics on display at Merrion Square. He was a devoted and astute observer of the game. ('He was always asking questions,' was how Johnny Byrne remembers Kerr when he was his assistant at Shelbourne in the 1980s.) Kerr was part of a new breed of football thinkers who hadn't played the game at a high level, but were intelligent and studied the game carefully and, as a result, were able to profoundly influence the game and its future when they got their chance at management level.

Noel O'Reilly was Kerr's long-time number two and he knows better than most what made the man tick:

'The reason for Brian's success throughout the 1990s with Pat's was an organisation and steely determination, the right players to do the right job for you. Pat's cleaned them up. They were all reserve players from teams that other teams didn't necessarily want, so Brian, who ran St Pat's for ten years, did so in his own way and revolutionised the League in many ways because of what he did. So I would like to think then that Brian, the way he came in and showed within a couple of years that a certain amount of planning, understanding players, not understanding their abilities but understanding players and coming up with a common-sense approach to football, influenced people.'

Although he won't admit it, O'Reilly was another vital ingredient in Kerr's success. Theirs had been a remarkably successful partnership because, O'Reilly says, it was based on mutual respect:

'I think you have to agree to disagree because if you have the situation that I saw, like when Graham Taylor was the English manager, when they did that documentary on him, and he said something and everybody on the bench agreed with him, that was f**king stupid stuff. You will say your piece, but he doesn't have to listen to you, or, if he does listen to you and it doesn't work, he will tell you, "For f**k's sake, what you are doing telling me that?" It is human nature, but human nature also says to you that when you don't know everything, you have to go and ask people questions.

I think Brian trusted me and I certainly would trust Brian in football terms and in going to look at a player, what is he like, and going to look at matches and going to see where we are playing the winners of the next round, I might go along and look at it and see who won and come up with something to talk about with the players. Building up this well of information about everybody in the League, who is good at corners, who takes them, who is in swingers, who is near the posts, where is the danger coming from. I would have thought in the early days that wasn't done, but Brian brought that to a fine art and people see that now.'

But the Kerr–O'Reilly double act, in spite of all its success, was fighting an uphill battle in trying to turn things around in the League of Ireland. The crowds still remained to be convinced and until they were, they weren't coming back. Dave Hannigan in his fine book on Irish football, *The Garrison Game,* tells a story that underlines where the League was at in 1997:

'Standing just inside the entrance to a National League of Ireland club on a Saturday evening in April 1997, the club secretary answered the enquiry about the expected gate with a hopeful air: "maybe 100". Talking to him again, two-and-a-half hours later, he was more exact. "Thirty-eight paid in".'

They weren't helped either, reckons Kerr, by all the chopping and changing that went on at the clubs:

> 'I had ten chairmen go through in the ten years I was manager of St Pat's. I remember my first season in 1986 and we were playing a game at 12.00 on a Sunday to avoid the 3.00 match on telly, then we didn't have lights until 1993. Coupled with our poor European results, people just didn't have as much respect for you in the League of Ireland.'

Such was the state of things.

Andy O'Callaghan, now Chairman of St Pat's, came back from London at this time and became very involved with the club he had supported alongside his Dad when he was growing up:

> 'We played, unfortunately, most of the time in Harold's Cross when Brian was there. In the early 1990s the fallout from the neglect of the 1980s was that the League was in bits in the early 1990s, so that when we won leagues with Brian the crowds were thin. It got bigger and it began to get better, in fairness, and when we went back to Richmond, initially crowds were good. That was a good era for us.'

Kerr's talent and achievements at St Pat's did not go unnoticed, and marked him out for greater things. He moved on to the Youths job in the FAI, which brought him the phenomenal success of managing the under-16s and the under-18s to European Championship victories, as well managing the under-20s squad that reached third place in the World Championships—a first in Irish footballing history. Kerr was on the fast track upwards, and it seemed inevitable when he eventually got the top job in 2003, succeeding Mick McCarthy as International Manager.

Was it inevitable, though? Noel O'Reilly isn't so sure:

> 'When Brian's name was thrown into the hat, I would say there would have been surprise at that stage. Would I have been surprised? I am not saying that I didn't think he could do the job, I would have been probably surprised when there was fifteen people in for the job that Brian would get it because of the FAI decision-making within a diplomacy process; but when it whittled its way down to a few bodies, I think people were able to read into it and

see what was going on. We played in a tournament in Malaysia seven years ago and since then the Spanish youth coach took over the Spanish international team, the Argentinean fella became their international manager and the Brazilian fella who was their manager also went on to the senior team. So in other countries it made and still makes sense, but it wasn't appearing that way with us, you know, until Brian got the job.'

Kerr's success with St Pat's and the Irish Youth teams struck an all-too-rare positive note for the League and the FAI in the 1990s, in a decade otherwise marked by controversy and infighting. At least, commentators assured themselves, the rise of Kerr meant the best *could* rise to the top through the morass of mediocrity and small-mindedness that sullied so much of Irish football. Or so we thought.

Just thirty-three months into the job, after failing to qualify for the 2006 World Cup, the FAI chose not to renew Brian Kerr's contract. While some lacklustre performances from the team led to calls for him to go, many felt he should have been given another chance. As one commentator remarked drily: if failing to qualify for a tournament becomes the benchmark for all future Irish managers, then standards have indeed been raised to a new high.

It wasn't just the ending of Kerr's international reign that saddened many in Irish football, but the fact that a role for someone of his undoubted ability could not be found within the upper echelons of Irish soccer. For the world looking on, Kerr had been sidelined and his talent lost to Irish soccer. Inevitably, rumours began to surface about the manoeuvrings of the FAI against Kerr, particularly John Delaney. Delaney was one member of the three-man committee that had appointed Kerr in 2002, and he was the lone dissenter; his preferred candidate was Bryan Robson. There were mutterings of conspiracy: was the Kerr sacking a case of moving on with the times and getting over disappointments, or was there still a sinister undercurrent of machinations and ulterior motives at play in the FAI?

VI. The Dublin Dons

The innovative and the experimental never really got much support in Irish football, as John Giles found out to his cost. But in

1996 a few hardy souls were willing to throw in their lot behind a new venture that might just resuscitate the League of Ireland. Football club owner Sam Hamann was looking into the possibility of relocating Wimbledon football club to Dublin. It was ambitious, but there were some who believed it was a Godsend— a once-off opportunity that should be grabbed with both hands. Over the next two years this became one of the most contentious issues ever to arise in Irish football. Suddenly, the League of Ireland had staunch defenders it didn't even recognise, and the numbers claiming the proposal put the League of Ireland's very existence at stake, and therefore was unthinkable, was staggering in comparison to the numbers who actually supported the game.

The contentiousness of the issue was fuelled in no small part by the fact that Eamon Dunphy became the public face and defender of the project, known as the Dublin Dons project. Dunphy had always had a knack of annoying Irish soccer fans, stretching back to his days as a journalist when he openly castigated the League of Ireland and then on to his infamous 'ashamed to be Irish' comment after the 0-0 draw against Egypt in Italia '90. After that outburst, Dunphy became the hate-figure of the soccer brigade, with Moore Street traders selling T-shirts depicting his head on a wasp's body—waiting to be swatted by Jack Charlton. Years later, many were forced to admit, reluctantly, that he was probably right in 1990, but the *Olé, Olé* band has never forgiven him for attempting to burst their big bubble.

Now here he was again, leading a charge to bring an English soccer team to Dublin to play against the other Premiership teams. For League of Ireland people, this was the final straw. English soccer was reviled as being responsible for taking away so many Irish fans; naturally if the Premiership didn't exist, League of Ireland grounds would be packed to the rafters every other week. The very thought of allowing an English soccer team to be based in the country, where the home league was struggling to survive, was unthinkable to them and would, they believed, have been the very last nail in the coffin of the League of Ireland. Whether or not that would have been a good thing is a moot point.

It was a potent combination: the old enemy and Dunphy. A

The Boys in Green. Fewer and fewer people cared about the League of Ireland, but over 200,000 fans turned out to see the triumphant Italia '90 squad.   (Inpho)

USA '94. More heroics — and the Irish fans were growing in numbers.   (Inpho)

Sealing the fate of Irish soccer? Jack Charlton, Ireland manager 1986–95.

(Inpho)

European champions! Brian Kerr masterminded under-16 and under-18 European triumphs in 1998. Just seven years later his tenure as senior manager ended in bitter circumstances.
(Inpho)

A place to call home. Bernard O'Byrne's vision for an Irish soccer stadium would result in his acrimonious departure from the FAI. (Inpho)

The biggest crisis of all: Saipan. Roy Keane and Mick McCarthy and the mess that was Irish football. (Inpho)

Irish football's greatest loss: 'The Doc' Tony O'Neill was Ireland's finest sports administrator; he died in 1999 aged only 54. (Sportsfile)

The commissioner experiment: 'On the one hand they wanted someone who would be chief executive, who would take decisions, and on the other hand they reserved themselves the right to contradict themselves or change.' Roy Dooney, the League's first and last commissioner in 2002. (Inpho)

Ollie Byrne, chief executive of Shelbourne FC: 'My headache today is somebody's debt tomorrow … no matter what, I will survive because that is the nature of the beast of the club. But some other club won't.' (Inpho)

Shelbourne's credible performance against Deportivo La Coruña in the Champions League in 2004 signalled an upturn in the League of Ireland's standards. (Inpho)

Croke Park. The constant redevelopment and upgrading of Jones Road showed
foresight and planning by the GAA.   (Inpho)

The king-maker: now the man in charge, what does the future hold for John Delaney and Irish soccer? (Inpho)

compelling argument was the picture of empty League of Ireland grounds, while down the road the Dublin Dons hosted 50,000 Irish soccer fans watching the likes of Manchester Utd or Arsenal. After all, how could an already struggling League survive with a Premiership team *in situ* just down the road? As had happened when the news of Rovers' departure from Milltown leaked out, closet fans stepped forward to declare loudly their undying love for the game. The League of Ireland, it seemed, could only garner big support when it was at death's door; otherwise, the humdrum existence of League titles and Cups was beyond the interest of these 'fans'.

So, what was all the fuss about? The plans for the Dublin Dons ran as follows. The £100 million project would provide for: the building of a 50,000 all-seater stadium at Neilstown, Clondalkin; the provision of road and rail links to the stadium; the installation of all safety and security features, such as surveillance cameras, etc; the creation of several Schools of Excellence placed strategically throughout the country to coach and train youngsters from nine years and upwards; the payment of £5 million to the FAI to be used for the development of the game; the payment of £5 million to the National League clubs, amounting to £250,000 per club; the remaining money to be used to cover general costs of relocation and signing established players.

Wimbledon claimed to have the approval of the other Premiership clubs and the backing of eighteen of the twenty-two National League clubs they had consulted. Their argument was simple: Wimbledon is a Premiership club without a home stadium and without a substantial audience. In the increasingly more professional world at the top, Wimbledon would collapse economically unless its problems were solved. Dublin could provide the solution to both problems: a 50,000 all-seater stadium, plus a regular audience of substantial proportions, if not always full capacity.

Despite tentative EU backing for the plan, the entrenched opposition of the FAI and FIFA ultimately killed the idea. The arguments raged back and forth as to the merits and demerits of the proposal. When it became apparent that it wasn't going to happen, some breathed a huge sigh of relief at having seen off the megalith of the Premiership, while others saw a once-in-a-lifetime opportunity thrown away.

Eamon Dunphy, typically, has no regrets, seeing it as yet another occasion when little Ireland shot down a good idea. He explains his own thinking on the matter:

'Well, it went back to the original thing of Shamrock Rovers that Dublin can support a professional soccer team of European class. There is no question about that because of the number of people who are playing here and because you could get 40,000 or 50,000 people in the ground every fortnight or more. That was what we were aiming for at Rovers and the chance arose again when the Wimbledon thing appeared as they were screwed and they had no fans. They didn't own their ground, but they had this priceless thing: a Premiership licence. They were looking to relocate and when I found out through Joe [Kinnear, manager of Wimbledon at the time] and Sam [Hamann, Wimbledon owner], I went to Paul McGuinness [U2's manager] to see would he be interested. He was a high-profile guy who would attract other high-profile guys and it would be a bit of buzz—U2 and all that, you need that sort of buzz about a project. Paul wasn't going to put fortunes into it, but he was extremely supportive of it and he saw the vision—he had a vision the same as he had a vision for U2. So at a certain point other people came in. I went and got Owen O'Callaghan, the property developer, because I knew he had planning permission for that site [out in CityWest] and knew that he wanted to build a stadium. I got him into the project because he had the real muscle and he was ready to go and build. I put him and Sam together and they were the key players.'

As soon as word of their plans got out, the criticism wasn't slow in coming:

'The biggest critics were the FAI, League of Ireland clubs and Pat Dolan was also prominent. I wouldn't single Pat out because he's a good fella, but they were saying if this comes in, no one will go to League of Ireland matches. My argument was if this comes in, you won't be able to sell enough tickets for League of Ireland matches because the people will be dying to come and see soccer.

The logic is very simple: if you live in Greater Manchester and you go to see Manchester Utd there is also Rochdale, Oldham, Bury, Stockport, Leicester around. If you go to Arsenal, does that mean that you are not going to go to Leyton Orient, Fulham, Charlton, Milwall? There is no argument. It develops a love of football but also the spill-over is that, first of all, the talented young players of the country don't have to leave the country to play—they can actually aspire to playing here. Secondly, you bring a load of pros into the country and in ten or twelve years time you turn them into coaches, high-profile quality players who can now coach in the League of Ireland. Soon you've got a massive facility up and running. Plus, we were going to upgrade every League of Ireland ground and give them fortunes to upgrade. We were going to make a fortune with 50,000 people watching Premiership football in Dublin with all the memorabilia, the shirts and all that.

But of course we got vilified. It never bothered me, however. You don't go into these things looking for glorification or vilification, you go into them looking to get your objective and the objective was to bring this massive money machine, this symbol of sporting excellence, this Premiership dream into Dublin free of charge.

Not only that but it was the big, big opportunity for Irish soccer to break through into Europe, to set new standards and to have a massive facility here for kids with huge benefits in terms of quality of life and not having to go to England. There was going to be massive investment in local football, massive investment in schoolboy football—massive. Now, to their credit, the schoolboys football were in favour, but there was a lot of opposition.

I wasn't surprised there was opposition to it, but I was surprised by the vehemence of it all. I don't know if I was personally opposed to someone who was building a national soccer stadium I would object to £500 million. It may be personal, but that is what I said when Giles came over and I came over with him in 1977—we encountered exactly the same thing. Now this time I brought in here the potential multi-billion-pound investment in Irish soccer and I was getting vilified for it. Now, I didn't have a huge personal stake in it because I said to the guys, "I can only do it this way" and it cost me a lot of money. I could only do this with integrity and if I didn't stand to gain from it. Paul McGuinness was very insistent that I get share options and stuff and I said, "At this stage I can only do it if I haven't got share options." You just don't have to be clean, you have to be seen to be clean. I said, "When we have it then we will talk."

Despite all the football opposition to it the government were supportive. Mary Harney was very supportive. Bertie was supportive, very supportive. Harney was supportive as it was in her constituency, but not just for that reason. Jim McDaid was supportive. Padraig Flynn was very supportive because we went to the EU—he was an EU commissioner at the time. And the EU was key to it. They set it up and they said, "Yes, this will happen." '

What about the other side of the argument? Pat Dolan, then St Pat's manager, was probably the most vocal and insistent critic of the Dublin Dons proposal. He outlined his reasoning in an article in the *Sunday Tribune* at the end of 1997:

'Wimbledonmania has dominated some sections of the Irish media in an attempt to condition the Irish soccer public that whatever the ethical, moral, or legal arguments against an English club abandoning their home to commercially exploit Ireland's love of sport, nothing or no one could stop it.

The game of soccer is the most popular globally, purely because it transcends social background, sex, colour, creed, age or nationality. People, supporters, are the integral fabric of soccer. If advocates of this scheme put commercial gains ahead of people and supporters, what is the future for football?

If Wimbledon's new football visionaries simply wish to benefit from being Ireland's representatives in a European Superleague, why not join the National League? A new National League club in Clondalkin in a 60,000-capacity stadium would be welcomed by St Pat's.

. . . Employment opportunities, that for the first time in a decade are available to young Irish professional players, would suddenly be limited to players vying for 11 places on one team. Thomas Morgan captained Ireland to glorious success in Malaysia where Irish players defied the odds and succeeded, coached and managed by Irish people. Thomas Morgan, Trevor Molloy and Colin Hawkins are new Irish soccer heroes who want to live and work in Ireland with St Patrick's Athletic. St Pat's are an integral part of the social fabric of West Dublin: our schoolboy teams provide a secure and constructive environment for hundreds of youngsters. Wimbledon's arrival would undermine this vital role and damage the social fabric of community life nationwide.

What about the great English export, the soccer lout? Does Dublin want to encourage hooligans who will undoubtedly impact negatively on our economic prosperity and consume police, court and prison resources? Our advice to Wimbledon's visionaries is to look elsewhere. Your scheme is morally, ethically and most crucially, legally wrong. For £2m or even £2bn, the Supersaints will never abandon the most important people in our football world— our supporters. Your future, our future, the future of Irish soccer is secure, as we will not allow Irish soccer to be destroyed for financial gain.

. . . Glamour is a perception, the reality is something different. People here are naïve about what the professional game in England entails, how hard it is to go over there and survive. That's why we need a strong game here. I'm not saying for one minute that players shouldn't go to England to play. If it's the right thing for them and their careers they definitely should. The problem is that for all players, it has become the only option. In that respect we have failed the Irish public, but we can change that.'

In private and in endless public media debates on the airwaves, on radio and in print, the pros and cons were thrown back and forth, with Irish football interests in one corner and the Dublin Dons campaigners in the other. Those in favour were labelled traitors to Irish football; those against were derided as narrow-minded parochialists, desperately trying to cling to a bygone age. When the project was finally defeated, the sigh of relief from the Irish soccer community was audible; those who had tried and failed shrugged their shoulders, unsurprised that another challenging idea had been shot down. Regardless of who was right and who was wrong, Dunphy is certain that Ireland will never again get the chance to host a Premiership club.

'It won't happen again because no Premiership club is going to be homeless again. These chances come once in a lifetime and if you look at the history of any great sports institution, it came on the back of people with financial muscle and someone with a vision

who could join the dots up and say Bang! go for it. You don't get
second opportunities and this was a moment—well, it was three
long solid years between the jigs and the reels. But of course the FAI
refused to say yes and wouldn't stop opposing it at FIFA level. But
UEFA were onside, the EU were onside as we are seeing every day of
the week and we will continue to see when it comes to a conflict
between soccer law and the EU. There is only one winner and we
were going to win. Of course we were going to win. The EU would
never have gone to court, but they just held out for a very long time
and that killed the project. The time element killed it.'

Pat Dolan, on the other hand, saw it as a victory to savour. For
a long time he had been a vociferous, outspoken and, some would
say, eccentric advocate of the League of Ireland, and this was an
especially pleasing victory because it meant the League could go
back to concentrating on improving its lot. What kind of lot that
was remained to be seen as another major row—even more bitter
and rancorous than Merriongate—was looming large on the
horizon.

VII. Clubs v players
On the pitch, St Pat's continued to dominate after Brian Kerr's
departure, winning the League again in 1997–98 and then retaining
the title—the first team to do so since Rovers in 1986–87; they
continued to do things right on and off the pitch and seemed to
represent the way forward for League of Ireland clubs. The club
actively used marketing and publicity to portray itself as the club
of the community and to re-establish its roots in Inchicore and
with the people. This approach is at the heart of St Pat's, says Andy
O'Callaghan, Chairman since 2002:

'You have got to make yourself part of your community, you really
do. It has to be on lots of levels: schoolboy level, inter-community
groups, into the hospitals, even the dynamics of Irish society are
changing in terms of the demographics, a lot more non-Irish
people living here. What do we do in each club to welcome those
people and make them feel like this is their club as well as anything
else? But then we really do need to almost rethink, and this is a

harder one, to rethink where we place professional sport in Irish society and in that context where we place professional football.'

The question of professionalism has always been a sticking point for the League. Time and again the detractors have pointed to the GAA and asked: if that was the League of Ireland, how well would it be doing? Instead of struggling to pay players' wages, the money could be spent on improving facilities, which would in turn bring more crowds in, which in turn would bring more money in, which would in turn … it's a reliable cycle. It is a compelling argument. As clubs sink deeper and deeper into debt, paying out more and more on players' wages, it seems that professionalism isn't really sustainable? O'Callaghan disagrees:

'I actually think you have no choice. We have debated this so many times; where sport is today, realistically, rugby has shown the way, while the GAA is unique because people are so passionate about their club and their county that they will support them. But they are not competing with other clubs, they won't get hockeyed by a professional club that comes over the water; whether it is Wasps or Man Utd in their sport. With the GAA the winners will always be an Irish team so there is a huge interest locally. If we chose to go amateur in this country, you would go back to the days when you would get stuffed by an Icelandic team. And the one chance we have is to be successful in Europe.'

One man who, predictably enough, rubbishes the notion of amateurism, or even a wage cap, is Fran Gavin, Secretary General of the Professional Footballers Association of Ireland (PFAI):

'It's a ludicrous notion. Just look at the GAA, the bastion of amateurism, which is even now talking about paying players. As for wage caps, that will never happen either as, firstly, every type of EU law forbids it, secondly the whole notion of putting a cap on a player's right to earn can never be acceptable and thirdly no club would ever abide by the rule, they would be trying to outdo each other and looking to pay players under the counter. It's exactly that sort of culture and mindset that we are trying to move on from.'

The situation changed in the 1990s. The Bosman ruling of 1995 fostered player power, wages were increasing and freedom of contract was a right within EU labour laws. While Roy Keane became Man Utd's first £50,000-per-week player and other high-profile footballers across Europe were receiving astronomical contracts, the grind in the less glamorous lower leagues meant players were engaged in a continual fight for proper wages and recognition. Fran Gavin has put much time and effort into making his members in the League of Ireland see themselves as workers, with every worker right that is their due:

> 'There is no such thing as loyalty. It makes me cringe when I hear people talk about player's loyalty to clubs, that it is not there anymore. There has never been loyalty from any club to players. It very, very rarely happens. Look at Beckham and United at the top level. You are a commodity at the end of the day, if you are not producing and if they are not interested, that is the way it is. Football is like that at the end of the day, it is transient. I have seen players more loyal to clubs and being more patient with clubs than I have ever seen clubs more patient with players. I deal with that everyday here in the office; clubs reneging on contracts, trying to pull the wool over players' eyes; trying to cancel players who are on two-year contracts because they don't think the player is right, or they don't fit or something.'

Yet in spite of all the progress made on footballers' rights, especially in the European game, Gavin reckons clubs' attitudes remain pretty much the same:

> 'They haven't got better, they have just got more serious. The stakes are higher, but at least we have made the players more aware. A lot of them are more aware of their rights and they will contact us quicker than they did before. Clubs have got very suspicious of the PFAI, but it is a good stick to have for the players if they can say to a club, "If you don't do it we will bring in the PFAI." They don't want us about the place, they don't like the way we do business. That is tough shit because we try and get the job done. We are not there to be popular, we are trying to support the players.'

It's fighting talk, but then, the changes secured have been very hard won. It has been very difficult to change attitudes towards players because the notion of them as commodities, rather than employees, is ingrained in football:

'I was a young lad at Derby and I remember signing and I brought my parents over and I was treated like a God and my parents were treated like the king and queen and when I signed, part of the deal was that they would fly me home at Christmas and Easter. So at Christmas I went to get the flight and at that stage you could only fly from Birmingham and I went up to get the money for the ticket and they said, "No, we are only giving you forty quid towards the flight." At that time a flight from Dublin was £140. I was only a sixteen-year-old and the club said, "Well, did you not read your contract?" and I said, "No", well I trusted everybody and I had to ring my father to send me the money to go home. That was the time I realised that, hold on, that is not right, there is exploitation here and I didn't want anybody else to be in that position. And teams today still do it. I will still support young players and make sure they are not exploited and I will defend them. Exploitation by clubs still goes on. Then they make you feel guilty for getting your wages and you had to fight for every penny you got in a lot of cases. Plus there's been a lot of reneging on contracts and I have seen a lot of that happening and I have built up my animosity towards the clubs on the back of such things.

People never realised that just because a footballer didn't build a shelf or paint a wall didn't mean they couldn't have the same rights. You didn't get paid just for turning up, you actually provided a service and that service was football and people paid for that service. It was trying to educate the players more than anything, that you have rights here because you are supplying a product and the product is your service as a footballer. But nobody ever saw it like that, they felt they were lucky to be playing.

I remember an incident when I was at St Pat's when Paul McGrath went to Manchester Utd and part of the deal was that we were to play a friendly against Manchester Utd. We were training the Monday before the game on the Tuesday and the manager told us all to turn up the next day at whatever time in Dalymount Park. I then asked were we getting some appearance money for this game? And he looked at me as if to say, "You mean you want to get paid for playing against Manchester Utd? Whereas my thing was Manchester Utd were getting paid to play against us, we are part-time players, why should we not have some sort of appearance money? I felt as a squad of fifteen players, if we were tied to £100 a game, £1,500 they wouldn't have missed. But typically we had to go and beg for it.

So we told Charlie Walker, the manager, that there wasn't going to be a match. We told him would he step out of the dressing room and we the players then had a vote that we wouldn't play the match if they wouldn't pay us. Thirteen of us people voted, two didn't vote because they were guest players, and, can you believe it, we lost it seven to six. When we counted the last vote I couldn't believe it, we were going to have to play for nothing. Then suddenly, the manager comes running back into the room and said, "Look I am after getting you £40 a man" and we said, "That's fine, we will take that!" And he still doesn't f**king know, but what annoyed me most is all the other c**ts said, "F**k the money". These players had only seen Manchester Utd on television and for them, for their families, to come along to Dalymount and see them play against Frank Stapleton and Ray Wilkins and all these guys, they weren't going to not let that happen. But personally, I wouldn't have given a f**k if the match hadn't taken place.'

VIII. Problems and answers

While players were beginning to receive more recognition, rights and power, the League was looking to move on from the bad old days of the 1980s. The question now was: were they too late? The introduction of Sky Sports and their deal with the Premiership on Sunday afternoons meant the FAI received in the region of £20 million from Sky in compensation for having TV games on at the same time. That windfall meant floodlights could be installed around the country, at all the grounds. The decision was finally taken to move League of Ireland football from its traditional Sunday afternoon time to a Friday evening. This, it was hoped, would re-invigorate the League.

Unfortunately, it came about twenty-five years too late. ITV's 'The Big Match', it should be remembered, first started broadcasting live Sunday afternoon games from the English First Division in 1968, and it was these broadcasts that many in the

League of Ireland point to as the real beginning of decline. It meant people could stay in the comfort of their own homes to watch a better calibre of football. And they did. In their thousands. True to form, though, the League clubs refused to budge from their tried-and-tested Sunday afternoon format, choosing instead to either go up against 'The Big Match' or kick-off a bit earlier. Even though some clubs already had floodlights by then and therefore had the option of switching to a Friday night, the consensus was to stick with Sundays because . . . well, just because that was the way it was always done.

Donal Crowther, Bohemians Secretary from 1985 to 1997 and League Secretary from 1997 to 2002 admits that the switch was tough for them to decide:

> 'The work that had to be done to get the members here [at Bohemians] to agree to it was unbelievable. We found the gates on a Sunday afternoon were being affected as we were competing with this and competing with that and it took a lot of hard work to move it from Sundays. There was a lot of resistance to it.'

Like most things, once the change has been made, the previous status quo is quickly forgotten. Now, Friday night is seen as the night for League of Ireland football, naturally. And it only took twenty-five years to get there.

Another solution put forward in 1994 was a merger of the League and FAI. Part of the problem has always been the fact that the League looked after itself through its clubs, while the FAI comprised an amalgam of all the various branches of soccer in the country, from the League to schoolboys to colleges and the women's game. While League of Ireland chairmen and secretaries would often be installed as Presidents and Secretaries of the FAI, the League of Ireland was still left to its own devices, with little or no interference from the bigger football family. In essence, what one had was a small, feuding family that was left to figure its own way out of its squabbles. There were twenty-two member clubs in 1994 and, remarkably, the one club–one vote mandate was still in place. Within these structures, the bigger clubs argued, they could never progress or move on as their proposals would always be voted down by the majority of smaller clubs, which had less ambition and less financial backing. They were content to let things float along as they were—once they weren't losing much money, that was fine with them. Given how much it took to move games to a Friday evening, it is obvious that any more grandiose ideas were unlikely to succeed in such an atmosphere.

Shelbourne's Chief Executive Ollie Byrne tries to explain the mentality that was prevalent:

'My headache today is somebody's debt tomorrow. If I have a problem today that a breach of the rules or a lack of adherence to the rules where it affects me and I argue it, I am the greatest bollocks since the sliced pan, but no matter what, I will survive because that is the nature of the beast of the club. But some other club won't. And that decision which affected us could destroy them and they don't realise it at this particular time because the mental approach is: if it doesn't affect me, don't get f**king involved.

The infighting and the internal structures of the game destroyed it. I am not saying that anybody deviously, maliciously or purposely set out to do it, but that is what happened. I am not going to name clubs because there are genuine great football people, but there are certain clubs in the League today that shouldn't be there. They are not ready for the growth of the game. But what happens is you get an occasional fairytale story like St Francis in the Cup in 1990. After that everybody said St Francis should be in the League and they came in and they couldn't draw dog's breath—no disrespect to them. But people moved and changed things and diminished the strength and appeal of the game in the way they did it.'

It was hoped that a merger between the League and the FAI would take the stultifying power of the smaller clubs out of their hands and centralise decision-making into a powerful FAI executive that could enforce change. In other words, the overly democratic one club–one vote rule would be gone and a decision-making body put in its place to change things around.

A working party consisting of Michael Hyland, FAI President, Louis Kilcoyne, FAI Vice President, Brendan Duffy, Honorary Secretary League of Ireland and Dr Tony O'Neill, Vice President League of Ireland was put together to examine the feasibility of merging the League with the FAI. Its report was brutally honest regarding the dire position of the League:

'The Football League of Ireland has survived decades of crises, falling attendances and declining media profile, but remains administratively strong. However, it has no resources for marketing purposes or general development, a poor bargaining position in regard to media coverage and no corporate commercial direction. The financial position of many of the member-clubs is precarious and almost all of the revenue generated by clubs finds its way to the semi-professional players in the League, rather than is spent on ground development, facility improvement or promotion of the League.

The League will find it very difficult to extricate itself from its current difficulties. Lack of resources render it impossible to execute the business strategy necessary to regain its former status. Competition from the National Team's activities and the focusing of interest on footballing activities in other countries further diminishes the status of the home game. Several clubs are under severe financial pressures, which are unlikely to dissipate if the situation remains unchanged.'

This was a grave indictment of where the League of Ireland stood in the grand scheme of things, with an open acknowledgment of its lowly place and a summation of the reasons for its failure. As had happened in the past, however, the ability to see the problems did not provide the solutions, and the imagination and creativity needed to come up with answers seemed sadly lacking—a lack that has been a constant throughout the history of the game in this country.

The report did make recommendations, but they were limited in scope. Its suggested action included: to devolve executive powers of the League, consisting of eight Council members; to make available to the League and Secretariat the full commercial and marketing resources of the FAI, with special emphasis on PR; to enlarge the League. These were not the solutions to decades' worth of ills. More paper-pushers and more PR wasn't going to save the League; it needed a better game and better environment

within which to play. The proposals simply weren't far-reaching
enough to be effective.

As it happened, all the debate and self-analysis was unnecessary:
the proposal for the merger fell on deaf ears and was allowed to lie
idle before eventually being forgotten.

IX. 'The Doc'

The biggest setback to the game in the 1990s came with the news
of the death of 'The Doc' Tony O'Neill, probably this country's
most able sporting administrator and a man whose vision and no-
nonsense approach had marked him out from the beginning. The
Doc had dominated the Irish soccer scene for over twenty years,
enjoying a career that covered many bases: from his association
with and management of the UCD soccer team, to establishing the
sports scholarships scheme, to rising to the top in Irish football
administration. Although he worked hard within the administration, he was very aware of the flaws in the system. He tried to solve
them, but even he fell foul of the frustration of trying to make a
difference in Irish football: he once described being involved in the
League as being like having maggots crawling all over you. The
Doc's passing served as a grim reminder that truly talented people
were few and far between in the game.

Brendan Dillon worked closely with The Doc at UCD, where he
appreciated just how talented this man was:

'You look back and you think, What was different about The Doc to
everybody else? I mean, everybody else you assume has a certain
amount of ability, but I think what marked The Doc out from
everybody else is that he was able to get on with people and had the
respect of people and yet have different opinions without people
seeing him as the enemy and that in football is very difficult. So he
was a very clever and very careful politician, but I don't mean that
in any malign way. He never—and I would have seen him
particularly in UCD in his position as sort of Director of Sport and
also before that he would have been Secretary of the Athletic Union
and Council—used his position to prefer the soccer club. Anyone
who showed any interest in enterprise, he was there to help them.
In terms of his attention to detail as an administrator he was

absolutely top class, but the best thing about him was that he was so humble, he was so understated, he was never out there spinning about what he did. He just went about and did his job; he was born of a very sharp mind and had a real passion for the game and I haven't seen that kind of real passion, to be honest with you, in any other. Obviously The Doc was completely devoted to UCD, but it didn't stop him seeing the bigger picture.

Even when he became President of the League, he still gave backing for the merger in 1994 between the League and the FAI, he was never in it for his own personal stake. He never allowed the pursuit of power to get in the way of what he thought was right and that is why I think he resigned as Chief Executive back then, I think he just saw it as a completely fruitless exercise in firefighting and never getting anywhere. So when he was approached by UCD and they said, "Look we are creating this new position of Director of Sport", it was just heaven because beneath it all—all the UEFA stuff and FAI stuff—it all boiled down to the fact that UCD and university sport was at the heart of what he was all about.'

It was The Doc's experience of and attitude towards the FAI that was most revealing:

'He was extremely cynical about the FAI,' continues Dillon, 'there would have been nights at the Montrose when we were talking about the FAI and we would have been openly cynical about them. I mean it was open and that was the only way he could deal with it. I think he saw the FAI for what it was. He saw the people in football largely for what they were and what he said was, "Well, I am just going to do my own thing". The Doc wasn't a committee person really. I mean, we sat on committees and we made decisions, but The Doc wanted to do his own thing. He was very much to that extent a bit of a dictator. Not that he came in and said, "I want this and I want that", he just had a very clever way of manoeuvring people to his own way of thinking. He had to work obviously within a committee structure, but I think he realised that within a committee structure he wasn't going to make any progress so he basically let that side of it just go on and then he did his own thing to a certain extent. I mean, he came following the era of Peadar O'Driscoll where nothing was done for years and years, so again I suppose anything he did was going to be seen as progress, but he would have been quite innovative in terms of the whole thing.'

So, the death of 'The Doc' Tony O'Neill at the end of the decade, the end of the century and the end of the millennium brought into sharp focus just how much the League needed outstanding sports administrators and visionaries in its ranks. This was the height of the Celtic Tiger, however, and optimism was running high. The new millennium promised a fresh new start and perhaps a better, brighter future for Irish football. As so often happened before, the new decade wasn't very old when all the hopes came crashing down. Eircom Park and the 'Bertie Bowl' were about to come to very public blows, and the post-Merriongate FAI, still in a fragile state, would be tested to its limits once more.

Part Six

The 2000s: New beginnings, or the final whistle?

THE FAN

'A lot of League fans would prefer to see Irish clubs do well in Europe than the Irish team do well. They feel more of a connection. It would mean more to me for a League of Ireland club to get through to the Champions League group stages than to see Ireland get to the quarter-finals of the World Cup.'

I. eircom Park

For anyone who had any doubts about just how deep politics runs within Irish sport—and Irish soccer, especially—the saga of eircom Park, which ran from 1998 to 2001, had all the ingredients for a series of 'The Sopranos': political intrigue, feuds, secret meetings, cabals and clashing agendas were all part of the mix in what should have been a simple story—the building of a sports stadium. In true Irish fashion, however, nothing could be straightforward; even the Taoiseach himself got involved. For the journalists it was manna from heaven as the soccer story was once again far from the pitch, with plenty of leaks to add spice to the proceedings, faction fights and back-stabbing. Merrion Square was once again a hub of intrigue and counterintelligence.

From the first year of his tenure as FAI Chief Executive in 1996, one of Bernard O'Byrne's primary aims was to build a stadium for the FAI. In 1998 a Stadium Committee was formed and plans for the project began to take shape, with finance and sites being drawn up. After the demise of Dalymount Park in the 1970s, the easiest alternative was Lansdowne Road. However, what was intended as a temporary stop-gap soon became a permanent arrangement, and Lansdowne became the home of Irish football. By the late 1990s it was embarrassingly clear that Lansdowne was a ramshackle, out-of-date stadium, an anachronism in the new world of sports entertainment and spectator comfort. Across the city, meanwhile, Croke Park's development into a truly world-class stadium stood as a remarkable achievement by the GAA—and a challenge to the FAI to look after its own in the same way.

O'Byrne was determined see the FAI in their own stadium, in control of its own finances instead of paying rent to a landlord and with the ability to exploit its own ground for all its corporate and entertainment possibilities. He used his initiative and forged ahead, putting out feelers to ascertain the feasibility and affordability of such a project. He made one crucial mistake, however: he kept much of what he planned to himself, rightly or wrongly believing that to get things done efficiently and expediently, the best way was to bypass the committees and the meetings and thus avoid being undermined by the factional groupings. O'Byrne was eager to get the project moving, but at the same time he was all too aware that there would be enemies across the table and they would gladly seek to bring down the project if he were part of the sacrifice as well. Such was the way of things.

The grand launch was held in early 1999, when Ireland manager Mick McCarthy flew over to be part of the announcement. eircom Park, a 45,000-seater stadium, which was estimated to cost £60 million, was planned for a site out at CityWest. There would be corporate boxes, bars and, most interestingly, a roll-out pitch so that concerts and the like could be held as well. Research visits had been undertaken to stadia around the world, and the model chosen as the inspiration for the Irish project was the Dutch stadium at Arnhem. This, it was proudly announced, was the future of Irish soccer: a home to call its own.

From the outside it may have looked like the FAI was finally pulling together to improve the lot of Irish football, but in reality the Association was divided on the plan. Many felt the cost of building the stadium would bankrupt the Association, which couldn't afford the potential overruns. Their question was: without cash in the bank, how could the future of Irish soccer be in safe hands? Brendan McKenna was Press Officer at the time and was pro-project, but he remembers the opposition to the plan:

'There was a lot of opposition to it from within the FAI. People were saying that it would be a millstone around their necks, that they would be paying for it for the next twenty-five years and it would take money out of the game, and maybe there was a certain element of truth in that. So they were against the building of it, but certainly Bernard O'Byrne for his part and Pat Quigley, they were totally committed to it . . . But they needed to get planning permission and South Dublin County Council dragged their heels on that and they didn't give them permission, so the delay naturally sent the costs soaring and it became improbable that it would be built because the cost almost doubled . . . And then Bertie [Ahern] came in and asked them to scupper the idea, that he would compensate them with money and also by building a stadium in Abbotstown.'

Ah yes, Abbotstown. Stadium Ireland. 'The Bertie Bowl'. Call it what you will, but quite unexpectedly the grandiose notion of a Taoiseach who had Napoleonic visions of a sporting Versailles were suddenly thrown into the pot. Instead of doing the usual and fighting amongst themselves about owning their own stadium, the FAI now had to contend with Bertie Ahern's dream of an 80,000-seater national stadium based on a sports campus where Irish sport would all come together. As a sweetener, Bertie was willing to overlook the FAI's silly plans to build their own stadium and to give them a few bob for switching to *his* plan. The first step was to convince the FAI that its plans for eircom Park were untenable.

At meetings with the FAI, the government kindly pointed out just how much in debt the Association would be as a result of such an undertaking, how the cost of eircom Park would run to over £100 million, and how there would be difficulties with planning permission and with the nearby aerodrome. Even Minister for Defence Michael Smith chipped in, saying he was opposed to the proposal because of the Baldonnel Aerodrome—even though the Air Corps had stated that it had no objection. Aside from the compelling arguments on offer, the government also held out the carrot of £11 million for League of Ireland ground redevelopment. It was a lose, lose situation for the FAI delegation: with all these elements conspiring against them, the FAI's own project was doomed to failure; and if they turned down Bertie's offer, they would be condemned by the public and their colleagues for ignoring the plight of the League grounds.

It was the height of the Celtic Tiger economy, so the notion of Bertie spending £1 billion on a stadium of his own didn't actually seem that extravagant. There was so much money floating around, the 'Bertie Bowl' was chalked down as just one more monument to our excellence. That was the first reaction; then reality hit. A 'Ceauçescu-era Olympic project' was how Attorney-General and PD President Michael McDowell described it; many wondered at the perverseness of spending £1 billion while homelessness was on the increase and the health service remained shambolic; some pointed to the fact that nobody actually needed an 80,000-seater stadium, especially on the outskirts of the city. Tom Humphries, writing in *The Irish Times,* summed it up in his unique way:

'Imagine this. A small island nation with no professional sports leagues. The soccer sultans, the doyens of the oul dickory docker, come up with a plan to build a stadium with a slidey roof and lots of parking in which half a dozen games per year (tops!) will be played. The rest of the year will be filled with Madonna concerts. Now, it so happens that the Government of the small island nation has 50 million punts from a donor. These to be put towards the cost of a stadium. The Government, too, is keen on sports stadiums. The Government has access to lots of land close to the city centre in a massive docklands development scheme. The solution is obvious! Enter Bertie. More cunning, more ruthless, more brilliant than all the others. And from the start what finesse! He sees that the FAI's proposed stadium is too big, too remote and too costly, so he sows confusion by suggesting a national stadium which is bigger, remoter, costlier. To the Stade Saint Bernard, a competitor, The Bertie Bowl. Two games a year and The Three Tenors for the other 363 evenings.

. . . Yet Bertie is too cunning to be seduced by the obvious. Does he say, let's build something together, something accessible and befitting our modest needs, something which will enhance the city and leave some money over for a proper grassroots sports policy which I have yet to formulate or even begin thinking about? Does he ever! Too brilliant! No! When bystanders point out that the emperor has no clothes, the Taoiseach just twirls his nipple tassles. You think I'm stark bollock naked? You think the Bertie Bowl is a white elephant? Well, I'm Lady Godiva, and squidbrain, not only is The Bowl a white elephant but it is modelled on the mother and father of all white elephants, Homebush Bay in Sydney, Australia. Yes, that's right, Homebush, the loneliest place on the planet. Homebush, through which the winds and the tumbleweeds and precious little else doth pass. So aren't you the fool! Get with the programme. Be proud of what we in our goosepimpled nakedness are trying to achieve.'

The Government wasn't going to be deflected easily, however. And it was not just the FAI that were to fall prey to Bertie's manoeuvres. On Friday 6 April 2001, the night before the GAA was to vote on whether to open up Croke Park to other sports, Bertie announced a windfall of £60 million towards their redevelopment of Croke Park. The implications of the funding went deeper than it seemed. The understanding was that by allowing the GAA continue to develop Croke Park for themselves and not open it up to other sports, then soccer and rugby would have to weigh in behind Bertie on his Stadium Ireland project. It was a clever move. At the next day's vote on Rule 42, Congress voted to maintain the rule, albeit by the slimmest of margins—one vote—and in the most controversial of circumstances, with some members missing from the vote and a recount ruled out. Bertie had bought out the GAA and was forcing the FAI's hand in the process.

Naturally, the introduction of the Bertie Bowl into the equation complicated things further and widened the divisions between the various parties at Merrion Square. It was calculated political manoeuvring on the part of the Government and in the face of it Bernard O'Byrne's plan was destined to fail. In the end, it was Irish soccer that suffered, and those in the League of Ireland who had supported eircom Park mourned it as another missed opportunity for the game.

The simple fact was that the FAI *needed* a home stadium. The 1990s had been a decade of firefighting and infighting and the Association badly needed something to restore pride. For a long time Irish soccer had been lacking a sense of pride, a sense of being in control of its own destiny. Instead, their plans were derailed by the Taoiseach's interference. As a result, after the Bertie Bowl had been consigned to the scrap heap and six years after plans for eircom Park were first mooted, Stadium Ireland was scrapped and the FAI and IRFU made a joint announcement that together they would redevelop and share Lansdowne Road. The revamping of the old ground will cost €300 million and won't be finished until 2008, at the earliest.

Looking back on the events and the final decision now, FAI officials are still divided in their opinions. Brendan Menton, who was General Secretary of the FAI at the time, was steadfastly against eircom Park, believing the financial implications of the project far outweighed the long-term gains of owning one's own stadium. In *Beyond the Green Door* he outlined the rows and divisiveness that attended the plan:

> 'I was continually asking for details and copies of documents and agreements but these were denied me, even at Board meetings of Centime [the company looking after eircom Park]. I had little support from any other director. Very often these meetings degenerated into rows . . . from February 2000 the arguments within the FAI intensified, but I was no nearer to persuading the Board of the FAI to seriously re-evaluate the project . . . The split was along traditional lines: League of Ireland (providing five members of the opposition group if I am included) versus junior football. The Schoolboys Association are perceived as mavericks within the Association and usually opposed most things as a matter of course.'

League Secretary Donal Crowther, from Bohemians, was firmly in favour of the plan:

> 'I think it is the biggest mistake they ever made, not going with it. They wouldn't give planning to eircom Park and yet they wanted to build one in Abbotstown that was practically at the end of a runway and the airport. It was a political thing and it blew up in their face . . . It never really came to the League to have a say in it. It was the FAI rather than the League that were involved, but Pat Quigley and Bernard [O'Byrne] were involved. He was another fella got himself into a job and then got himself out of it. He would have been there for life if he had played his cards right.'

Pat Quigley, President of the FAI at the time, was another supporter of O'Byrne:

'The biggest problem Bernard had was that he kept a lot of the information to himself. He probably did that for his own good reasons—if he didn't tell anybody, nobody could go along and harm the situation. But he kept some things a little too tight to himself. He had a great vision for eircom Park and I gave him 100% support on that and was often hung out to dry because I supported that particular thing. But I think that we did need a place of our own and I still think we do need a place of our own, the Taoiseach put a stop to that—plus some of our own members, unfortunately.

We had spent hours and days meeting all the right people and we got the land and the site, the plans were ready; we did get some interference from the Department of [Environment] and the people that were involved with the airport [Baldonnel] they made all kinds of excuses on that. And yet we had got the professionals from England and Europe to explain what they were complaining about. It took us nine months to a year to get a meeting with the Minister at the time, it was crazy—you would get a meeting with the Pope in between . . . Then, once the Taoiseach came out and wanted his own one, that was the end for us. Other people could see that it wasn't going to cost us any money then, while we had a couple of million spent on eircom Park trying to get it together. Some of our own people were against it and it is amazing. All of those people or some of them have now gone from the FAI and ended up not talking to one another. They were against every move that we made.'

Then, as expected, things started to turn bitter and personal between the different factions:

'Things were said to me as President at the time. I wasn't behind the door in letting people know and a lot of these people have now gone and at that particular time they would hardly bid me the time of day or bid other people that were pushing for eircom Park and yet these people are now gone and looked for support themselves when they ran into trouble. And they came to me looking for support when they were in trouble . . . [at the time] there were horrendous meetings going on for four, five, six hours, it was very hard to keep your concentration and to keep your cool. To put it mildly they would be pretty bad, maybe vicious at times. A lot of it would be personal: where do you think you are going? and do you realise what you are doing? kind of thing.

. . . There was bitterness down the line, but this was the worst. The Night of the Long Knives was fairly bitter and acrimonious, but eircom Park for me was the worst. I used to dread going to meetings. You never knew what was going to happen. You would look at the agenda and you would say, Okay, there shouldn't be any major problems here, we will get through everything, but then something would come up. And it was all well orchestrated. There were meetings I would say between the other group making sure that every angle was covered. You would know by the way they started asking the question that there was something coming and it left bad feelings between an awful lot of people. It wasn't really looking at the future of football, it was a way of figuring out how can we bring down these people that have this idea in their mind of having our own stadium? We have to bring that down and get rid of it. So at that stage we weren't looking to the future element of football. It was very much, in my personal opinion, to stop eircom Park going ahead.

The lowest point was the night we had to give in for eircom Park. That was one of the lowest nights for me. They went on and on and kept at it and at it. Every angle that you would go for they always had an angle against it. I suppose the government didn't help the situation either by them going for their stadium. And then that fell by the wayside . . . In fairness, no one asked me to step down as President because I had only six months to go, so there was no real sense in saying goodbye and I wasn't going to offer to step down at that particular time. I just felt it would put more pressure on the Association by having more turmoil and I accepted the decision as best I could, but for me it was very hurtful as it was for other people that had given a lot of time and a lot of effort.'

The defeat of the eircom Park plan meant that Bernard O'Byrne's future in charge of the Association was in danger. Within weeks the anti-eircom Park/O'Byrne faction found a means to force him out. Brendan Menton discovered that O'Byrne used his company credit card for non-company items. It provided just enough ammunition, and soon an investigation by the

Association's financial sub-committee held that O'Byrne had mis-used the credit card on a number of occasions during his four-and-a-half years in office. O'Byrne denied any impropriety regarding the use of the credit card, but did admit to a number of clerical errors. It wasn't enough. He was given an early retirement package and shown the door. O'Byrne had ruffled too many feathers during his tenure and had lived or died by his stance on eircom Park. Once more, another head had been chopped off the block in Merrion Square, and the Menton–Delaney faction was moving ever closer to gaining control. Perhaps this would have been the way of things if the FAI had gone ahead with eircom Park, but as it stood, the plans and O'Byrne were jeopardised by a politician with a plan.

II. GAA Inc.

The Bertie Bowl was very much a sign of the times. Ireland was giddy with its economic successes, but success can breed discontent. The explosion of property prices, the transport gridlock, the cost of living and the increasing divide between the haves and have-nots have contributed to creating a society of unequals, and one that is fattening itself on food, alcohol and drug excesses. The Bertie Bowl, then, can be seen as a rather apt symbol of turn-of-the-century Ireland: bloated, excessive, vulgar and excessively expensive, it pretty much sums up the state we are in. People have begun to question who we are now and what kind of a society we are becoming. Historian Diarmaid Ferriter sees it as a quest for something beyond material wealth:

'There are certain things that we could still see as being distinctively Irish in terms of our sense of place, in terms of certain parts of the country, in terms of how we speak, in terms of how we write and in terms of how we think. But that is becoming more and more a pale shadow when set against vast consumerism. It's the old argument about a very poor country becoming very rich very quickly and how we manage it and whether it is a good thing or a bad thing. There is an awful lot of bubbling resentment in Ireland; it's a mixture of all sorts of things: it is a huge resentment about divide in Irish society, about housing and I would argue that the exact same issues that are important in Ireland, that are still important today, if you take seven or eight specific themes like housing, transport, jobs, the status of people in society, poverty in Irish society, all those debates are still there. Now the parameters of the debates have hugely changed, but we still haven't solved the underlying problems and we have created new ones.

It is about long-term planning as well so that when there is that amount of money around, how do we manage it and how far ahead do you look? There is more of that going on now with people trying to look at getting a proper infrastructure in the country and the fundamental question is: why are there still people lying on hospital trolleys and why is there so much poverty? And then, how are they linked into a question of identity? We used to always blame outsiders for what had gone wrong and there is a degree of legitimacy about certain things, but it was quickly discovered that we were in charge of our own destiny, especially if we weren't doing things particularly well. Then you could argue that Ireland became a kind of, Europe's shining light, as one publication put it in terms of creating money and encouraging enterprise, but that is of course only one side of the story. The other side of the story is what do you lose in the process. And then the flipside of course is how good is it to see Irish identity now in terms of the wider world, in terms of having so many more people over here from different countries?

But in terms of identity and what we have lost, just about everything is thrown into the consumer pot. There is an utter pragmatism there now. Things are being measured constantly in terms of monetary value and all that. I do wonder about kids when I see them, because I am teaching them now as well, who are growing up with nothing but economic boom; obviously you would be delighted for them in some ways in that they don't have to think in terms of emigration, but at the same time you would be worried that they would lose that knowledge of their country's history. I would always worry that you will have a generation growing up who won't really have a knowledge of Ireland before the 1990s.'

One effect of this questioning of Irishness and Irish identity has been the re-affirmation of the place of Gaelic games in Irish society. As people begin to get lost in the globalisation of economies and societies, a positive symbol of oneself and one's country is needed as a badge and marker to stand out from the rest of the world. In searching for that, the GAA was perfect territory. The GAA is essentially a return to the local, to the parish and to the community, which is then represented on the national stage in the All-Ireland Championships, in an amphitheatre of which any country in the world would be envious. Coupled with the corporate management of the games through sponsorship from brands such as Vodafone and Guinness, the GAA has become not only an identifying symbol but a brilliantly marketed one that encourages glamour and appeals to a new brand of fan. Perhaps it is, as sportswriter Eamonn Sweeney calls it, a golden age for the GAA?

In contrast, while Croke Park gets 80,000-plus full-houses, the League of Ireland is currently at its lowest ebb in terms of popular support. It has lost that connection to the local areas. Shelbourne was homeless for so long, Drumcondra disappeared, Shamrock Rovers lost their home: these sorts of upsets have prevented the League of Ireland from putting down roots in communities, and you don't get GAA levels of passion and devotion without very solid roots. In fact, for most soccer fans and players, it is the junior club that is the bedrock of the local community and around which the soccer community volunteers and supports. Outside Dublin, the junior soccer scene is also as strong, but, tellingly, there the League of Ireland is associated with a 'lower-class' of organisation and there is a tacit understanding that it represents the old Ireland of working-class notions and factory work. In the 2000s, the GAA is the only one that has remained a fixed point, able to portray itself in a way that fits in with the New Ireland of money and designer brands and success.

Eamonn Sweeney sums up the difference between being a GAA fan and a League of Ireland fan:

'The big difference between the rural areas where League of Ireland [promotes] soccer and the GAA is basically that soccer is for people that don't own their own houses. That is not being snobbish about it, although there is a snobbery in GAA County Boards about soccer in that soccer is played by people who live in terraces and that is the unsaid thing, which is why, for example, the GAA would not have a great problem sharing their grounds with rugby. There is a certain amount of touching with your betters when it is rugby and there is the same with soccer, which leaves the League of Ireland in a terrible position in the Celtic Tiger era where everything is glam and image and success and when you even had an arch conservative running for the President of the GAA in Christy Cooney, who said things like, "I don't want soccer or rugby in Croke Park because it would sully the brand image of GAA." In the Celtic Tiger age there is no worse thing you can throw at someone than being losers and, to be honest, the League of Ireland measured by those things is a loser in the game. There is no JP McManus, Dermot Desmond backing going on in the League of Ireland and there never will be.

You see, coming from a small town in the countryside, there is always that thing that the guy who even has the smallest of farms would consider himself to be vastly superior to the guy that doesn't own even his own house, for example, and there has always been that. That is the thing about soccer and the League of Ireland—even look where the grounds are, if you look where the Showgrounds are, or you look where St Mel's Park is, the grounds are generally in working-class areas of a town. The League of Ireland is the untrendiest thing, the least fashionable thing and it suffers because of that.'

Thus it has been proved that the GAA's approach—like that of the Church—of putting down its foundations through an immense building programme into the new Dublin suburbs of the late 1960s and early 1970s was the right approach. In doing so it maintained its relationship and link with the community throughout the changing years, and therefore remained a reliable focal point for communities, no matter how much was changing around them.

This fundamental difference between the vision of the GAA and the lack of vision of the League of Ireland is that of being able to maintain the link to the community. This can be illustrated by a trip to an Irish bar in America, strange as that may sound. The Irish bars across America are community centres of sorts for the Irish living there, who are so keen to hold onto their primary connections with home. And what are those primary connections? Dave Hannigan, former *Sunday Tribune* sportswriter and now based in New York, noticed the trend:

> 'I go to bars to watch the GAA in the summer and I go to bars to watch the Ireland Internationals. At an Irish soccer international in a bar you wouldn't actually meet very many, if any, who will say to you, "What about City? How do you think Cork City are fixed this year?" You are much more likely to get somebody sitting there with an Irish jersey on watching Ireland play Israel and say, "How are the Cork hurlers fixed for the summer?"'

III. The Commissioner

As the New Ireland establishes itself firmly in the 2000s, the FAI is anxious to prevent scandals emerging that suggest incompetency in Irish football. Every time the FAI gets negative coverage, it reinforces the general perception that it is an old-style organisation with old-style attitudes and problems. In order to move on in perception and in reality, the FAI is very aware that it needs to keep its house in order. The problem is, it seems to be a magnet for scandal.

Hot on the heels of the eircom Park saga and its unsavoury internal feuding came another unwelcome scandal that strained relations between two League of Ireland clubs, showed up the administration for just what it was and ultimately saw the League end up in the High Court. It all started with a new idea: the concept of a League Commissioner. It seemed sensible enough: employ an overseer to lead the way and keep the ship slick and serene. The appointment was duly made, but as everyone congratulated themselves and the new Commissioner slipped into his new surroundings, no one realised a time bomb had been planted at the heart of Merrion Square.

The new Commissioner, Roy Dooney, was a man who had previously worked in political circles in an advisory capacity and thought he had seen it all in the world of politics; nothing prepared him for what lay in store at the offices of the League of Ireland. He describes it as a place encumbered by basic structural problems, understaffed, with key people past retirement age, where IT systems were antiquated and there were little or no stored databases for all the information accumulated over the years.

Merrion Square might be a salubrious address in the city centre, but inside No. 80 it was a cramped, tired old building that did little to encourage good work practices. It is a long, narrow building with a central corridor running horizontally across it, where people communicated through shouts across open doors—and communicated very little with those on the other levels. It was into this environment that Roy Dooney stepped as the latest great white hope, a time he remembers with very mixed emotions:

'I would have thought that when they got a commissioner the first thing they should have done was invested in IT and people, basic-level office staff. There was no budget for it, you would get a sort of a PC or you would get a disk drive and then three weeks later you would get a screen. It was all piecemeal, there was no integration of the systems or anything. The database package—even the player registration database package was some sort of an off-standard package—it wasn't anything mainstream like Microsoft or anything like that, it was sort of a one-off package that somebody had bought.'

From the outset there was no clear chain of command, and even his job spec. was undefined:

'You were answerable to the Board of Control, but that was never clarified. Part of the problem was that, on the one hand, they wanted someone who would be Chief Executive, who would take decisions, and on the other hand they reserved themselves the right to contradict themselves or change. Here's just one small example: eircom noticed with photographs of League matches when the players weren't wearing the eircom League sleeve patches. I was constantly on at the clubs asking them, will you get them to wear the sleeve patches? And all these excuses would be given, "This is old kit, this is new kit, this is the kit that somebody had in the washing machine". The excuses were like something you would get from a Sunday morning team in the Phoenix Park. So on one occasion, after several warnings, I decided I would fine, I think it was Shamrock Rovers, £200—some Mickey Mouse sum of money—for not wearing their sleeve patches after several warnings. But at the following Board of Control meeting they voted to overturn the fine on the basis that it is them this week, it will be us next week. That is only a low-level example, but the whole time there would be repeated rows over things like rearranging matches. It was meant to be that the Commissioner had power to re-fix matches if they were called off, but that was regularly being subverted by the clubs, who were doing it themselves.'

In his short time there and in his involvement with the League clubs, it was an eye-opener for Dooney. Looking back, he doesn't bear grudges, but he is extremely critical of the way things are run, with the clubs' interests over-riding any sense of reality:

'In theory, with the title "Commissioner" the word sort of conveys basketball, or baseball or football in America, but no, it was nothing like that, it was a kind of a silly title in a way because they didn't have a structure in place. But the clubs are constantly looking for a quick and easy solution. They are constantly looking for something that will deliver them a crowd of 10,000 per match. It is all short term. There is no doubt these fellas love their clubs and they love what they are doing—they wouldn't do it otherwise; take Ronan Seery in Dublin City, Ronan is a nice fella, but that club is like some sort of extension of a PlayStation game. You are the manager of a scabby little club a mile from Tolka Park and Dalymount Park, your biggest neighbours. You have a crappy little stadium and, okay, you have a great idea to call yourselves the Vikings and play in the Dublin county colours, but you just go nowhere and yet the fellas, they do love it. Another chairman I heard had more or less frittered all his money away back into the club. I was told that he sold his wife's car and he took a second mortgage on his home just to pay a players' wage bill. It is just mad.'

While Dooney was getting to know the lie of the land, he could never have imagined what was about to blow up in his face. Where do you start when your job spec. is unclear and your authority is being undermined? What do you do when the IT systems are outdated and basic structures non-existent? In Dooney's book, you start at the beginning: he decided to make a start on player registrations, little realising the hornets' nest he was stirring up:

'It emerged that one player wasn't registered properly—Paul
Marney at St Pat's—and I took the view that it was a genuine error,
the player had been with them and it wasn't an attempt to deceive
or defraud or get the player in under false pretences. So I took the
view, okay, we will let it go through, but then it just rumbled on and
on.

Ollie [Byrne of Shelbourne] was getting fed information from
Pat's by somebody in there who didn't like [Pat] Dolan [St Pat's
manager], as I recall it, and with my political background I had
always found chasing leaks to be an entirely futile exercise, you just
waste huge amounts of effort. But Ollie Byrne came into the offices
about a second registration and he had obviously been tipped off.
This was in September—just three months into the job.

It just rumbled on and on and then there was the second case,
the Livingstone [a second St Pat's player] case which I was aware of,
but again I still believed it was a genuine mistake. Then when I went
looking into the registration thing, it was chaotic. There were all
sorts of discrepancies and inaccuracies in the registration system.
At that stage the electronic database was very clunky and inaccurate
so the real database was a paper file, a brown A4 folder, and you
would have all these pink forms in it with the players' registration
forms in it. Then, the rule book itself was a complete mess because
it was like a lot of rulebooks over the years, bits had been added into
it so you ended up with a series of both very and mildly
contradictory elements; there was no flow to it and there were badly
worded amendments—things would have been rushed through at
eight o'clock at night when everybody wanted to go home. So that
was in need of a major overhaul as well.'

As a result of the flawed rules, inaccuracies and inconsistencies,
the League penalised St Pat's by deducting nine points for fielding
an illegal player (Marney) in three games. Adding to the confusion,
a FAI arbitrator ruled, on appeal, that the points should be
reinstated on the basis that, given the regularity with which the
rule of the registration of players was being breached in one way
or another, a strict interpretation would result in a large number
of players being declared ineligible to play. Shelbourne, who were

fighting St Pat's for the title, took a case against the appeal ruling to the High Court; they were unsuccessful and St Pat's kept their reinstated points. Just a few weeks later, in March 2002, news of the second failed registration by St Pat's came out, with an admission from Dooney that he had been aware of it since the previous September. The controversy continued when St Pat's were then deducted fifteen points for their registration irregularities to which, in true League of Ireland fashion, Pat's responded by demanding an examination of all 1,200 registrations at every club, arguing that the three-point deduction be applied in each and every case that was not according to the rulebook. St Pat's appeal was not upheld and Shelbourne were named League Champions after St Pat's point deduction brought them from first to third place. To this day Pat's still claim that the League title 2001–02 was rightly theirs to claim.

What a first season for Dooney! Registration irregularities, appeals, court appearances, media leaks, intrigue and clubs setting against each other mid-season. What was shocking to him as a newcomer was that seasoned League of Ireland observers shrugged their shoulders and said, 'What's new?' In fact, the League, its image and its competency had taken yet another bashing—and all of this just two months before the über scandal of Saipan erupted. Dooney knew that his tenure was not going to last the full three years—he had been compromised and undermined, and already the media was reporting that the clubs wanted him gone.

'The upshot of the registration thing that ultimately precipitated my departure was that I went to the League AGM in Spring 2002 and I said, "Look, I made mistakes, I apologise." I took the genuine view that it was an administrative error, but Dolan has a lot of enemies within the League and that is what really got them. Dolan was permanently lecturing everybody else about how the League should be run and how it should do its business. So, in the end, they produced a report which in time-honoured fashion was leaked to the media and more or less said that I had lied about what I knew and when I knew it. I didn't lie, but what happened was that some of the people gave evidence that I knew to be wrong.

But when this report was leaked and it basically was implying that I was a liar, so at this stage I was getting seriously pissed off and I got legal advice on it which was very strongly that I had definitely been slandered and this was not done according to due process and so on. The advice I got was that I should contest the findings or contest the process. And when I did this, my solicitor said to me, "You realise that what you are embarking on here probably marks the end of the road—you don't start sending legal letters to your employer, you know." So I said at that stage I recognised this and I said I cannot see how this is going to work. The arguments between the lawyers were going backwards and forwards all summer and the season had just started again. At this stage I just wanted to get out as quickly as possible. I was due to go back on the Tuesday and I sent a letter in saying I was going back in, which was unreplied to and literally at about quarter to twelve on the Monday night I got a phone call at home from Michael Hyland saying you needn't come in tomorrow, we have agreed a deal. Within a couple of weeks then the whole thing was tied up.'

After just fourteen months, the League's brave new step in appointing its first and last Commissioner ended in disgrace, scandal and ignominy. Dooney feels that what happened to him is an indictment of League practices:

'It was an interesting life experience. I have said it before, of all the places I have worked in my life, I have never met so many unpleasant and stupid people in the same place all at once. They might say the same about me, but there was a meanness and nastiness there that I have never come across before.'

IV. Destination: Europe

Amidst all the off-pitch battles, the only positives were coming from the pitch itself. Shelbourne began to emerge as the dominant club again, remaining in the top two and winning titles in 1999–00, 2001–02, 2003 and 2004, as well as coming runner-up in 2000–01 and 2002–03. Since then, Shelbourne have struggled on the pitch, with Cork City and Derry City now coming to the fore at their expense, while off the pitch the Dublin club has been struggling financially without major European football to bring in the big money.

Doing well at domestic is level is all well and good, but League clubs are very aware that to make a real impact and be taken seriously as players, they need to compete in Europe. That has always been the real test, but it has proved impossible to pass. Over the years clubs couldn't even make it past the likes of Omonia of Cyprus—defeats the critics of the League would crow over. In technical terms, UEFA ranked the League's standing in Europe as forty of fifty-two, behind even the likes of Liechtenstein and Belarus.

One breakthrough. That was all that was needed to get the ball rolling. A good European run, qualification through to the group stages against the likes of Real Madrid, Manchester Utd and AC Milan and suddenly people would sit up and take notice. Would it happen, though? Could it happen? After all, there have been famous nights when Real Madrid visited Limerick or Liverpool visited Dundalk, and it hadn't amounted to anything in the end.

Shelbourne's European Cup run in 2004 gave a teasing taste of what could lie ahead for League clubs if they could progress to the next level. They won a tense and taut victory over Hadjuk Split in the second qualifying round, then got one of the plum draws for the next round, being drawn against Spanish giants Deportivo la Coruña. A victory would put Shels into the group stages of the Champions League, where they could have been competing against the likes of Chelsea, Manchester Utd and Barcelona. Of course, against a team like Deportivo, even a draw would be considered a worthy outcome.

Shels moved the tie to Lansdowne, hoping to cash in on a big attendance, and sure enough, despite a downpour that evening, 25,000 came to see them take on Deportivo. This was big-time soccer in Dublin and the fans were interested. It was reminiscent of the days of Manchester Utd and Celtic's visit to Lansdowne Road, where they met Waterford Utd and full houses, and it showed there was life in the League yet. For ninety minutes Shels held the Spanish stars 0-0, but in the second tie at Deportivo the hosts won 3-0. Nonetheless, Shels had been just ninety minutes from the Holy Grail of the group stages of the Champions League.

That August night at Lansdowne saw 25,000 football fans go

home drenched from an unexpected downpour, but still happy. It was a red-letter day for the League. Shels had done themselves and their League proud. Most importantly, they had shown the thousands of neutrals—many of whom may never have been to see Shelbourne before in their lives, or even been to Tolka before—that Irish clubs were finally reaching a level where they could compete. They had shown that standards had indeed risen and that those who had derided Irish soccer for so long now needed to take stock of their criticisms.

Of course, there have been one-off success stories for the League in Europe before, but what is needed now, more than ever, is sustained progress in Europe over the next few years, with the ultimate goal of reaching the Champions League group stages. If that can be achieved on a regular basis and football fans can expect to see the European giants of Manchester Utd, Milan and Madrid coming to these shores each year, then the League of Ireland can move into a new golden age. The League's best hope of future success is through its connection to football's biggest product: the Champions League. Progress in this competition is the key to attracting more fans to the game—if they don't have to travel to England to see Manchester Utd or Liverpool and can instead travel across to Lansdowne to see them and other European teams in action against League of Ireland clubs, well, then a new audience will be found for Irish football. The fickle fans may not return every week to League of Ireland clashes, but at least European nights will give them more of an awareness and a reason to support their club and, hopefully, the League can then move out of the shadow of the success of the GAA and the international team and ditch the loser, backwater tag it has borne for so long.

The signs are there that it is happening, slowly. The decision to move the League to Summer Soccer—a decision that, unlike the move to Friday nights, was taken over a much shorter period of time—has helped clubs be better prepared for Europe by starting the League in March and finishing up in November. More full-time set-ups and better coaching and training methods have also been steps in the right direction, as has the agreed merger between the FAI and the League of Ireland. After sticking so long with their stagnant ways, things are finally moving forward and progress is being made. It is as if the clubs have woken from a forty-year slumber, recognised the changed world they now inhabit, acknowledged the empty terraces around them and finally figured out the action that must be taken.

There are, of course, still things to worry about and it is far from rosy in the League's garden. Shelbourne's recent improvements have come at an expensive price, with a rise in turnover and player wages, and because other clubs hope to compete with them, spending throughout the League has risen accordingly. They are all banking on success to see them through, but it is an expensive gamble. Just take the example of Leeds Utd's spectacular fall from grace, which shows what can happen when everything is bankrolled on possible future success. Clubs are reporting weekly losses of up to €10,000, while turnstile takings are still extremely low. Some things haven't changed yet: weekly lottos, raffles and goodwill is sometimes all that keeps clubs afloat. Andy O'Callaghan, St Pat's Chairman, is an old hand on the question of financing:

'I have found it hugely frustrating and it almost comes back to the point that the lack of resources in football in this country generally means that it is a struggle. It is a struggle to pay your own wages. It is also a struggle to raise the profile of the game. It is a struggle to convince people that this game is our number one game. Yet it is seen as somebody else's game, there isn't a collective view towards it. I think there is a collective view about our hurling and GAA teams and about our rugby team and certainly our international team and even the provinces, but there isn't that kind of collective unity and support towards the League.'

Even though Ireland is now a wealthy country with its fair share of millionaires, unfortunately Irish Abramovichs have not stepped forward to invest in football. Even an Irish Malcolm Glazer would probably be welcomed at this stage! Instead, the Dermot Desmonds and the JP McManuses of this world invest in the Celtics and the Manchester Utds—and who can blame them? They are shrewd investors, looking for a good return on their money and at the moment, who can see where profits in a League of Ireland club can come from? Even so, the known bankrolling of GAA county set-ups highlights how far back the League of Ireland has slipped in the consciousness of the business community. Where are the millionaires who want to invest for the local pride and honour in their club and the League?

It brings us back to the problem of behaviour and perception. To observers, for over two generations the League members have shown themselves as self-serving men of little vision and action, stuck in their out-dated ways, happy to focus on old feuds that will one day be brought to bear on the men sitting across the table from them. This crass attitude has dragged down the name of soccer in this country, allowing it to be associated with cabals, scandals and small-minded pettiness. Who, in these circumstances, would want to get involved with it? And all the while, the GAA and IRFU have stormed ahead, portraying an image of sports associations that are visionary, long-sighted and in control of their affairs—all qualities that bring blue-chip sponsors on board. The winning mentality fostered by the Celtic Tiger is here to stay, and people want it in their sporting spheres as well; backwater leagues will remain just that.

Of course, clubs could wait around for a millionaire to walk through the door and prop them up, but in reality they have to sustain themselves. While coaching and training methods have been revised, it is in the area of finances and proper accounting that there is most reluctance to change. Brendan Dillon, former UCD and League Chairman and an oft-frustrated advocate for change, explains:

'One of the things that we recommended was the whole issue of clubs having accounts and of clubs having a proper legal footing. I would have seen that as prerequisite to any structure and once you have got the structure right, then you can take it to the next step. In 2000 we produced the document that said clubs had to present audited accounts every year, they had to provide a budget as to how they were going to finance themselves and if there was a shortfall in the previous year they had to show how they were going to make it up; this was going to be applied and most of my entire year as

Chairman of the League we spent pursuing this particular rule. I mean we spent nine months making sure that Drogheda kept trading in terms of business and it took about six months before they finally admitted that, yeah, there was a whole load of revenue debts, debts that they basically wanted just to forget about, but we stuck to it and every club effectively did have to get their accounts in order. Since I suppose my whole training as a lawyer is about regulation as a way of doing things, to me just having rules that people ignored, you just can't tolerate, but over a period of time you realise everybody just talks about the game and then when you get to the end of the edge nobody wants to jump. It is just like everybody asks, "What's in this for me?" and nobody can see the bigger picture.

We have never seen the value of having a very good national soccer league. We have never really as a country valued any of these sports—it has been down to the associations themselves. The difference is that the GAA has been a very well-run association; that is why it has been so good, plus it hasn't had that amateur versus professional type dimension, so they can just get on with running their games instead of having to say, how are we going to pay our wages next week? which has largely been the focus of soccer clubs. The idea of investing in your facilities was just a pipe dream for most clubs for the past thirty or forty years and in many cases still is. That is only beginning to change now because of the grant funding, and it is taking longer than it should but you can see it start to come through. You are beginning to see the grounds are getting a bit better and training facilities are starting to improve.

But that is only half the problem; the other half is that as a country, I don't think we have seen the value in the League. We are beginning to say, well, why can't we have a Rosenberg? Why can't we have an Irish club that can do well in the Champions League? Shelbourne's achievements have woken people up and they are saying, well, maybe we can do this, maybe we can succeed. But unfortunately, we, the people who are in football, have shot ourselves in the foot so many times. We don't market ourselves well; we don't work together well; and we haven't really seen ourselves, as I think we should do—as custodians of the world's biggest sport in Ireland. That is what we are.

I think we need a full merger, we need full integration and we need John Delaney calling the shots . . . I genuinely think they do want to succeed. They do want to see Irish clubs do well in Europe, they want to see Irish clubs being successful and they do want to see people at games. I am just not sure they know how to do it. The greater challenge at the moment is to get everybody to agree to a common strategy and a common way forward and I think all the will in the world isn't going to make that happen. And I think that is where the real issue is.

I remember we played Liverpool once in a thing called the Carlsberg Tournament in 1998 and one of the senior FAI officials at the time was asked what his view was on the Carlsberg Tournament and he said, "Well I don't know, but I am glad to see that my club was playing." This was an Irish guy and I think he was on an English Channel and they said, "Oh right, that is St Pat's then?" And he said, "Oh no, my team is Liverpool." I remember hearing that and thinking we have got it so wrong. I remember thinking, what other country in the world would have that situation? But now, I do think that it has started to shift. I think in fairness that was the end of the old view, that very demeaning view towards Irish soccer.'

V. Saipan: the watershed

The event of earthquake proportions that finally shifted Irish soccer from its apathy was not something that occurred on a football pitch, a club boardroom—or even in Ireland. Instead, it happened on a little island in the Pacific Ocean, an island more famous as the place where thousands of Japanese committed suicide at the end of World War II by jumping off the cliff edges into the sea rather than face the coming Americans. This was Saipan.

In 2002, on Saipan, Irish football crossed its Rubicon. In the most public, most humiliating and most Irish of ways, the storm that erupted between Irish manager Mick McCarthy and captain Roy Keane made front-page headlines around the world and sent reverberations through the sport that are still being felt to this day. Keane was sent home on the eve of the World Cup as a result of an interview he gave to Tom Humphries of *The Irish Times*.

'I spoke to Roy Keane in Saipan and he was quite affable,' explains Brendan McKenna, who was one of only three FAI officers on the island at the time. 'He asked me would I set up a suitable time for him to do an interview with Paul Kimmage from the *Sunday Independent*. He said, "I'm easy, but talk to Kimmage to find out what time and come back to me," and I did that. Tom [Humphries] then appeared in the hotel after training one day. I saw him because we had already had a press conference at that stage and Tom appeared in the team hotel and I went over to him and I said, "Tom are you alright?" And he said, "Ah yeah, I am okay, I kind of have half an arrangement to talk to Roy Keane, you know." But I told him, "Just to mark your card," I said, "Roy has already arranged to talk to Paul Kimmage." "That won't cut across me, I'll do my own thing," Tom replied and off he went and arranged his own thing. When that interview appeared, then the whole bomb went off.'

There is no point in recapping the events that led up to and caused Keane to go home. The entire country played out the drama on the airwaves, TV screens and newspaper pages, and we can all remember the too-hard pitch and the other inadequacies that sent Keane into a rage. The upshot was another investigation and yet another report, the infamous *Genesis Report*, which was a serious indictment of the sport. If it wasn't bad enough, Irish football had humiliated itself on the global stage. The FAI, through its own incompetencies, was headline news again—but this time it was on Sky, CNN and news channels around the world. The Association's mistakes and maladministration were revealed in the most public of ways: the culture of malignancy that had been allowed fester for so long was finally outed in the most public and most embarrassing way possible.

It was a David and Goliath battle between Old Ireland and New Ireland. Roy Keane saw himself as just doing things right, as being serious about the matter at hand and ditching the old Irish attitude of being there just for the *craic*. Here was a man who had worked his socks off to get to captain Manchester Utd, and he had done so through talent, force of will, dedication and a winner's attitude—all the things that Irish people were now associated with in the days of the Celtic Tiger. Irish society was now a society of success, of entrepreneurs, of results. So the Roy Keane attitude of 'fail-to-prepare, prepare-to-fail' rang true. Against Keane was the sturdy Mick McCarthy, a man not given to complaining, a man who belonged to the old order, which saw Ireland as the underdog. The pitting of these two stubborn forces brought into sharper focus the widening gap between this new breed of Irishness and that of the migrant diaspora. Mick McCarthy, son of a lorry-driver from Waterford, was a proud Irishman, brought up on stories of migration, unemployment and struggles. Was he truly aware of the sea-change in Ireland at the time?

Fintan O'Toole summed up the 'underdog' attitude in *The Guardian*:

> 'Low expectations are the ultimate guarantee of pleasure. If we got beaten, we were proud and happy to have been there at all. If we won, as we did so gloriously against Italy at USA '94, it was a moment of pure ecstasy, God doing us a favour we hardly deserved. Whereas England hounded and jeered managers who were moderately successful at big tournaments, Ireland all but deified Charlton, whose sides recorded a grand total of one victory in normal time from two World Cups.'

What was perhaps most interesting of all about the whole affair was the change in public opinion between the immediate aftermath and the present. Now that there's plenty of water flowing under the bridge, more and more people are counting themselves on the side of Keane. If it came to a popular vote between Keane and McCarthy, Keane would win it. Even the massively popular musical, 'I, Keano', which portrayed Keane and McCarthy in a sympathetic light, had the crowds on their feet at the end of the night, chanting Keane's name. Keane had been reworked in the poplar mindset as the hero figure who was right all along; it bears a striking similarity to the furore that surrounded the criticisms of Jack Charlton's style at Italia '90, criticisms which are now generally accepted as valid. For some, it has meant a reassessment of what it means to be Irish and admitting that we have, of old, pandered to our notions of inferiority. For us to maintain our winning ways, to keep our New York shopping trips and foreign properties, we know, deep down, that it is necessary to stick with the attitude as shown by Keane.

In the fallout from soccer's biggest argument, it was inevitable hat a new investigation would have to recommend real change. The *Genesis Report* duly arrived in November 2002, and promised to be the blueprint for a new future for the FAI. When the knives came out, it was General Secretary Brendan Menton whose head was to fall, but everyone else remained in place at the FAI top table and preached the good word of *Genesis*.

How much of it, though, was propaganda, bluff and bluster? It was a bone of contention that while radical change was preached and expected, many of the same faces that saw Merriongate, the Night of the Long Knives, eircom Park and the Marney Affair were still there, around the table. And what about the recommended changes themselves, proposals for a new executive structure to administer football and the appointment of a Chief Executive, a Director of Performance, a Director of Football Operations, a Director of Marketing and Communications and a Director of Finance and Administration and the reduction of the Board of Management from twenty-three to ten—just how far-reaching were they? Brendan Menton, who now works for the Asian Football Confederation, has been the most ardent critic of *Genesis*, claiming that only when the old culture that exists in Merrion Square has been edged out can real change be effected. Delivering his resignation speech to a press conference, he remained critical:

'Some of the fundamental problems associated with the administration of football in Ireland are not just about Saipan. I took the reins eighteen months ago, and, while I have made many changes across various disciplines within the association and the game, the review indicates that the issues impacting negatively on the FAI span a long period and, more importantly, looking to the future, require the type of radical and genuine reform of which some of you in this room have recently written. We are talking about a new organisation, not just a service and overhaul. This will take a certain type of leadership, not necessarily someone steeped in football.'

Writing in his book, *Beyond the Green Door*, Menton elaborated on what he saw as the flawed basis to *Genesis* and gave a clear

impression of just how deep the malaise runs in the corridors of
Irish football—and this, remember, from a man who had been
involved with Home Farm from boyhood and whose father was
one of the founders of the famous soccer nursery:

'The flaws within the structure and culture of the FAI run deep. I
did not have the ability and strength to change the organisation.
Does anyone? . . . *Genesis* addresses none of the fundamental issues.
Widespread political reform is needed. Political reform is only
marginally on the *Genesis* agenda, which is why the FAI have
seemingly embraced it with enthusiasm . . . Irish football thrives
despite the FAI. The FAI seldom discusses important football issues.
Its meetings are dominated by petty politics. The rows are more
important than the issues. Dealing with matters arising from the
previous meeting's minutes can take hours as people try to score
points off each other. The Association's committees simply do not
function and achieve nothing positive for the game. Neither
[President and General Secretary] can give constructive leadership
because as soon as they come up with a good proposal it is knocked
. . . I came to hate the organisation and its poisonous atmosphere
. . . It took me six years to realise that if you want to achieve
something for Irish football, you have to stay away from the FAI.'

On *Genesis* he says:

'*Genesis* did not look at the political structure of the FAI. The *Cass*
recommendations were far more radical. The politicians were
happy with *Genesis* because apart from a reduction in the Board
numbers, it left their structures, representation and privileges
untouched. The main impact would be on the executive staff at
Merrion Square. The FAI will not fundamentally change until the
political structures are reformed. Most problems arise at the
political level rather than the administrative level . . . My biggest
criticism of the *Genesis Report* was that it did not deal with the
culture of the FAI. If you are going to change an organisation like
the FAI, you have to change their culture. We can all see that this has
not happened, hence nothing will really change . . . The report has
stranded the FAI in no man's land. The FAI politicians are happy
with this as it is not threatening to them. They will endorse *Genesis*
with enthusiasm as it ultimately protects their interests.'

Tom Humphries described events in 2002 as the 'beloved soap opera down in Merrion Square' and he wasn't far wrong. There always seemed to be rows, resignations, departures, sackings and investigations. All that was missing to complete its 'Eastenders' script were the murders and sexual intrigue . . .

Here then, six years on from the *Cass Report*, which had also been highly critical of the FAI for its lack of planning, vision and structure, *Genesis* was reporting that 'most basic management disciplines were non-existent' in the FAI and 'fail to recognise good organisation practice employed elsewhere in sport, including Ireland'. There was, it said, no 'culture of discipline in the management of the FAI' and even such basics as 'better planning and attention to detail' and 'all training facilities and equipment to be checked and delivered on time' were lacking in 2002.

Would anything really change, people wondered? Menton was the only one from the FAI management level to go, and while promises of hiring a new Chief Executive, finance director and performance director were bandied about, it took another two years, and Government threats to their funding, before the FAI appeared to act on the matter. And, of course, the blight of scandal continued to spread.

Fran Rooney was appointed CEO in June 2003, but lasted little more than eighteen months before resigning with three years left on his contract. The words 'internal row' arose once more, this time centering around Rooney's management style, and clashes with Merrion Square and League of Ireland officials led to just three of the sixty-strong FAI Board of Management supporting him in the end. But in true FAI style, it wasn't to be a quiet departure either. With his tenure about to come to a premature end, Rooney went on 'Liveline' in a public appeal to the 'ordinary football fans', declaring his capabilities and love of the game. Once again, Irish football's dirty linen was being washed in public.

Former Honorary Treasurer and long-time football official John Delaney (whose father, Joe, had had a chequered career as Honorary Treasurer and was implicated in the Merriongate scandal of 1996, but who has been, according to son John, a 'big influence on my life') then took temporary charge before being forced to publicly advertise the CEO position under threat from the Government. In March 2005 John Delaney was formally appointed as permanent Chief Executive of the FAI. Is this what he had been planning all along, some asked? Had this been his father's ultimate goal back, way back in 1996? Was this the Delaney plan finally coming to fruition? In the background there were mutterings that it was his Machiavellian-like manoeuvrings that had ensured he would eventually take over the Football Association of Ireland. On his rise to the top, any potential enemies were sidelined, or put out of the organisation. Some even alleged it was his father, Joe, who had been pulling the strings all along, determined to exact his revenge on all those who made him the scapegoat of Merriongate. As Tom Humphries said, soap opera stuff.

Now, after nine long years, John Delaney had gone one step further than his father and was in charge of the whole Association—and, most importantly, he had arrived there without any more enemies in his sights. The mutterings weren't stilled by the decision to appoint Delaney. While he celebrated his promotion, words in the ears of journalists were enlightening them as to what may have been going on and what this could all really mean.

VI. John Delaney: the future of Irish soccer in his hands

Opinion on John Delaney differs hugely, depending on who you are talking to. In the 2000s so far we have seen multi-million-euro sponsorship deals, revenue surpluses and increased attendances, but that hasn't brought harmony to Merrion Sqaure because many feel that the man in charge has two faces: public and private. What you see isn't necessarily what you get with John Delaney. FAI sources and men who have worked closely with him over time say he is first and foremost a politician, a man who understands the human frailties and who knows what it takes to survive. As the FAI enters its most critical stage, a time when it needs to regain the credibility and respectability lost over the last ten years, when it needs to put in place the structures and administrations to deal with professional sport in the twenty-first century and when, crucially, it needs to answer the challenges being thrown down by the GAA and IRFU, the question that arises again and again is: is CEO John Delaney the right man for the job? Is Irish football safe in his hands? Opinions are deeply divided.

'John is the most Machiavellian character I have ever met in my life,' says one FAI source who has worked with and knows Delaney through their football dealings, 'and I have to say that is exactly what the FAI doesn't need. What the FAI needs is a Liam Mulvihill, a Philip Browne, an administrator; someone with an attention to detail who will go into the office and who will manage the people within the office and that is something that hasn't been done before. I would have had a lot of time for Brendan Menton [previous General Secretary] as an individual and I think that Brendan did some very good things, but he was completely undermined and shafted by John Delaney in an absolutely nasty, appalling way. I was only recently looking over minutes of FAI meetings and it is appalling how Delaney just spent the entire two years while Brendan was there just undermining him; he was having finance meetings where they were bringing up these issues and just at every turn Brendan met with opposition.'

Others point to Delaney's successes and astuteness in his business career, suggesting there are the qualities needed to bring the FAI forward. Again, the counter-arguments are quick to surface. His critics point out that he was previously Chief Executive of QC Logistics, which was then taken over by ABX Logistics, while his other interests in operations, such as a coffee-making vending machine, furniture business and a bakery, have all shown accumulated losses over time—€200,000, €36,000 and €460,000, respectively.

'I have had discussions with people who were in business with John,' says another source, 'and he told me of an acquaintance who had business dealings with him. To cut a long story short, this particular business was serviced by one particular client and this guy just wasn't happy with the way things were going and as far as he was concerned he just didn't want to continue doing business whereas John wanted to continue. John wanted to do the deal and the guy said to him, "I'll do it on two counts. One, you give me all

the shares I gave you and secondly that I never see you ever again."
If you were to talk to people, they would tell you such stories. I have
spoken to people and people have contacted me because they
obviously know that I have been in a war with the FAI and that I
have checked out John Delaney's business background.

What he does is, he goes into companies, bought into
companies, and then it kind of all falls apart again. I don't think he
is a millionaire. I mean he would spin you, for instance, that this
logistics company he sold for €8 million, he was telling us effectively
that this was what he got, but again the word was that he only got
about 10% of that. Now why would you go about telling people that
you got €8 million? He is just a Walter Mitty-type character and by
all accounts there would be no serious money there. I am not saying
he would be penniless—he would be fairly wealthy, but certainly
not a millionaire in terms of things.'

When the conversation turns to John Delaney and the FAI,
inevitably the name of his father crops up almost immediately:

'His father had huge charm but he was a control freak. Joe would be
up in Merrion Square five days a week; now I don't know what he
did for money, but he was up there five days a week. One guy told
me a story about him when he was in a hotel in Sardinia in 1990. "I
was doing business with people from Chile," he told me, "and I was
bringing them out for the match and an Irish fella asked me, do you
know Joe Delaney? He is supposed to be coming in with tickets for
me." So he decided to hang about anyway and the next thing Joe
comes in and he wasn't carrying one of these suitcases, he had one
of those wheelie trolleys and he sat down in the foyer and it was
packed to the brim with tickets. He was there for three hours that
night and then came back the following morning until the case was
empty and he didn't take one cheque, everything was cash.'

Joe Delaney's role in the Merriongate affair in 1996 tarnished his
reputation and led to his enforced resignation. However, critics are
suspicious of his role in his son's career, suggesting that when Fran
Rooney was in place as CEO and Brendan Menton was being
undermined, it could have all been part of the long-term plan to
get John the CEO job. It sounds like paranoia, but there is, say his

critics, a series of victims of the 'Delaney plan' that can be traced back in logical progression. John Delaney is quick to dismiss such notions, claiming that shafting people

'... became part of our culture . . . I think what shouldn't happen really is that voluntary people shouldn't really be removed from office going forward from now. I think if you are not doing your job, an executive is measured in terms of how you go and how you don't go. A voluntary person is appointed for a term and they should be reappointed or not based on a vote, but removals and all that had happened over the last number of years—and we were all part of that and we all saw different moves and different parts—I think that is something that we all have to leave now and I think there is an acceptance of that within the game. There is a real sense of unity at the moment today and we don't really want to go back to the days of certainly having our internal rows externally exposed. All national governing bodies have, I suppose, people within their game who don't get on with each other. That happens in life. Your own family is like that. But you have to ensure that if you are going to have difficulties that they remain internal, you sort them out internally and get on with life . . . It is nine or ten years ago now when all that happened. It is a lifetime ago and I have a lot of lessons learned—I was just a young guy of twenty-six, twenty-seven years of age back then.'

His critics beg to differ:

'If you go back to John when the whole eircom Park thing happened, John would have jumped on the back of Brendan Menton and John Byrne who were in the anti-camp,' explains one source who has been intimate with the inner workings of Merrion Square. 'He obviously saw this as a way of getting Byrne to trash the eircom Park issue. You see that went back to the famous night when Joe [Delaney] was shafted and Bernard [O'Byrne, CEO at the time of the eircom Park saga] had got the nine LFA guys to vote against Joe. So John would have obviously had a sort of a very long memory in that respect.

As O'Byrne moved on, Brendan [Menton] went in as General Secretary. Now, Brendan was a decent guy—I am not saying he was the best administrator insofar as I think that at times his attention

to detail let him down and he took on too much and he didn't
delegate things, but he brought in very good people and he had a
good team who did work well for him—but John Delaney just
spent his entire two years there just basically undermining him and
shafting him. Why? Well, Brendan writes in his book how when Joe
[Delaney] got f**ked out of the FAI and he came back in looking for
his hundred grand back, Brendan told him to f**k off. Now
whether that was being stored in the memory bank, we just don't
know but he was being treated in a most appalling, dreadful way.

Then there was the issue of Mick McCarthy's bonus. I have seen
Liam Gaskin's [McCarthy's agent] affidavit on the matter and I
would have been very strong against John on that. Ultimately we all
agreed to do a deal and we said, we don't need another purge, but
John Delaney should never have been allowed administer it. He just
went up to Gaskin and McCarthy and said, "I think you are doing a
great job and you should be getting a bonus," and McCarthy said,
"What do you think I should be getting?" and he said, "A hundred
grand," and McCarthy says, "A hundred grand sterling and that's
fine," and Gaskin agrees to sit down with the officers to sign it.
Then, Delaney goes back to the office and says McCarthy is looking
for a hundred grand bonus because the contract wasn't signed and
so they meet the following week and Delaney says to Gaskin, "Don't
tell them that we had this conversation".

So the FAI have this meeting about this one hundred grand, let's
say, and they agree to it because they can't afford to lose McCarthy.
It is the night before the Spanish game [in the second round of the
2002 World Cup] and they come back to Dublin and what does
Delaney do? He says, "We had to pay", he puts it in the minutes that
an hundred grand extra bonus should be paid and then, of course,
he has one of his lads lined up to ask the question, "How did that
come about? Because the contract with Mick McCarthy hadn't been
signed." Now all of this came out in an affidavit which I have seen
and read. So why did he do it? Because he wanted to get rid of
Brendan Menton. Because Delaney always wanted the top job.'

O'Byrne and Menton were out of the way, but the top job was
still not Delaney's. Fran Rooney, former CEO of Baltimore
Technologies, was appointed as the next FAI Chief Executive:

'The Rooney thing I just couldn't figure out,' says the source, 'I mean, within two weeks of Fran Rooney's appointment, himself and John were just like that—it was just extraordinary how two people could become aligned so quickly. I actually think that Rooney was set up. I think what happened was that Rooney would have been seen as having the huge profile—Baltimore Technologies and all that—and Delaney would have been advised to go with him. A guy called Gary Owens, a guy from insurance, was a shoe-in for the job we were told. The job was his and then suddenly two weeks later, Delaney says, "Ah we gave it to the other fella". I just didn't think anything of it at the time, but then Rooney came in and spun his way in a second interview about what they would do and what they could do.'

Rooney's appointment, coming so soon after the criticisms of *Genesis*, was announced as a fresh new beginning for the FAI, but, as usual, things went awry shortly after he took over:

'Rooney had good ideas, but he was out of his depth when it came to putting the ideas into actual reality,' according to one FAI source. 'He had a mantra that clearly believed that as a CEO it is the CEO who is out there shafting people and firing people. He definitely believed in confrontation and that is how to get your way. He didn't get on with people from day one and that was clearly just his way. That is all very well if you are backing that up with results and work and you are saying, well in fairness he has brought this fella in to replace him and you can't argue with what he has done, but in reality, he was doing nothing. There were meetings after meetings and basic questions would be asked and nothing would be done. But quite apart from that, the biggest issue I would have with John Delaney is that Fran Rooney made decisions, told lies and shafted people. He was a complete disgrace and John Delaney defended every single thing that he did until he was able to get rid of him. Then you see, getting rid of Kevin Fahy was part of the plan because if he got rid of Rooney and Kevin was still General Secretary, then Kevin would have taken over as interim CEO.

Oh I do think this was a long-term plan. I think that Delaney was very, very clever. Getting rid of Kevin Fahy, what they did to him was just the most disgusting thing. Again I saw the letters that Milo [Corcoran, FAI President at the time] wrote about in his minutes and it was just appalling stuff; there was a sixty-man council that were bought off and told that Kevin Fahy is trouble and you need to get rid of him. This is the frightening thing: that one or two people can get control—and they did—and they were effectively in complete control and able to manipulate things. So Delaney gets rid of Fahy. He then shafts Rooney, obviously. Michael Cody then, who is now brought in as a sort of a lackey to be undersecretary, who is now retired, says, "Oh, I have no interest in taking over the position of CEO". This despite the fact that the rule says the Honorary Secretary shall step into the CEO's shoes. Suddenly, the door is opened and our knight in shining armour walks in.'

Thus began Delaney's tenure as CEO of the FAI:

'I would say that the only benefit of John Delaney coming in as CEO is that he won't have a John Delaney shafting him at every turn. That is the only benefit that I can see. He might now actually be allowed to do the job and he also won't be able to hide behind in the shadows, which he was able to do as treasurer. I believe his stewardship as treasurer was appalling as well. It had been the politics of the cheque book and of the ballot box. It had been a case with the cheque book where basically clubs and affiliates have just been written money for any old project and there had been no proper policy in terms of funding. He was on the Strategy Committee for the Technical Plan, for instance, so he knew for three years that the technical plan was coming down the track yet there wasn't one euro set aside over that time for funding it. Now obviously money has become available and that is fine but that, in truth, is just short-term politics.

I would be frightened. I think John is sharp. He has a very sharp mind and he is very skilful. He would be saying one thing to your face and then going to the club saying, "Listen, you know we cannot work with him and you know we will give you this and we will do this." And I have no doubt that rules were being breached. I am not saying that he has been feathering his own nest, but certainly there are a lot of stories out there about tickets and extra tickets being printed for matches and no accountability and so on. All I can say is that it will be interesting to see who gets the finance job because if somebody goes into finance and starts poring over the past . . .

Delaney, you see, is not a detailed man. He is careless and he does leave trails behind him and I think he will get careless. But the problem is that means there will be another f**king shaft in a few years time and we are back to square one again. He shouldn't be CEO because he is certainly not a Liam Mulvihill or a Philip Browne, who are there because of a passion. I don't think he has a passion for football. I think he has a passion for power and this is the only way he will get power.'

Even on the question of *Genesis*—the FAI blueprint for success—the sources claim it was a stitch-up in its implementation. Certainly, for once, Delaney was caught making promises in public that he couldn't keep, declaring in 2002 that 'if the recommendations are not implemented in one full year, I will be out of this place. End of story.' Three years later the FAI was still in the process of implementing *Genesis*' recommendations—and Delaney was still CEO.

'If you follow the recommendations of *Genesis* you couldn't go wrong, but the whole board thing was just completely hijacked,' says the former official. 'What everybody missed and what everybody has forgotten about was *Genesis* said that on the board that there should be two non-executive directors—that is without a shadow of a doubt the most important recommendation of *Genesis*—yet that was completely forgotten about. I remember, on the night before the AGM in Galway when *Genesis* was put through and they were putting their ten-man board forward, there was a list of things that we hadn't addressed simply because we hadn't the time and the whole thing was, let's get this through, and this was only stage one. But they got their ten-man board. They had their control. They completely hijacked the voting process and they just got their own people on the board.'

It would seem that concerns about Delaney went beyond Merrion Square; a source claims he was a talking point in Government Buildings:

'People in the Department of Sport would have huge concerns about Delaney, but it's a case of, if they have got to work with him, they have got to work with him. What John O'Donoghue was saying in December 2004 about not going to tolerate a 12–18-month picture of employment was very interesting in that he was saying, "Watch out Delaney as CEO". But because Delaney is the only CEO in town I think that O'Donoghue realises that politically he cannot stop him. Even in the Sports Council [which is responsible for government funding to sports bodies] they didn't want to know. Treacy [John Treacy, Sports Council Chief Executive] was handing out money, increasing their grant and *Genesis* just wasn't being implemented. Then John Curran in the Dáil Public Accounts Committee started asking questions and the whole thing starting blowing up around Treacy. All he has got is a job where all he has to do is follow a process. Instead he got sucked into this game with Rooney and Delaney. I remember having a conversation with Treacy when the whole contract row with Rooney broke out. Treacy rang me and he said, "We cannot afford this, we cannot afford to have another row, this is just terrible, we are looking for more funding to govern," etc., etc. I said, "John, there are serious issues here," and he said he didn't want to know, he just didn't want to know. I told him, "You have got to understand that this is far deeper than money." But he didn't want to know.'

The litany of accusations and allegations against Delaney goes on and on, but we can't ignore the fact that the FAI isn't pure as the driven snow either. There are always a few sides to every story, and the same is true of the Delaney tale.

'People just can't—and don't—grasp how dirty things really are in Merrion Square and what does go on,' explains one former official. 'There are people there who, because something is not their idea, are undermining it at every turn. Just go back to the *Cass Report* in 1996, which Brendan Menton instigated and which looked into the whole structure internally. Yet the John Delaneys threw it out because it was Brendan Menton's report. They f**ked it out saying, "No, you can't do that, you couldn't do that". Once you have that mentality in there it is very difficult to see how things can change. Before I got involved at the deep end I used to hear stories and didn't think people could be so malign. I still think that any human grouping can work, but it depends on leadership and if your leaders are John Delaney, Milo Corcoran and Michael Cody, f**k me! Forget it, you're in trouble. Just look at the FAI ten years ago and look at the FAI now.

I think the problem for the FAI simply boils down to people's egos, and in any political organisation you are always going to have it. I mean, let's be honest, you don't want to become President of the FAI, Chairman of the League whatever, if you don't have some ego and you like some power. But it should be born of a desire to change things and do things. And it is a problem because if you sit there and do nothing, nothing happens. If you go in there and you try, people will say, "Who the hell do you think you are?" A huge amount of criticism has to be levelled at the leadership of the FAI consistently as I think that the quality of people who go into administrative positions is appalling.

It is because, especially if you look at the junior legislators, for a lot of them becoming a Council member or a Board member of the FAI is the highest position they will ever command but yet, a lot of them wouldn't even know how to run a business; they don't know what corporate governance, making decisions or abiding by rules is because in their leagues or in their little kingdoms they are not challenged. They are gods within their league and they have grown up in this culture that by the time they get to the FAI it is ingrained in them. Most of them are working at it so long they've got thirty years, possibly more, of ingrained culture, in terms of how to do business. They are not going to change all of a sudden because he/she is now the President or Vice President of the FAI. My experience is that most of them spend so long climbing up the ladder that they are certainly not going to put their head up and have it chopped off and lose that power. Power is a drug that, unfortunately for a lot of these people, is far more important than making the right decisions. The FAI and power-broking now goes hand in hand but, the biggest problem is the juniors who are very fixed in their ways; they are very difficult to get on with and very difficult to bring change about. Attitudes at this stage, if you go back to 1996, they are so ingrained we are talking about ten years of shaft followed by counter-shaft.'

So who, then, is John Delaney? A Machiavellian spin doctor with an insatiable appetite for power, or a man pitted against the obstacles of FAI narrow-mindedness and fighting the good fight on behalf of the game? We have seen what his critics say of him. His supporters, on the other hand, also make a compelling argument. They see the positive developments, such as the Technical

Development Plan, full-time professionalism, better facilities and better training and coaching methods. They see John Delaney as a strong CEO, a man who knows the League of Ireland inside out having worked his way up from club level at Waterford Utd.

The only way to reach an objective decision on John Delaney is to talk to the man himself. In person he is an accommodating and affable man, someone who will give freely of his time if he thinks it will help in putting his and the FAI's message across. And there is much he wants to say:

'There is a huge passive interest today, as we speak, in the eircom League. I know so many people who can tell me who is winning games by watching the Aertel, reading the papers or whatever, but they don't physically go to a match. An interesting figure is that 150,000–160,000 people watched the FAI Senior Cup final on the box this year, but yet there was less than 10,000 people at it. That was the same day that Arsenal played Manchester Utd and it was the same day that the Aussie Rules match was on in Dublin. So there is a huge passive interest in the game, but getting people to go to the matches is a difficulty. That is actually the real difficulty, but having said that, 400,000 people went to our matches this year in totality. In the eircom League we need to build on that and to benchmark that. What you need, I believe, in this social society that we live in now, you need to be able to bring the wife and the kids, it is not just about the guy going to the match on his own or with his mates. That is part of it, but it is certainly not all of it.

If you take a step back to the 1950s and the 1960s, people were prepared to stand out in the rain. I remember going to see the FAI Senior Cup final in 1980 when Waterford won it. My Dad was Chairman and it was packed; even though it rained that day people were prepared to stand out in the rain with their paper hats or whatever it was back then. And they were there with the flask and the cut sandwiches on the way up on the side of the road. But now, people's expectations have moved on from that, be it the Celtic Tiger, be it the revolutionising of the game that Sky brought with the money they brought in the 1990s. People expect to be entertained not only on the pitch now but also around at the facilities, they want facilities that match their expectations. And that has been the change as I see it in that now it becomes an idea for the eircom League clubs that you actually provide facilities for the clubs to meet the expectations of the supporters.'

On the issue of the clashes between League of Ireland clubs and the inability to achieve consensus, he is at least cognisant of the problems existing between the clubs and aware that a tougher approach is required:

'I think the Association must accept that it deserved certain criticisms over the last number of years—there is no question of that. If you hear some of the stories about the international team around the 1960s/1970s/1980s, that is not pretty stuff to read. But I don't think it was that different to some of the other countries at the time, be it across Europe or certainly some of our other home nations. But we left ourselves more open to exposure to it probably by being closer to the media in a lot of what we did. I think the criticisms of our professional planning over the last couple of years are unfair because I do believe they are well organised. Our planning now is top notch and I always make the point that we are twelfth in the world so we must be doing something right. Three World Cups and the European Championships, so we must be doing something right in Irish soccer. I think some of the criticisms are fair enough to criticise us on certain aspects but not in total.'

The burning question, of course, is how can change, definitive change, be brought about?

'Part of the problem has been that twenty-one or twenty-two people were arriving to a board meeting of the FAI on a monthly basis having to protect their own interests, and then going away and having their own problems with their own clubs and having their own issues to solve, and then coming up and having to solve the League's issues. It doesn't give a cohesive structure to the development of the game. I was one of those twenty-two delegates. I used to be that Waterford delegate coming up every month and if I got five grand or a grand towards the under-21 team, I was delighted going back down the road because I had my five grand got. I wasn't thinking strategically about how the League should go forward because I had my own issues to deal with on a parochial level. What I am suggesting is that to drive the League forward, and there is no magic wand here, this will only be done over a course of time, over a course of benchmarking, it needs a couple of issues which I identified: one was live television to create awareness, and we have succeeded, in that the twenty-nine or thirty matches live matches to be shown is a tremendous rise previously from five or six. I also felt that we the FAI had to treat the League seriously if we wanted people to invest in our game. You must have a significant prize fund and what we have delivered on is a minimum of €400,000. In terms of running the League on a monthly basis, it is a smaller committee of six or eight people with three or four from the clubs and three or four from FAI, simple as that. And then it is executively driven under the direction of the FAI, no dotted line, just a straight line to the FAI. So, what you have is a smaller number of people deciding in the League so the clubs are involved and the FAI are involved. You have an executive team reporting directly to the FAI and you have participation agreements whereby the clubs are governed by a legally binding agreement.'

It all seems reasonable and practicable in print, but it is also reminiscent of the type of language used by An Taoiseach, Bertie Ahern, when discussing benchmarking and agreements and executive decisions. Even Delaney's honest appraisal of the various relations within the game, while being frank, has a conciliatory tone:

'Previously, the FAI had enough of its own issues and the League kind of went about its own business. I think it was always known that politically there was always—I suppose it is probably too strong to say ill feeling, but there was certainly the junior strand of the game and the senior strand of the game didn't get on as well as they should. I would say that the Association probably wasn't ready for what we are talking about now and it is true in a sense that politically twenty-two clubs giving up its power base in terms of running its affairs is something that they would trust the Juniors to do. The timing is right now. The clubs are certainly realising that they have to get administratively up to speed and they should concentrate on their own issues. They should leave it to other people to advance their League and they can see that the FAI can do that. If people like myself are there, then the trust will actually come. With the twenty-two clubs, I grew up with them. I know them and understand them.'

Given all the tumultuous staff changes, resignations and severance packages, the FAI has been in constant turmoil for the best part of ten years and, what's worse, has been playing out these incestuous power struggles in the public spotlight of the media. But enough is enough, says Delaney. It is time to call a halt to all the bloodletting, to move on and grow, with him at the helm; there must be no more *coups*.

> 'What we need more than anything is a stability period. We need to be stable for a period to actually see the benefits of all these items. And I think if we get a stable period, I think we will be in great shape in five years time. I really believe that we will be in great shape in five years time if we get a stable period. I couldn't emphasise a period of stability enough—if we get that, our credibility will be restored . . . I think in every national governing body or major organisation there are always going to be issues. You must be aware of them, certainly I am aware of them and have been in the past but I think that particularly in the last CEO the difficulty wasn't political and I don't think that political issues are high on the agenda in the game today. I really believe that.'

Now firmly in control of the FAI, and with close friend Steve Staunton appointed as the new International Manager, John Delaney will continue his family's long tradition of involvement with the game in Ireland. Like many an Irish politician, soccer officials in this country are handed down the role and title from father to son, like a heraldic badge of honour to maintain their line of succession. In time-honoured fashion, John Delaney is continuing on what was given to him by his father:

> 'It is part of your heritage. I will never forget as a kid being brought to all the matches. It is part of how you are brought up, it is part of you. In 1979 Waterford were beaten by Dundalk in the Cup final and I remember my Dad being very upset at losing the game, but you went on and in 1980 we won the Cup [beating St Pat's 1-0 in the final]. It was who you were. This was just something that was part

of you and was part of your heritage. There is no other better way to describe it. Waterford was just something that you did that you were delighted to do and so you would take on that challenge. There were some really difficult low points when you were trying to raise money and all that, but you got through it. It was like a baton and you were grabbing the baton and nobody else gets it.'

The baton is firmly in his grasp now, but how long can he hold on to it? How long before the unnamed enemies emerge from the shadows to carry on the FAI's proud tradition of back-stabbing and the unexpected *coup*?

Conclusion:
Too little, too late?

As I write this concluding chapter, the country has just witnessed one of the greatest achievements in Irish sport, with Munster winning the European Rugby Cup. In other words, an Irish team has taken rugby's equivalent of the Champions League. In just ten years Irish rugby has gone from amateur to professional and has not only made that transition successfully but has managed to hold onto its finest talent and reform ideas about how sport should be run in this country.

In the same period, the GAA has gone from strength to strength. Millions of euro are pouring into its coffers from multi-national businesses, all wanting to be identified with the hugely successful brand that is Gaelic games. Thousands of people come through the turnstiles in record numbers every year, all wanting to be part of the GAA summer. It is a mammoth achievement for the organisation and it continues to plot its way intelligently, capitalising on every opportunity and asset. Its future looks as rosy as rugby's does.

And soccer? Well, that's a different story. We have seen and read about Merriongate, the Night of the Long Knives, the Commissioner, the Marney Affair, the *Cass Report*, Saipan and *Genesis*. Admittedly the international team have remained hugely popular, but even appearing at the 2002 World Cup was tinged with embarrassment after the row between Mick McCarthy and Roy Keane. Worse still, there haven't been many high moments for the League of Ireland. While League fans will undoubtedly take umbrage at this, they must ask themselves just how many people care about the League of Ireland season anymore? To their credit, the fans will defend the League to the hilt, but with the leaps and bounds being taken by Irish rugby and the GAA, the League's fans, as well as the League itself, are more and more being viewed as an anachronism.

The Irish soccer team is the only draw for Irish fans these days— but if they fall any further in the rankings, it would not be hard to envisage a future, revamped Lansdowne Road only half-full for meaningless World Cup qualifiers. That is why it is ever more important to make the effort to improve the offerings of the League of Ireland. The rapid changes in Irish society over recent years means the people are looking to hold on to some part of their 'original' identity, hence the resurgence of the GAA and the strong identification with local clubs. The question for League of Ireland clubs is: can they sell their grounds, those shards of history, and start anew on the outskirts of the city, such as Bohemians are doing?

If there is a single metaphor for the downfall of the League, it is surely the beleaguered Shamrock Rovers. How long can this once great club survive outside of the top flight, without a home and reliant on the goodwill of the fans running the club? The demise of Rovers, from being the Manchester Utd of the League to going into examinership in 2005, casts a dark cloud over the future of League of Ireland soccer.

It is John Delaney who now has Irish soccer in his hands. While some commentators believe he is just the latest in a long line of FAI executives who have connived their way to the top through *coups* and bloodletting, others see his manoeuvrings as necessary to the survival of the League. Taking power away from the clubs is paramount, and the merger between the FAI and the clubs announced in May 2006 is a step in the right direction. Other 'radical' proposals are more questionable, such as renaming the Premier Division the 'Premiership', reducing division size from twelve to ten, or increasing the prize money. Whether these tactics prove useful remains to be seen. Nonetheless, it is to be hoped that the clubs will no longer veto change for the better, or stand in the way of progress just because they don't like it or don't understand it. Hopefully, the recent development and success of the cross-border Setanta Cup and the FAI–League of Ireland merger are proof of a new willingness to change.

Once upon a time the League of Ireland was a place packed to the rafters, where fans celebrated local rivalries and players were revered as gods. Then, over a forty-year period, and through a poisonous mixture of mismanagement, small-mindedness and lack of planning, the League fell out of favour with the Irish people. The managers had forty years to correct what was obviously and fundamentally wrong. They failed.

The reality now is that the League doesn't have time to mess around anymore, trying more half-baked ideas in the hope that a Paddy Abramovich will come riding over the hill with 20,000 spectators in tow. As the clubs and their officials finally cede power to John Delaney in the hope that miracles can be worked, one wonders if it is too little, too late. Will the real legacy of the League of Ireland be the 'Sold' sign at Dalymount, just as the bulldozers move in?

Index

Morris, Michael, 169
Morrow, Edward R, 164
Morton Stadium, 21
Mulligan, Paddy, 141
Mullins, Brian, 101, 106
Mulvihill, Liam, 162
Mulville, Billy, 20
Murphy, Brian, 136
Murphy, Jim, 65
Murphy, WP, 18, 19, 20

Neill, Terry, 141
Neilstown stadium proposal, 179, 180, 182
Newcastle United, 127
'Night of the Long Knives', 171–2, 204
Nolan, Ronnie, 17, 30
Noonan, Austin, 62
Northern Ireland international team, 140
Northern Ireland Troubles, 106, 109, 112–16
Norway v. Ireland (1985), 140

O'Brien, Seamus, 125
O'Byrne, Bernard, 157, 171
 eircom Park, 197, 198–9, 210–15, 229
O'Callaghan, Andy, 176, 184–5, 217
O'Callaghan, Owen, 180
Ó Ceallacháin, Seán Óg, 39
O'Dea, Jimmy, 63–4
Odense Select XI, 31
O'Donoghue, Fr, 135
O'Donoghue, John, 233–4
O'Driscoll, Peadar, 88, 193
O'Dwyer, Mick, 105
O'Gorman, Paddy, 5, 120
O'Hara, Maureen, 134
O'Hehir, Micheál, 27, 38, 39, 40–41, 105–6
O'Keeffe, Paddy, 28, 54, 109
O'Kelly, Seán T, 33, 36
O'Leary, David, 140
Olympic Games (1956), 30
Omonia, 215
O'Muiri, Alf, 109, 112

O'Neill, Frank, 71
O'Neill, Liam, 40
O'Neill, Tony, 'The Doc', 89, 90, 190
 Charlton appointment, 140–42
 tribute, 192–4
O'Regan, Fr, 33–4
O'Reilly, Noel, 39, 149–50, 175
 on administrators, 168
 on junior football, 159–60
 on Kerr, 174–5, 176–7
Oriel Park, 65, 96
O'Toole, Fintan, 49–50, 53, 107, 111, 151–2, 153, 166, 222
Owens, Gary, 231

paedophilia, 166
Paisley, Bob, 140, 141–2
Paley, William, 164
Pat Grace Kentucky Fried Chicken League, 125
Pelé, 52, 85, 86
Peyton, Noel, 15, 17
PFAI, 60, 66, 185–6
pitches, condition of, 67, 99, 100, 121, 123
Pius XII, Pope, 37
players
 freedom of contracts, 66, 186
 loyalty, 186
 registrations, 211–13
 second-class treatment of internationals, 60–62, 126
 sleeve patches, 210–11
 see also professional status; wages of players
points system changed, 125
Poland, 126
Portadown, 114
Pownall, Stan, 17
prize money, 91–2, 238
Professional Footballers Association of Ireland (PFAI), 60, 66, 185–6
professional status, 23, 60, 66, 83, 185–8
 ban on professionals suggested, 58
Prole, Robert, 23, 24, 81–2
Prole, Royden, 18, 81–2